BE YOUR OWN PSYCHIC

BE YOUR OWN PSYCHIC

The new interactive guide to TUNING IN your psychic
abilities and transforming your life

Sherron Mayes

Hodder & Stoughton

Copyright © 2003 by Sherron Mayes

First published in Great Britain in 2003 by Hodder and Stoughton
A division of Hodder Headline

The right of Sherron Mayes to be identified as the Author of the Work has been
asserted by her in accordance with the Copyright, Designs and Patents Act 1988.

A Mobius paperback

1 3 5 7 9 10 8 6 4 2

A CIP catalogue record for this title is available from the British Library

ISBN 0 340 82477 8

Typeset in Electra by Palimpsest Book Production Limited,
Polmont, Stirlingshire

Printed and bound in Great Britain by
Clays Ltd, St Ives plc

Hodder and Stoughton
A division of Hodder Headline
338 Euston Road
London NW1 3BH

To my daughter Isabel
My inspiration

Acknowledgements

A big thank you to Carolyn Hicks in giving me her steady flow of support, humour and feedback for this book. Thanks to my agent Andrew Lownie for acting with lightning speed and giving me great confidence. Thanks to everyone who helped bring this book together with their wonderful intuitive stories. And finally a huge thank you to everyone at Hodder & Stoughton publishers who instinctively knew this was a great idea.

Contents

1

Discover Your Potential to Change Your Life

There is no cure for birth and death save to enjoy the interval.
George Santayana, 1863–1952, American philosopher

Have you ever yearned to be psychic? Did you wonder how great it would be if you knew with total conviction whether you'd get offered that fabulous job, sensed totally that you'd met the love of your life, instead of just another time-waster, or had an instinct for buying the right house? Well, guess what: you already know the answers.

Like it or not we all use some of our psychic ability every day to a greater or lesser degree. Having a 'nose' for business, feeling inspired, acting on a hunch or a strong gut instinct are all phrases we use in day-to-day language and with good reason. If you see someone who is successful in their job, not just a pen-pusher, but a property magnate, a great salesman, or a brilliant teacher, look at their behaviour. You can bet they're acting on more than just basic educational skills. What they're doing naturally is tapping into their inherent psychic abilities.

Now you can dismiss my claims all you like. If you don't feel you have an intuitive bone in your body, don't despair. Just as we need to exercise physically to improve our muscle tone, we also need to exercise our psychic muscle to unlock our own powerful potential.

It is true that some of you will find it easier than others to

1

develop these abilities and have a special talent for it. You may feel that you are already psychic but want to strengthen and hone your sixth sense. To anyone at any level of under-standing the simple answer is always the same. Just like learning any kind of craft, the more you do it, the better you will get. And the only ingredients you need to make a start are curiosity and an open mind.

Through many years of learning about my own awareness, let me tell you something that I know is absolutely true. Psychic abilities are not a gift that is given to the highly evolved or to special people who have a mission to the save the world. You may want to change the world, but, believe me, whatever your path in life, you are naturally psychic. Some of you may have had a glimpse of 'special' powers, such as acting on a hunch that pays off or having a premonition, but fob it off as a fluke or a 'one-off' experience. But that is just the tip of the iceberg. You actually have access to all the answers about anything you could want to know. And it is your right as a human being to nurture the gift you were born with. You can pretend it doesn't exist and plead ignorance, in which case your explosive potential will simply lie dor-mant until you decide to unlock it.

If you're still not sure, think back to your childhood experi-ences, where you may have faint memories of telepathy, out-of-body sensations, a sense of spirit people and amazing dreams. That is where the roots of intuition are. We were fear-less, open-minded and full of adventure – until we grew up.

I should know. It happened to me. Seven years ago my life changed dramatically and I was propelled from a mundane existence into a new and magical world where anything was possible.

From working in a monotonous job that I could do standing on my head, I found a career I genuinely loved and became a successful journalist on a lucrative contract to a major national newspaper, the *Daily Mail*. People thought I was lucky, but I knew different.

But before my new life took off, I went through a crisis that changed me beyond recognition.

At the time I had a job as a medical secretary, a mortgage on a flat, enough money, and a plodding relationship that I knew wasn't going anywhere. I was in a comfortable rut but I also felt a sense of innate frustration, of not knowing what direction to take with my life. I chose to believe that this was my fate and probably as good as things were ever going to get. But buried deep down inside was the feeling that I had unexplored potential and at times, if I dared admit it to myself, I wanted more. Was it possible that at the age of twenty-nine I could have a job that inspired me and a life that fulfilled me? Not much to ask. But I could have blindly trudged along into old age accepting that my existence was fated to be the way it was, until suddenly out of the blue the universe gave me a sharp smack in the face, and I was forced to re-evaluate my life.

It was a series of traumatic events that led to what some might consider a complete emotional breakdown. One spring morning I was taking a short cut to the station on my way to work. On what was normally a quiet side street in New Cross, south-east London, a car unexpectedly sped round the corner and drove into the back of my legs as I was crossing the road. I was thrown up into the air, landed on the bonnet and then flopped down on to the road. The driver was just about to race off when several passers-by stopped him.

I felt shocked and on the verge of hysteria as I was helped

to the pavement by a young chap. As the police were called, an ambulance came and the same man accompanied me to the hospital and sat with me until I was checked over. Fortunately, the doctors said that because the accident happened so suddenly, my body was relaxed and hadn't tensed up, so I hadn't been seriously hurt physically, apart from some whiplash. But I was in deep shock. I'm not the sort of person to feel sorry for myself, and so I returned to work that afternoon, not realising the state I was in. The next day my handbag was stolen from my office. I had a new pin number in my purse and by the time I realise what had happened the contents of my bank account had been emptied. I felt so fragile; it was as if I wanted to cocoon myself away from the dangers of a life that seemed frighteningly out of control. Yet in a few days' time I was due to start a new job working for a private doctor in Wimpole Street as office manager. Things did not bode well.

Over the next few weeks I began to feel nervous about venturing outside the house, wondering what else could hurt me. Although I continued going to work, my new job proved to be a nightmare with my boss apparently assuming that manager meant slave and expecting me to do everything, including cleaning the floor.

Every night I went home desperate to know why all this was happening to me and wondering whether the future held any hope. It was causing problems with my relationship as I quickly deteriorated from being witty and fun-loving to the equivalent of a frightened animal cowering in the corner. I didn't even have the confidence to communicate properly. One evening my boyfriend Anthony said that he was concerned when I kept edging away from him into the corner of the living room. Every inch he took towards me,

I shrank back. 'I want to kiss you and you keep moving away,' he said softly. I remained silent and hung my head. I was in turmoil and words couldn't express what I was going through. Although I wanted and needed comfort, I felt there was nothing in life I could trust in and an invisible shield seemed to be enveloping me. When bad things keep happening out of the blue, it creates a sense of powerlessness and fear that makes you feel paralysed and unable to enjoy the moment.

In abject desperation I decided to seek some guidance from a clairvoyant medium, who I had met at the local spiritualist church. I had gone there a few times out of curiosity, but didn't think much else about it.

The clairvoyant, Jean, was middle-aged, but slightly unconventional in that she was also a journalist for car magazines. When I arrived at her terraced house in Lewisham, I walked upstairs and sat in her cluttered living room. I didn't know what she'd say, but I hoped it would be something simple like, 'You'll come into a great deal of money without having to work for it and live happily ever after with 2.2 children and a loving husband.' I certainly wasn't anticipating the message she gave me. 'You're wondering if these bad things that are happening to you are ever going to end,' she said rather seriously. 'But you have a strong psychic and healing ability. And you're quite clearly not using it.' Much to my apprehension she continued, 'You have been experiencing difficult times and I can tell you now that if you don't use these gifts, your life will continue in this way. But if you do use them, whatever you decide to do will bring you immense success. If I were you,' she said, staring at me with intense dark eyes, 'I would set about developing your psychic talents post haste. You are already gifted, so it won't take you long. Within a few months you'll have abilities as good as any established psychic.'

What she said struck a chord deep inside. But if I wasn't already terrified with what was happening, I left her house that day feeling scared witless, yet with an urgent need to discover how I could develop myself. However, I knew I didn't want to be associated with a spiritualist movement. I wanted a straightforward approach with no religious associations, with which I might or might not agree. I was anxious to make contacts and within weeks I discovered a medium who took classes in psychic studies and my life began to be transformed.

In retrospect, it should have been easy for me to recognise my psychic gifts. I was always very open-minded as a child and an adult. I've had amazing intuitive dreams throughout my life, sensed presences around me and read any book I could find on esoteric subjects from witchcraft to reincarnation. But like many of us who occasionally pick up on things intuitively, I just couldn't recognise my own potential. Now I know the reasons why. I was brought up by my mother, who believed in Eastern philosophy, meditation, homeopathy and reincarnation. She also believed in psychics and mediums and occasionally consulted them. But the flip side was that she was also filled with resentment, fear and insecurity, and often repeated, through her own misery, negative messages that I absorbed mentally like a sponge. Messages that I know now were entirely her perception of life and nothing to do with me. She told me that life was destined to make you unhappy, that I was ugly and that I would never be successful. Painful words, which when repeated often enough mould the way we see ourselves as adults. In my case I'd become a victim, dogged by depression, who could never realise her dreams or have what she wanted. I just couldn't trust my own thoughts or feelings about anything, and because I had no confidence in my abilities, I was unwilling to accept that I could help myself.

But this life-changing insight, if a little unnerving, was a real breakthrough. For the first time I could see my circumstances with clarity. Although I know that our parents mould us, I couldn't live my life blaming the past or my mother. I had to accept her weaknesses and her strengths and that she had done the best she could. As an adult, I also had to realise that I alone had to take responsibility for the path my life was to take if I was ever going to be happy.

I was like an excited child with a new toy when I finally understood the language of my sixth sense. I was amazed when I suddenly had information about a situation or person that appeared to me like magic.

In a development circle of around twelve people in a small room in Kensington, west London, we sat in silence to experiment with intuition. I remember focusing on a plump middle-aged man sitting opposite me. The first thing that came to me was that he had a major problem in his life. That's all I knew, so I mentioned this and he nodded. Then it came to me in a flash. 'Is it redundancy?' I asked.

'That's exactly what it is,' came the reply.

I was thrilled. How on earth did I know that? Then I saw a picture in my mind of ice cream and a sense of being abroad.

'But you're going on holiday to Italy,' I said.

'Yes, we are,' he said with a smile.

I was astonished. I just couldn't believe that I was able to pick up such accurate information.

Another time I focused on a woman in her forties. I saw a picture in my mind of her sitting in a kitchen looking out on to a garden. I described the scene and she confirmed that she often chose this room in which to think about things. Then I sensed her emotions, which were of overwhelming sadness.

'It's as if you're feeling that you've given up on life?' I continued.

'Yes,' she replied quietly, and she suddenly put her head down and cried.

And I knew I'd relayed a truth. I saw her life, like mine had been, was in a rut. Plodding on day to day without any real meaning to existence. Ruts might be seemingly comfortable, but they are in fact desperate circumstances, where we put our lives on hold.

Many similar situations revealed that I was not only able to pick up the surface problems of someone's life, but also be a mirror for the deep emotional issues that were buried inside. The feedback gave my confidence a much needed boost and I knew that at last I was heading in the right direction.

As part of my continued studies, I would meet up with another like-minded girl friend, Sandra. I soon discovered it was no irrelevant coincidence that she was also a journalist for *Elle* magazine. She'd overcome dyslexia to do the job she loved and, like me at that time, she was petite and blonde and always wore a mini skirt: the antithesis of what most people would expect of a budding psychic. We both eventually confessed that we'd hated each other on sight, until we realised that we had rather a lot in common. At her flat in the King's Road we would practise tuning in to each other while we nibbled on tacos and chilli sauce until the early hours. As with anything new, continued practice is an absolute necessity if you want to learn your craft well.

One thing I've learned about uncovering the psychic self is that once you ask a question in your mind the answers come, but not always in the way you expect. I remember confiding to Sandra the one thing I knew I was desperate to achieve: to work for myself. Writing was something I had wanted to do since I was fifteen, but how could I break into such a competitive business without studying for years? And make a living from it. Particularly in the cut-throat world of media journalism.

I knew I had to take action. So I enrolled on a two-hour-per-week session for a feature-writing course at City Lit in Holborn. Fortunately, I never needed to attend more than twice. That was October 1995. After three months, by January 1996, everything was to change and my new career would unfold faster than anyone would ever have believed possible.

On one of our psychic evenings I discovered Sandra had an old computer that she hadn't wanted to get rid of for nostalgic reasons. But she suddenly said, 'Sherron, would you like this?' as she handed me her machine. Apparently a voice in her head said firmly, 'Give it to Sherron,' while I was sitting in her flat and she simply felt she had to. I was amazed and grateful, and stored the computer in my flat, not planning to do anything with it just yet.

Then a few weeks later my first published story was handed to me on a plate. I was sitting on the Tube in central London. We were told we would be waiting there for some time. For anyone who travels frequently on the Underground, there was the familiar message that someone had jumped on to the tracks and there would be delays. But this particular day I had the recurring thought: Why would anyone want to die like that, in such a gruesome way? Later that evening as I walked from the station to my Victorian terraced flat in New Cross I reflected on the Underground suicides again. I then heard a distinct voice in my head say, 'Write about it.' It was so insistent that I felt inspired to follow it up the very next day, and phoned the London Underground press office to get some facts. It was fair to say that their response was pretty unhelpful and off-putting for a new writer.

'The story has been done to death,' was the irritated reply. 'The train drivers have given their view.'

'But what about the victims' stories?' I asked with keen curiosity.

'I don't know about that,' said the abrupt voice on the phone. 'Fifty per cent of them die anyway.'

That means 50 per cent are living and maimed in some way, I thought. I immediately phoned *Time Out* and asked if they'd like to commission me to write a feature on the subject, not really understanding what a commission was. (But I'd discovered from my tutor on my two sessions at City Lit that this was the starting point, as it was considered to be a verbal contract.) Perhaps I was being a little over-confident in approaching a mainstream publication with no experience, but it just seemed the right place to start. *Time Out* wanted an outline and then asked me to go ahead. My article was published a month later.

From then on, an endless stream of feature ideas would come into my head, and once I focused on a subject I found I could match it immediately with a suitable publication. The appropriate journal would simply flash through my mind. Anyone who has ever done any freelance writing knows how much research can go into putting the right idea to the right title. But whatever newspaper or magazine I rang with a feature suggestion, they instantly commissioned it. I was amazed. Doors seemed to open up in front of me. I must confess I had none of the donkeywork of researching where to place work as my own intuition was telling me loud and clear. Of course I still needed to use my logic, but there had to be a balance. When my rational mind took over and I forgot my intuition, I would sometimes persist with a particular newspaper. But my sixth sense quickly overrode such attempts. On one occasion I took something else to *Time Out* and distinctly heard the words, 'Nip it in the bud.' It wasn't going to work and didn't.

To continue exercising my abilities I did psychic readings for people and got many recommendations. Often someone would cry at simple things I had said and say, 'No one has ever known that before.' I was genuinely pleased that I was able to do something useful that seemed to be working. And, more than anything, suddenly the depression that had stalked me for most of my life vanished as if I had released pent-up mental energy by helping others in this particular way. But more of that later.

My career took off so quickly that after a year of working for many of the mainstream magazines, I was getting an article published in the *Daily Mail* almost every week. Within eighteen months I was offered a contract with them.

It made me realise something very important: now that I had developed these new skills, I didn't have to struggle as I had before. I suddenly had an extra sense activated that was smoothing my path ahead. Many people couldn't believe my good fortune. 'You must know somebody or just be lucky' was the general consensus. And I took great delight in telling anybody who would listen that not only had I left school at fifteen with no qualifications, but I had no training as a writer.

I was proud of that for one reason: it proves beyond doubt that by listening to your own inner voice you can achieve anything you want to.

Make a real commitment to yourself

The tools I learned in development circles are simple and straightforward. The different tasks I will give you in this book are a way of focusing your mind to allow your intuition to flow. But you will also learn a whole new inner language of the psyche. And once you unlock the codes, information will be as easily available to you as breathing in and out. Soon I went on to teach my own courses. And I've seen everyone from housewives to sales executives surprise themselves that they are indeed telepathic, intuitive and with a pool of answers to many questions. I will explain all you need to know about tapping into the powerhouse that exists inside you.

So let's make a pact. If you promise to keep an open mind, then your life can improve 100 per cent. Within these pages are the tools for you to sharpen your intuition and be one step ahead of the game of life. You don't have to be the next Mother Teresa, or turn into a new-age hippie who yearns to travel the world and live in a commune. You can simply become much more successful at everything you do. And as we go through each step, I promise you will become more confident of your own abilities. Of course, there will be times when you feel frustrated and I will remind you that you are simply trying too hard and you need to relax. Through my own valuable lessons, I will help you use the specific techniques and the many visualisation exercises in this book to learn how to develop and strengthen your innate sixth sense. You will discover that the outcome isn't just about becoming your own psychic but also becoming a master magician of your own destiny. Using the powers of your mind, you will have the knowledge to create successfully the life you want; make money from a job you love and enjoy the relationship you always dreamed of.

Within three months, with these intuitive tools, your life can improve dramatically. You will learn about true independence and discover that the best teacher in your life is you. You don't need to resign yourself to fate. You can create good fortune and opportunities by sensing with your own inner radar which direction to take in work, love and friendships for the best possible outcome.

But before you go any further you need to begin the process of unlearning. When we do an exam we memorise information and then use it logically. But understanding how intuition works is very different from learning through our rational intellect. As you will soon discover.

2

Balance Your Yin Yang Energy and Understand the Dynamics of Your Aura

We have to free half of the human race, the women,
so that they can help to free the other half.
Emmeline Pankhurst, 1858–1928, English suffragette

Before you begin developing your psychic abilities, there's something very important that you need to take on board. You can become highly intuitive, but you also need to learn how to use that new-found talent in your everyday life. You may discover all the inspiration and inner guidance you want, but you need to act on it and make it work for you. So it's essential to discover your strengths and weaknesses so that you can work on them to optimise your psychic powers.

Some of you will inevitably find it a lot easier than others to develop these intuitive skills, thanks to the development of our minds. As many philosophers and scientists have said over the years, we only use a small part of our brain. The way we think and react coupled with our childhood and adult experiences will stimulate some parts of our brain more than others. A go-getting stockbroker who plays competitive sport in his spare time will develop different parts of his brain compared to a sensitive artist who spends a lot of time alone.

To explain fully, we first need to understand that every living entity has cosmic energy called chi within them. This energy is polarised into forceful and receptive aspects, known as yin and yang. When we operate from both, these energies flow easily and we have perfect balance in our mind, body and emotions. Balance is essential to all aspects of our health, because it keeps you rooted within yourself. This feeling of being grounded brings an inner harmony that means we learn to respond consciously to events in our lives, however problematic, with control and awareness, rather than simply reacting thoughtlessly. A balanced mind and body means you are more generous and kind. You think more positively and, because you feel secure within, you take other people's feelings into account – even in a crisis. Imbalance, on the other hand, makes you ungrounded and weak. Because you are stressed and reactive, your energies become blocked in your body, mind and emotions, which leads to a release of toxic chemicals that cause ill health. You react in a self-centred manner because you can only respond through your own mental state, whether fear, insecurity or depression. Oriental thereapies such as acupuncture, reflexology, shiatsu and acupressure are known for rebalancing these energies, removing the blockages to create healing in the body and mind. This is why after one of these treatments patients often experience a feeling of inner calm.

Yin energy is feminine and introspective and dominates the right side of the brain, which holds the key to our creative, sensitive and intuitive qualities. Yang energy is masculine, bringing logic, assertiveness and practicality, and relates to the left side of the brain. In order to use our creative psychic gifts fully, we need to have them balanced, integrating both sides of our brain. Too much yin energy can mean you're a dreamer who lacks motivation. You may have flashes of inspiration, creative and intuitive thoughts but be unable to use them constructively. Too much forceful yang energy may mean you're very pragmatic and assertive, but can never relax and be receptive enough to listen to what your inner voice has to say. This is how much of society has progressed. Many of us have become too yang-orientated, reliant on every sort of technology from the dishwasher in the kitchen to the spellcheck on our computers at work. We analyse all our problems. But we've forgotten how simply to feel.

How you are predisposed will match your response to this book. Being psychic is one thing, but the skill is being able to use that ability to make things work for you. The extreme yang people among you will be determined to succeed, frustrated if your psychic awareness doesn't develop quickly enough. You will need to discover that it isn't a race. The extreme yin people may get lost in the psychic exercises and possibly lose sight of their objective. But you can learn to become more balanced to get the best out of your own potential.

The perfect quote to express how we can integrate our masculine and feminine energies comes from Iona Marsaa Teeguarden, an acupressure specialist, who says: 'The Taoist idea of psychological balance is to embrace both the female and male sides of our natures – to be both receptive and active accordingly to circumstance.

'The most masculine man is not only strong and active, but also gentle and receptive – strong meaning assertive not aggressive. The most feminine woman is not only gentle and receptive but also strong and active – receptive meaning accepting not dependent.'

Yin or yang: your personality traits revealed

To discover exactly where you are now, I have devised a quiz that will show you how yin (right-brained) or yang (left-brained) you are.

1. You go to a favourite restaurant and find the special dish you always order is not up to the usual standard. Do you send it back?
   - ☐ a) Definitely – after all you're paying for it.
   - ☐ b) No – it's easier to eat it.
   - ☑ c) Possibly – but you'd rather not make a fuss.

2. You have an interview for a highly paid new job. How successful a candidate do you feel you will be?
   - ☑ a) You feel it's unlikely you'll get the job. But you're going out of interest.
   - ☐ b) You want the job and you'll prove that you're what they're looking for.
   - ☐ c) It could go either way.

3. What exercise are you most interested in doing?
   - ☐ a) You're interested in more gentle forms of exercise like yoga, walking or t'ai chi.
   - ☑ b) Active competitive sports.
   - ☐ c) You love all types of sport and exercise.

4. Do you remember your dreams clearly?
   - ☑ a) Sometimes, depending on how quickly you wake up.
   - ☐ b) Nearly always, sometimes even in colour.
   - ☐ c) Not aware that you dream at all.

5. If asked to organise a function for thirty people – arranging food, venue etc. – how confident would you feel about doing it?
   - ☑ a) You'd immediately get on the phone and start organising.
   - ☐ b) Act flustered and panic.
   - ☐ c) Relax, do your best and enjoy the experience.

6. When reading about astrology, reincarnation or things that can't be easily proved are you:

☑ a) Open-minded? The universe is a strange place and you are fascinated by anything different.

☐ b) Cynical? You believe only in the scientific approach.

☐ c) Totally open? You have often felt you have psychic abilities yourself.

7. In a group discussion do you sit back and let others say their piece?

☐ a) Yes; if everyone's talking you'd rather not interrupt.

☑ b) Definitely not; if you have a point, you'll make it. That's what discussions are for.

☐ c) You say something if it's necessary.

8. In a dilemma would you follow your gut feelings or hunches?

☐ a) What feelings? You just think things through.

☐ b) You try to listen to your feelings. They're often more accurate than your logical views.

☑ c) You're aware of your feelings, but you don't always trust them and prefer the logical approach.

9. If asked to work a computer that you'd never seen or used before, how would you react?

☑ a) Confidently. Look at the manual and follow the instructions.

☐ b) Not very confidently. But if in doubt you'd ask for help.

☐ c) You wouldn't know what to do, computers make you nervous.

10. When you feel emotional or upset, do you bottle things up?

☑ a) No. You need to talk to get things off your chest.

☐ b) Your volatility makes you say things you eventually regret.

☐ c) You'd rather forget about it. Discussing it opens up more problems.

11. Do people often tell you that you're pushy or dominant?

☑ a) Yes, all the time. But that's how you get things done.

☐ b) No, they have no reason to.

☐ c) Depends on your mood.

12. Have your partners generally been outgoing, assertive types who take control?

☐ a) Definitely not. You tend to attract analytical, unambitious types.

☑ b) No, you attract calm but assertive types.

☐ c) Yes, most of the people you have attracted have been outgoing and assertive.

13. How would you feel about attending a meditation class?

☐ a) You like the idea, it would calm you down a bit.

☐ b) Not interested. You wouldn't be able to sit still.

☑ c) You'd consider it.

14. Would you describe yourself as easy-going and laid back?

☐ a) Yes, nothing worries you too much.

☐ b) No, you're a born worrier and prefer to be in control.

☑ c) Sometimes; you can appear calm to others but inside you panic.

15. Do people describe you as having a fun-loving personality?

☐ a) No, you're serious and can be introverted.

☐ b) Yes, most of the time you're extrovert and gregarious.

☑ c) It depends on your mood.

Scoring

1. a) 10	b) 0	c) 5		9. a) 10	b) 5	c) 0
2. a) 0	b) 10	c) 5		10. a) 5	b) 10	c) 0
3. a) 0	b) 10	c) 5		11. a) 10	b) 0	c) 5
4. a) 5	b) 0	c) 10		12. a) 10	b) 5	c) 0
5. a) 10	b) 0	c) 5		13. a) 5	b) 10	c) 0
6. a) 5	b) 10	c) 0		14. a) 0	b) 10	c) 5
7. a) 0	b) 10	c) 5		15. a) 0	b) 10	c) 5
8. a) 10	b) 0	c) 5				

What your score means

0–45

You are very yin-orientated (right-brain tendency). You tend to be dreamy, sensitive and hide your feelings rather than express them. You may be creative and intuitive but find it hard to put your ideas into practice. You may lack energy and have no inclination to exercise because you are living more in your head and not feeling grounded in your own body. You could find it hard to mix socially in large crowds, preferring your own company or that of a few close friends. This will depend on how yin your energy is. The lower the score in this category, the more yin you will be. You may experience a lot of other-worldly happenings, but lack the motivation and abilities to use your intuition in everyday life. You need to focus on your logical pragmatic thoughts, as well as your feelings. They are equally important. If you have a creative idea for a book or a whacky invention, make sure you do something about it. Learn to be more assertive when asking for what you want. Make a point of expressing yourself clearly, so you feel you are being heard. Assertiveness classes could be useful and more active sports such as tennis or aerobics may invigorate you.

50–75

You are fairly balanced with a good measure of yin and yang energy. This means that you can combine logic and intuition in equal measure and are not extreme in introversion or extroversion. You will be able to develop your abilities easily and use them wisely as you have a good understanding of people and come across as an easy person to communicate with. You may find that you lean to the yin or yang more predominantly according to the stress or circumstances in your life. Become aware of your reactions at that time. Relax and if you feel you can't solve a problem turn to your intuitive responses.

80–150

You are very yang (left-brained). You tend to be extrovert, logical and ambitious, even dynamic. Of course you still have the yin right-brained qualities of intuition, but your overall energy is the forceful yang that can override your sixth sense at times. How can you listen to your inner voice when you are rushing through life, barely pausing for breath?

You need to balance yourself to bring more harmony into your life and access your potent power. You must find time to relax. Yoga, t'ai chi, reflexology or shiatsu will help you to become more centred. Try not to be too dominating in your relationships at work or home. Make a point of tuning in to what you feel rather than what you think and be more aware of others' responses to things you say. Creativity is also very balancing, bringing out the yin intuitive side, so take up a hobby that helps you such as painting, writing or poetry. The key to becoming more yin is to go with the flow, whereas extreme yang energy will manipulate and try to control.

To illustrate how balanced energies influence our everyday

lives, these stories on Louise and Julian are good examples of the problems that can occur when you have an imbalance of yin and yang. They both show how they overcame obstacles by balancing these energies, which changed their reactions to circumstances and brought them success.

Louise's story

Louise was a creative sculptor who was never short of ideas or inspiration. At the age of forty-four her yin energy (right brain) was highly developed, but when it came to trying to run her own business and sell her sculptures successfully it was a different ball game. She came to me to develop her psychic skills so she could improve her creativity and earn more money. Her psychic abilities weren't a problem. Within weeks she felt very 'fired up' and inspired about a new range of figurines she wanted to produce. Good contacts would swim into her mind and her dreams were telling her where to go next in the market.

But months later she came back feeling miserable. She had a major problem: she wasn't assertive enough. People would take advantage and cut her down in price, so she wasn't making enough money to earn a living. And despite doing the job she loved, she was having problems taking control in a business world dominated by men. If she wanted to succeed as an artist, her creativity and intuition were not going to be enough. She had to learn to develop her more masculine yang energy. Many artists are like Louise. Their energy is too yin and they find it a struggle to make a living from their work. Some can even be exploited by their own agents and galleries. I advised her to go on an assertiveness course to deal with her unresolved issues about taking control. And also to be aware about being submissive and not getting what she wanted for herself.

Now she's changed dramatically. She hasn't given up her womanly attributes like wearing make-up and feminine clothes, but she can stand up for herself in the business world and experience real equality. Now she names the price she feels is right (yin energy), but won't be beaten down (yang). She also says how this new-found assertiveness has brought the balance she needed but has altered her relationships with men. Some of them, she says, now feel threatened because she won't dance to their tune. But now she's changed, she's realised they're not the type of man she wants to be with any longer.

Julian's story

Julian was a typical 'yang' high-flyer. At the age of thirty-eight he was married with two daughters and over eighteen years had worked his way up to being a director for a chain of estate agents. Like a lot of ambitious men, when presented with problems he always thought of a logical solution. He attended one of my courses when he felt he wanted to learn how to do things differently. He was finding it hard to recruit people who, as he put it, would be 'stayers'. He'd had a bad run with people leaving within weeks of starting the job or being unmotivated and it was affecting company morale.

After regularly focusing on stimulating his psychic abilities, he learned to enhance his intuitive responses and trust his gut feelings. He noticed that interviewing someone can be a real problem if you leave it entirely to logic. The process could be very false, taking someone at purely face value. He agreed he'd often gone on appearances only and discovered that just because a person has the perfect CV and is immaculately dressed doesn't necessarily mean they're right for the job. Now he concentrates on how he feels with them, despite the fact that they might be nervous or seem inexperienced. If he feels uncomfortable with them, he trusts that feeling and considers how a customer might respond and how that could also create a bad atmosphere at work. Recruitment since then has been much more successful with a lower turnover of staff and newcomers who are eager to get on with their jobs. So these days, at work, before any recruitment starts, he makes sure that all his personnel first check into their 'antennae' as he calls it.

Julian discovered that without dismissing his logical approach he merely rebalanced his yin energy and allowed both sides of his brain to work for him. The effect has changed his personality, as he says that he feels calmer and more centred. He goes with the flow instead of overreacting. Recently a chap left their company to work for the opposition. In the past Julian would have had a sleepless night analysing the situation and worrying about it (very yang). Now his yin energy is more activated he realises that he can't control everything and whatever happens happens.

An important point to remember is that our yin yang energies often become unbalanced due to events in our lives and how we respond to them. And rebalancing our energy is an ongoing process that we need to remain aware of if we are to get the best out of ourselves and our lives.

Travel back in time

Now that you are more aware how you tend to respond and think, you will be able to maximise how to get the best out of yourself. If you're concerned that you're simply too pragmatic, logical and yang-thinking then become a little more yin – and relax. We all have instinctive, intuitive psychic abilities buried within us. They are the seeds of our true potential, waiting to be explored. We have just forgotten how to use them. Certainly our sixth sense has been with us since the beginning of time. Knowing how to feel was something our primitive ancestors knew a great deal more about than we do. They may have been light years behind us in sophisticated thinking, but their senses were alert to the slightest danger as they survived on their wits. They weren't daydreamers, but instinctive men and women of action, in tune with nature and their surroundings, because they had to be. And that primitive instinctive sense was naturally there in your childhood.

So in your mind travel back to that time of innocence as a child, when you believed in magic. Like many of us, I saw the world with very different eyes to the adults around me. The universe was an exciting and mysterious place and I took it for granted that I could feel and see the presence of spirit people. There were no debates or arguments to tell me any different. I wasn't afraid of death: I knew with total certainty that the real me lived inside my body and could never be destroyed.

Many of us experienced this so-called 'make-believe' world. We may have had special friends whom we talked to, or suddenly said something philosophical out of the blue that stunned the adults around us. But this magical world filled with pixies, angels and 'special friends' is not a naïve fantasy. As children we naturally used our imagination and creativity all the time. We had natural psychic gifts. But as we become adults we are subtly programmed by the world around us to believe that logical, pragmatic thinking is the grown-up way to live. Very quickly cynical attitudes and the need to conform chip away our childhood confidence in that intuitive voice. And is it any surprise? Children soon learn to shut up and switch off when they're called silly for having visions or imaginary playmates.

Children have a special talent that we can all learn from. They are open-minded enough to believe anything. I was certain that my dolls must surely come alive and play together once I had gone to sleep. That fantasy life is such a creative part of the development of our minds (the right-sided yin aspect) but it is seen as our innocent gullibility. Harmless fun, which must be shaken off once we're old enough to be sensible.

A memory that shows the strength of my childlike convictions was when I was only eight years old and was playing with my toys in the front room of our bungalow in Plymouth. I took one of my floppy rag dolls and closed my eyes and focused on it with all my concentration. Come alive, I was thinking, dance. I tried again and again before I threw the doll aside with frustration. I really believed that somehow if I could concentrate all my powers I could put life into that inanimate object. What that memory showed me was this: that as a child I had total belief in my ability to influence my surroundings. I had absolute conviction of my own power. I just didn't know how to make it happen. And therein lies the contrast between our child and adult perceptions. As children we are born with open minds and a desire to explore. Everything in life seems possible. But as adults we become so fearful that we focus on the limitations and we allow cynicism to cloud our views. Slowly our psychic gifts are suppressed and we forget how to tap into our own inner guidance and knowledge for help.

Now, however, we have the possibility of creating a new future. Imagine a world in which our children are encouraged to use and develop these natural gifts. Imagine a world where logic and intuition are intertwined. And just think for a minute about the explosive potential that we would have as human beings if we were encouraged to be our true selves: the knowledge that would be awakened within us and the cures that we could find for disease; the new ideas, discoveries and inventions that would be created that could help mankind. This book is for exactly that, whether your children grow up developing the intuitive intelligence they were born with to make a new future, or whether you suddenly decide to change your life and fulfil a new potential. This is how to reawaken that instinctive spirit within and be your own psychic. You may not be able to make dolls come to life, but you can discover the pool of potential within you to create the life you want.

How psychic development works:
The dynamics of energy and how our auras reveal everything

There are many different ways in which energy works. Developing ourselves psychically affects our entire being, altering our brain wave patterns and the energy field that surrounds us, which in turn develops and strengthens our higher mind.

To explain further, Dr Robert Beck, a nuclear physicist, travelled all over the world measuring the brain waves of healers, ESP readers and psychics. He discovered that when we use our psychic and healing powers, our brain waves register a 7.8–8 Hz alpha rhythm, which synchronises exactly with the fluctuations of the earth's magnetic field, known as Schumann waves.

This means that the psychic's or healer's brain waves pulse at the same time and frequency as the earth's Schumann waves. It was also discovered by Dr John Zimmerman, president of the Bio-Electro-Magnetics Institute of Reno, Nevada, that once a psychic or healer has linked up with the Schumann waves, the right (yin) and left (yang) hemispheres of the brain automatically become more balanced with each other. Using our psychic abilities therefore links us with the earth's magnetic field pulses, which connect us to a powerful healing energy source. This brings us better health and harmony.

When we 'tune' in psychically to someone (just as the earth

has a magnetic field), we are sensing information held in the human magnetic field, which is also known as an aura. This energy surrounds us and can be seen as a light or grey colour, but some 'sensitives' see its myriad colours.

There are seven different levels of the auric field (see page 30) and, just like an invisible map, it contains all the information about us, such as whether we suffer from a back problem, unresolved issues, low self-esteem or have a strong work ethic. Everything about our physicality and all our thoughts and feelings – good and bad – show up in our energy field. Even a creative idea can be seen in our aura.

As soon as someone walks into a room, their energy field will speak volumes about who they really are. This electro-magnetic field can sometimes reach up to three and a half feet in healthy individuals and that is why some people are described as charismatic or dynamic. They really make their presence felt. In certain very psychic, creative or spiritually aware individuals, the field can treble in size. But the life force in our aura works a bit like a battery that over the years begins to run down. Children have a strong, vital aura. But we only have so much life force. Therefore, in the unhealthy, or the elderly, the aura can shrink back to just an outline around the physical body.

Our energy field also explains why we can take an instant dislike to someone or immediately feel an affinity. One girl friend of mine said that an estate agent had sent someone round to view her property, which she was trying to sell. She opened the door to an impeccably dressed, handsome man. But she said for some reason she felt instantly that there was no way she would let him into her house. He evoked a sense of terror in her and she couldn't imagine walking round the house with him following behind. She made her excuses and closed the door quickly. Her sixth sense picked up from his energy field that something loud and clear was giving her danger signs.

But fortunately, more often than not, if we feel uncomfortable around someone it can be because they are unhappy with themselves. It is not necessarily because they are evil or nasty. For example, if the second level of someone's aura is unhealthy, which relates to feelings about themselves, the person may be depressed or full of self-hate. If you feel positive about yourself, then their field will be vibrating at a different frequency from yours and you will naturally feel uncomfortable around this person. And the other person will feel uneasy about you. Thoughts are energy and that is why there is a lot of truth in the saying 'Birds of a feather flock together', meaning that people of like-minded energy are drawn to each other. We often get a sense of someone straight away, but we are usually too preoccupied with our own selves to notice or we choose not to pay attention to the 'vibes'.

Unfortunately, it is a fact of today's fast society that our minds are too noisy to pick up on subtle information when we have more pressing matters to think about. It is the same as being in the countryside and listening to loud music on the radio. The sounds of the birds, the crickets and the leaves rustling on the trees are all there. But it's only when we turn the radio down that we actually take notice of the often quite loud effects of nature. The same happens when we turn down the internal chattering in our heads.

It is by strengthening the fifth, sixth and seventh levels of our aura, which relate to the higher mind, that we are able to develop our psychic abilities and pick up more clearly on all this information. If you're confused – don't be. Just know

that by trying out the exercises in this book that enable you
to quieten your mind, you will be activating the yin (right)
side of your brain and building up those levels. And as you
begin to hear your own definite inner voice that has previously been drowned out, your aura will reflect your new-found
knowledge.

There is a great deal of information about the human aura.
It could make an entire book in itself. But for clarification of
the seven levels of the aura please refer to the box below.

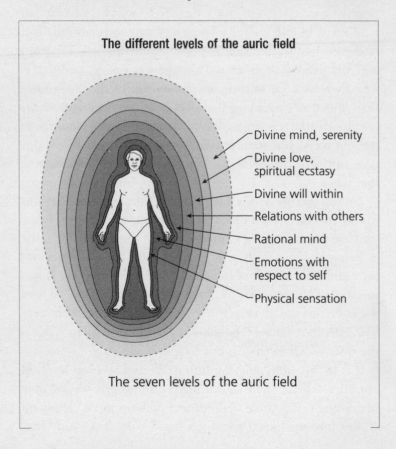

The different levels of the auric field

- Divine mind, serenity
- Divine love, spiritual ecstasy
- Divine will within
- Relations with others
- Rational mind
- Emotions with respect to self
- Physical sensation

The seven levels of the auric field

First Level – Physical sensation

This relates to all the physical sensations that are painful and pleasurable. Any discomfort or disease in the body shows up in this inner part of the aura. If this level is weak, you dislike physical activity, which may include exercise and eating. Anorexics would suffer with a weak first level as well as someone who might be desk-bound at work, and who goes straight home and slumps on the settee. *The more you take care of your body with exercise and healthy eating, the stronger this level will be.*

Second level – Emotions about ourselves

This level relates to our own feelings of self-worth. This level is strong if you feel comfortable with yourself, and like and love yourself in a healthy way. But if this level is not functioning well, you are suppressing negative feelings about yourself or may even hate yourself. This would relate to someone who may be depressed or feel suicidal because of low self-worth. *The more you learn to nurture yourself by thinking about yourself positively and constructively, the stronger the level will be.*

Third level – Rational mind

If this level is healthy, you have a strong, clear mind and may enjoy studying different things. You are rational and have mental clarity. But if this area is unhealthy, you may think too much, particularly about negative thoughts and you are not interested in any intellectual pursuits. *Learning and studying different things will improve this level as well as a balance of yin and yang mind energy (intuitive and rational thought).*

Fourth level – Relations with others

If you have a strong and healthy fourth level, you have many positive friendships with people and enjoy healthy intimate relationships. You like to be around people and may work in the caring industry. If this level is undercharged, you may be a loner. You may be celibate, preferring not to have intimate relationships. Or you may think relationships are more trouble than they are worth. *To strengthen this level you need to learn to give more love to develop your heart with friends, family, lovers and children.*

Fifth level – Divine will within

If this level is functioning properly then you like a sense of order in your life. Your house is clean and tidy, you do your job well and you are always punctual. You feel connected to the greater purpose or pattern in your life. If your divine will is not functioning well, you do not have a sense of purpose. The 'rebels' in our society have a weak fifth level. They may resent so-called 'society's rules'. They do not keep their homes clean and tidy and always turn up late. These people need to discover their true path in life. *This level is strengthened by learning to use your intuition.*

Sixth level – Higher spiritual love, spiritual ecstasy

If this level is healthy you often feel inspired and have had many spiritual experiences. It is experienced as a sense of elation or bliss. If it is weak, you may not understand what people are talking about when they discuss esoteric experiences. You may think they are all deluded and living in a fantasy world. Cynics and atheists would have a weak sixth level. *Strengthening this level can be done by actively doing visualisations/meditations to still the mind and raise your awareness.*

Seventh level – Divine mind, serenity

This is the level of the creative, divine mind. I say creative because artistic ability comes from this higher source. When it is healthy this outer level of the aura extends from your body by about three feet and you feel spiritually protected. When it is strong and we connect with someone else's strong seventh level, we can learn to communicate telepathically. You have many creative ideas and know what to do with them to make them work. You have a strong understanding of God. You may be a teacher of philosophical subjects, an inventor, a scientist or work in the creative industries. If this level is weak you do not understand what life is about. You are not able to think creatively or come up with good ideas. You may strive for unreasonable personal perfection because you cannot accept yourself. *The best way to strengthen this level is to be creative, still your mind with visualisations and meditations and learn how to access your dreams and guides for help.*

The scientific proof of the aura

Even for the sceptics among you there is an enormous amount of scientific evidence proving that we all have an energy field around us. Dr W.J. Kilner of St Thomas's Hospital, London accepted that the aura existed and began to experiment to make it visible to the human eye, so that anyone could see it. He developed the 'dicyanin screen' before the First World War, which is a lens painted with a coal-tar dye. This has an amazing effect on vision and enables the eye to perceive the ultra-violet range and therefore see the aura as a luminous grey/blue emanation surrounding the body. He published a book called *The Human Atmosphere* which showed that any doctor could check the condition of a patient with his Kilner screen, as the field showed a dark or discoloured mark over any unhealthy area.

Kirlian photography is now well known and you can usually get an aura photograph taken at many new-age shops. It is most commonly used to depict the different colours in our aura that show our emotional state, which changes subtly on a daily basis, depending on how we feel. It was invented in the early 1900s by Semjon Kirlian, a Soviet scientist, and involves a process that uses high frequencies and electron streams. Peter Mandal, the German naturopath and acupuncturist, has since clinically researched Kirlian photography as a serious method of diagnosis for the last thirty years. This energy field has also been measured by devices such as the electroencephalograph (EEG), electro-cardiogram (ECG) and a highly sensitive magnetometer known as SQUID.

We thus have real proof that an aura exists around every living thing whether it is a plant or your pet budgie, and that information ranging from our health, creativity and our future can be picked up from it.

The very basis of your psychic development, therefore, is the dynamics of energy. Discovering how yin or yang your energy is, along with in-depth knowledge of your auric field will demystify these extraordinary powers and help heighten your understanding. This chapter has now provided you with the foundation material, and you are ready to move forward to the techniques that can transform your life.

3

The Power of Imagination: Your Launch Pad
to a Higher Awareness

*Discovery consists of seeing what everybody else has seen
and thinking what no one else has thought.*
Albert Szent-Gyorgyi, 1893–1986, Hungarian scientist

In this chapter we look at the first link in the chain to psychic awareness, the much underrated powerhouse of our minds: our imagination. I use the word 'underrated' because using our imagination is something most of us take for granted, but through your mind adventures you'll learn never to underestimate it again.

The truth is that this simple mental process has unlimited potential. It is, in fact, the very bridge we need to cross to reach a heightened state of consciousness that will ignite our psychic powers. And make no mistake about it, our imagination is a potent tool. We only need to visualise a plate of hot chocolate fudge cake and we start to feel hungry, or focus on an erotic fantasy to see how our heart automatically beats faster and our temperature rises.

So why not use this creative faculty to relax into a deep state of peace, expand your mind energy and lift your vibrational frequency so you are able not only to 'receive' information but listen to your inner voice.

Of course anyone in the creative field, such as advertising executives, writers or designers, knows imagination is absolutely essential to their livelihoods. Even for the accountants and tax inspectors among you – and indeed for all of us –

don't be surprised if by strengthening this part of your mind your artistic side really starts to flow. When it does, be ready. Write down anything that comes into your head; paint or make something. Who knows? You could become a great novelist, film-maker or a poet. If your culinary skills aren't great, you might suddenly surprise yourself and rustle up a tasty dish. Even if no one ever gets to see your creation it could change your life in the smallest of ways, by just giving you a sense of fulfilment.

Let's face it, where would modern society be today without the great geniuses of our time if these inspired men and women hadn't tapped into their imagination to help mankind? It is through their creative 'flashes' and 'insights' that some of the great ideas and inventions exist. In fact, nothing in life can be materialised or set in motion without it first existing in our imagination. Think about that. Thoughts are powerful. And you just might get what you wish for!

There is also a cosmic surprise in store for anyone embarking on these exploratory journeys into the imagination. A golden reward awaits your efforts that is an additional bonus to unleashing your hidden powers. Once you open the door to your higher mind, you will find you are granted access to the most precious treasure of all: the gift of grace.

In case you are confused and wondering what I am on about, I shall explain. I still remember with complete clarity a vivid dream I had over ten years ago. I was having a question and answer session with a man in a suit who seemed to be acting as a teacher, prompting me as his student. There were many questions, but the one that stuck in my mind was when he asked, 'And what comes with imagination?' and my reply was simply, 'Grace.' It may seem like a strange answer, but I intuitively knew exactly what it meant. That is what imagination does. It provides the springboard to the higher realms of your mind that allow grace to flow into your life. Without wishing to offend any atheists among you, grace comes from the universal source that some people call God. In short, it is the divine opportunity to begin again, to start over.

Of course just like energy, or emotion, grace is invisible to the human eye. But we know these things exist by how we feel. And we know grace is active in our lives by the magical ways in which it manifests itself. Grace can fill us with much needed energy, create the right coincidences to support us in our lives, or ensure that the right person crosses our path just when we need it most.

So why is it that imagination holds the key to these higher levels? It is simply because our minds are pure energy that can be programmed by us like a computer. Although we can't see mind energy, make no mistake about it, everything is stored there – good and bad – hidden away in that Pandora's box of our subconscious: traumatic memories that can linger and still affect our behaviour, and positive thoughts that drive us on with hope and encouragement. Our current thoughts are creating our future and affecting our mental and physical health. When we think about ourselves and our problems, our mind energy funnels inwards creating a pressure and sometimes depression. But when we visualise images designed to raise our consciousness, our state of mind is naturally changed to become more positive and expansive. This is why (as I mentioned in chapter one) I discovered that my recurring depression suddenly lifted when I began to develop my psychic powers. The constant visualising to expand my mind energy meant I felt an optimism and lightness of spirit instead of the oppressive feeling of melancholy. I believe this is one of the greatest cures for chronic depressive sufferers and can benefit everyone's health through thinking more positively.

With the skills you are about to learn, you too will discover the many benefits of imaginative travelling. Instead of allowing your thoughts to control you, from now on you will be learning how to master your mind computer. By focusing this vast energy, you can not only learn to be your own psychic, but you will find it easier to make use of your mind in your everyday life. You will be able to concentrate more fully on whatever tasks you undertake throughout the day, as well as relax at night, simply because you are harnessing this energy, instead of being a slave to its antics as it whizzes from thought to thought.

Discover your predominant sense

Before we begin this creative journey it is important to know how to build strong mental images. The stronger the image, the more efficiently you can access the higher mind and tap in to your intuitive powers. When I first taught my development courses some people were concerned that they couldn't 'see' things well or couldn't hold on to a picture in their minds, yet they could still get a sense of what was happening. Others could visualise easily but couldn't bring in the sounds and feeling with it. And of course, using all your senses well in visualisations helps you to create sharp and focused mental pictures that will allow the receptive aspects of your mind to become more flexible and powerful.

The first step is to discover how your mind operates in terms of mental imagery. We all think in a visual, auditory or kinesthetic/feeling way. (In these circumstances we will include taste and touch under the category of feelings.) We have one sense that is called the 'driver' and we think and communicate in this preferred way quite unconsciously. Once you have identified your predominant way of thinking, you can begin to sharpen up the other senses in order to improve your visualisations. Here are the definitions of the three senses.

Visual

You think in terms of pictures and mental images.

Auditory

You think in terms of noises, which could be anything from background music to the noise of a bath running.

Kinesthetic feeling

Your thoughts are represented as internal emotion or physical touch.

There are many ways to identify your dominant sense. But just because you work as a photographer, surprisingly, might not mean you are visual. It is the words we use, our body language and preferences that really define how we think. Other generalisations can give you pointers, too.

Look at the list of phrases below, which give examples of how we constantly use words depicting all five senses in our communication. Become aware of the words you use most in conversation and letter-writing.

Visual language

I get the picture.

Things are looking up.

That looks good.

Do you see what I mean?

That's colourful.

Out of the blue.

See you soon.

Auditory language

That sounds good.

I hear what you're saying.

Things clicked into place.

That's a belter.

That rings a bell.

We're in harmony.

Listen to me.

Kinesthetic feeling language

That feels good.

I get a good feeling.

Hand on heart.

It feels right.

Get a taste of success.

We should keep in touch.

It was a pleasure.

Taste

It was a bitter-sweet moment.

She seems sour.

Smell

There was the scent of fear.

Here is a simple questionnaire that will act as a guideline. For each question, see which picture comes into your mind first that sums up whether it is a visual, auditory or feeling sense and tick the one that applies to you.

1. *A pleasant scene – a waterfall*

☐ a) Do you see it clearly, with water cascading down a rock face?

☐ b) Or maybe you hear the sound of trickling water?

☐ c) Or perhaps you feel the water running all over you as you stand underneath it?

2. *An everyday habit – think of making coffee*

☐ a) Can you hear the sound of a coffee percolator?

☐ b) Do you see a cup of frothy cappuccino?

☐ c) Or can you taste that distinct aroma as it's brewing and the feeling of holding the cup?

3. *How do you see yourself relaxing in a bath?*

☐ a) Do you immediately think of lying in a warm bath?

☐ b) Do you see a picture of a bath or imagine turning on the taps?

☐ c) Do you hear the water running into the bath and the sound of splashing?

4. *Picture a social event*

☐ a) Do you hear music?

☐ b) Do you imagine the surroundings, people?

☐ c) Do you feel the vibration of the music or the atmosphere?

5. *Think about eating out*

☐ a) Do you see your surroundings, the food and who you're with?

☐ b) Do you hear music and people's voices chattering?

☐ c) Do you smell/taste the food and how you feel being there?

6. *Think of a good friend*
- [ ] a) Do you hear the sound of their voice?
- [ ] b) Do you see an image of them or somewhere you were together?
- [ ] c) Are you reminded of how you feel when you are with them?

7. *Think of last Christmas*
- [ ] a) Can you smell food or are any emotions evoked about how you felt?
- [ ] b) Do you see your surroundings and who you were with?
- [ ] c) Do you hear any conversation or music in the background?

8. *Going shopping*
- [ ] a) Can you hear any background noise or conversations?
- [ ] b) Can you see what you are buying and who you are with?
- [ ] c) Do you get an immediate sense of the stress and hassle or whether you feel an adrenaline buzz?

9. *Think about your work*
- [ ] a) Do you instantly see the setting, sitting in front of your computer or being in an office?
- [ ] b) Do you get a feeling of how it makes you feel, depressed or happy?
- [ ] c) Can you hear the sounds of anything like the phone ringing, or people's voices?

10. *Last time you went on a first date*
- [ ] a) Do you instantly recall the conversation or background noises?
- [ ] b) Do you see the person you were with or where you were together?

☐   c)   Do you get a sense of any emotion, such as butterflies or dread? Perhaps it was happiness that it worked out or misery at the thought?

11. *A memory of going on holiday*
☐   a)   Do you picture a scene?
☐   b)   Do you feel any emotions?
☐   c)   Do you hear any sounds?

12. *Last time you had a quarrel with someone*
☐   a)   Do you recall any feelings?
☐   b)   Do you hear the conversation?
☐   c)   Do you picture the scene?

Scoring

	Visual	Auditory	Feelings		Visual	Auditory	Feelings
1.	a	b	c	**7.**	b	c	a
2.	b	a	c	**8.**	b	a	c
3.	b	c	a	**9.**	a	c	b
4.	b	a	c	**10.**	b	a	c
5.	a	b	c	**11.**	a	c	b
6.	b	a	c	**12.**	c	b	a

Now check the number of letters you ticked in each column. The highest score will be that of your dominant sense.

The visual type

Visual types think in terms of mental images and pictures. Visual people are easy to spot. They love aesthetics and beauty around them. They like things that look good and their conversation is scattered with words that describe something visually such as colour, hazy, see, focus. They may prefer going to the cinema or theatre than to a concert. For example, Carolyn is forty-three and runs an advertising agency in London. She is typically visual. She uses phrases like 'See you soon', 'That looks great', 'That's attractive' and 'I see what you mean'. Her own image is also of vital importance to her. A trip to the hairdresser's once a week to get her hair washed and blow-dried to perfection is imperative. She has even been known to pay over £100 for a loo seat, just because it looked good. She hates any kind of clutter and insists on excessive amounts of storage space to keep it at bay. She always notices details like your hair, fingernails and skin. And when she goes to a restaurant she prefers her food beautifully presented, nouvelle cuisine style.

Visual eye position

You can tell when the visual person is thinking or talking as their eyes often look up to the right or the left as they focus on a picture in their mind. If not they look straight ahead. Were you ever told in the classroom that you wouldn't find the answer written on the ceiling? Well, you probably could, as your eye movements reveal how you think in pictures.

Visual type physical signs

Predominantly visual types have a slim, tense body with hunched shoulders. Victoria (aka Posh Spice) and David Beckham are typical. They hold tension particularly in the shoulders and abdomen. They tend to breathe with shallow breaths high in the chest. Their skin colour is pale and their voice tends to be high-pitched with a nasal tone. They talk fast with quick bursts of words. They tend to point a finger or extend an arm in conversation.

The auditory type

Auditory people are less common. They think in terms of sounds, which could be noises, or conversation. They may put the stereo or television on as soon as they come in. Singing, dancing or physical activity to music appeal to them. Their conversation is scattered with hearing-type words such as rhythm, harmony, click, resonate. For example, Sandra, age thirty-eight, is a fitness instructor. She has music or the radio on all the time, whether in her car or as soon as she walks through her front door. She's always on her mobile phone and when listening to someone she often uses the phrase 'I hear you' and 'Sounds good'. She also loves writing poetry and reading it out loud. People often tell her that she loves the sound of her own voice. Socially she likes to eat out in loud, busy places where there's lots going on.

Auditory eye position
When the auditory type is thinking they tend to look sideways towards their ears, left or right.

Auditory type physical signs
Predominantly auditory types have a softer body than the thin visual types, and tend to fidget a lot and to lean back or forward rather than stand up straight. Robbie Williams is true of this type. They breathe evenly using the whole chest with a typical long exhale. They have more colour in their faces than pale visual types. They talk at an even pace and their voice tends to be clear, resonant and melodic. Their body

language shows them with their arms folded or in a telephone posture with their head tilted and their hand touching their mouth or chin.

The kinesthetic/feeling type

They think in sensual, emotive terms that include touch, taste and smell. Kinesthetic people tend to be more tactile and might like to dance because they 'feel' the vibration of the music, or have regular massages or other bodily treatment as they need to be reassured through touch. Or they do a lot of physical sport. Their conversation is scattered with words such as feel, sense, enjoy and touch. They could really enjoy eating a meal more than most because they find the texture and smell of food very pleasurable. For example, James is thirty years old and a journalist. He seems on first impression to be a visual person because of his profession and that he likes to dress smartly and has an eye for interior design. But when you listen to his language he is obviously predominantly kinesthetic. His conversation is scattered with feeling language such as 'That feels right' and 'We must keep in touch', 'With all my heart' and 'It was a pleasure to see you'. He moves sensually and loves nothing better than long, lingering dinner parties where he can take time to enjoy different food. He is notoriously untidy and tends to have things everywhere, which is typical of the kinesthetic type. His favourite pastime is going salsa dancing, which isn't just about dance, but sensual slow movements.

Kinesthetic/feeling eye position

When the kinesthetic type is thinking, their eyes are lowered as they draw on their feeling and emotion. Their teachers may have told them at school to look up when they are speaking or to look someone in the eye.

Kinesthetic/feeling type physical signs

Predominantly kinesthetic types have a full soft body with a tendency towards being overweight. Their shoulders tend to droop. Nigella Lawson is a true depiction of this type. Their breathing is deep, slow and low in the abdomen. They have more colour in their faces than the other two types. Their voice is breathy and soft with slower speech, which may have long pauses. Sometimes their voice may be low with a deep tonality. They move languorously and they may curl up or sprawl on a settee. Even sitting on a chair they might pull their legs up under them or have an arm across their stomach.

Once you have a fairly good idea what your predominant sense is you can start to strengthen the others. You may even have a second sense that is pretty well tuned, the third one being clearly the weakest. If, for example, you know you have a problem visualising, then start by simply focusing on objects.

Start with something simple like an apple.

If you have problems picturing it clearly then place an apple physically in front of you. Then close your eyes and visualise the colour. Is it red or green and what size is it? It might be hard at first but keep focusing on the outline and then fill in the colour. You could then think of a plate of lasagne. What does it look like in the dish? Can you visualise the colour of the cheese? Is it slightly browned on the top?

The same pictures can apply if you want to strengthen your feelings, which include taste and smell. Imagine tasting the apple. Is it crunchy or soft? Is it sweet or bitter? How are you feeling when you are eating? Happy or sad? And again with the lasagne. Get a sense of whether it is warm, having just come out of the oven.

And if it's hearing you want to improve imagine the crunch of the apple as you first bite into it. You can reproduce the sound of thunder or a police siren going by.

Whatever your weakest sense is you can keep improving it with different picture settings. Soon your mental dexterity will sharpen up. Although all three senses may not equalise, you will certainly find that they become well honed.

Exercises to engage the imagination

You are now going to put your senses to use in some visualising exercises to help strengthen your imagination and expand your mind energy.

Now you've identified your own most active 'sense', before you start on the exercises please remember these words: *'Don't worry.'* You do not have to get everything right. Just go with what works for you for now. As long as you get some sort of picture impression to begin with you *will* start strengthening and expanding your mind and releasing tension. The rest will come with time.

And do keep a sense of humour. In fact you should relax and enjoy the process. When embarking on psychic studies you must do the opposite from the norm. Trying too hard to achieve results is a complete turn-off to the higher mind. Have fun. This is about experimentation.

Remember, daydreaming, which we all do for short bursts every day, is a natural way of relaxing our minds and letting go of mental tension. You might have already discovered that it is often in this daydream state that new ideas and creative thoughts come to us, just as they do on the verge of sleep.

Setting the scene

First find a comfortable quiet spot where you can be alone. It might be lying on your bed, or – if you have a noisy family – some time in the bath with the door locked might be the best place. Take the phone off the hook and use the objects around you that help you to relax. You can light candles and incense and play background music. Then make sure you are comfortably warm as you concentrate on your breathing. All the exercises will make full use of all your senses and help you on to the launch pad for flight into your new inner world. But I have also added some stress-buster visualisations that will help you get rid of tension and still help to focus your mind.

If it is hard to recall what I've said from the written word, you can always record your voice reading the different exercises, so then you can relax and play it back. But if you do, remember to speak calmly and clearly, so that you don't hinder your own ability to concentrate.

Exercise one: a deep cleanse

Before you start on the other exercises, it would be a good idea to prepare by relaxing and getting rid of some of the mental and psychological junk that we carry around. Every day things happen to us that can make us tense, whether it's a row with a partner, problems at work, a traffic jam or just a well of deep-seated anxiety that colours the way we see things. This makes the mind energy funnel inwards and we start to feel tired and irritable. Actively using our imagination is a great way of relieving stress in our lives as well as expanding our mind energy.

49

Angela, age forty-eight, works in the antique business and found that visualising in a particular way helped with the stress of dealing with her work and her divorce – as well as making her more intuitively aware. She says that her imaginative travels are so important to her in life that they've probably made her the optimist she is today as they are such a relief for depression. She told me, 'When I get stressed I get digestive problems and feel sick. It makes it hard for me to get out of bed in the morning, because I feel so tired all the time. Particularly when I was getting divorced from my husband and moving house, I literally couldn't eat from nervous tension and became so thin my family were very concerned about me.'

She found out how to visualise through her local spiritualist church development circle nearly twenty years ago. She now finds a particular mental exercise helps to release stress. This one is a wonderful starting point, as it helps to wash away all the tension, anxiety or negativity that we accumulate throughout our lives, enabling you to feel rejuvenated and cleansed.

Imagine you are standing naked underneath a waterfall in a secluded woodland clearing. Visualise the top of your head opening up and the clean, spring water pouring in and running through your body, washing away any stress, physical tension and negative emotions. See all these negative energies as dirty water pouring through the soles of your feet and fingertips, with all the old tensions and thought forms going with it. Once all the dirty water has been washed away, imagine crystal-clear water filling you up and flowing over your head and all around your body, building up until it reaches your shoulders. This will make you feel clean and light and very refreshed as if you've been liberated from all your problems. Afterwards, picture yourself surrounded in a cloak of white light.

This is something that you can do easily whenever you feel

drained and need a mind-boosting tonic even if you are travelling on the Tube or train going home from work or after a business meeting. Or waiting for a delayed flight at the airport can provide a perfect opportunity to rid yourself of tiredness and irritability. It's also a very pleasant way of drifting off to sleep.

It will also help you to feel cleaner and lighter for other reasons apart from just thinking differently. The stress and tension that we hold on to accumulates in our auras and literally looks like dark negative energy. If left, this is what would turn into shoulder and neck pain or other physical conditions. Once you have cleared away the tension with a vision of clean water or white light, this cleanses this negative energy before it has a chance to take hold and affect you physically. You will be left feeling restored and healthier in mind and body.

Exercise two: rising above

To begin your foray into this new imaginary world, I would like you to jump right in at the deep end. I am using a scene that most people will feel relaxed with. But later on you can use other scenarios that you find pleasing such as a green meadow, or a beautiful forest clearing. Afterwards I will explain exactly what has happened to your mind energy.

Imagine you are walking down a winding path towards a warm, secluded beach. You can see the bright orange sun in the midst of a clear blue sky. Its golden rays shimmer on the sea and the beach seems to stretch for miles. As you step on to the sand it feels warm beneath your feet. It's totally peaceful apart from the sound of each wave breaking and you watch as one wave breaks on top of the other. There's a cool breeze and you take three deep breaths in. You can smell the salty water and taste the salt on your lips. As you sit down on the sand, you look up into the sky when you hear the noise of seagulls as they glide overhead. Then you notice the clouds floating across the deep blue colour that joins with the sea. Take a few minutes to watch the clouds and see the different shapes they make. Then focus on the waves slowly ebbing and flowing into the shore. Lie down on the sand and as you feel the warm sun on your skin, start to focus on your breath as you breathe in and out.

(If you continually relax into this vision, your mind energy will gradually expand outwards into the universe where it becomes more receptive to connecting up with a network of thought energies. It works a bit like finding the right frequency to link into a radio station. But this process is also a meditation which will bring about a sense of deep calm that allows us to be more in touch with our own inner voice.)

Imagine then that you suddenly feel the you lying on the beach rising above your body and heading towards the clouds in the sky, until you feel you are sitting on top of one and looking down at yourself. Your body lying on the beach seems so small from this distance. Take a minute to relax and look around at the panoramic view. You can see the beach, and the sea and cliffs surrounding the beach. Take in a deep breath of the salty air. When you are ready, imagine yourself back in your body lying on the beach, otherwise you may feel a little light-headed. As you slowly get up and walk back towards the rough pathway you feel a deep sense of peace. Take another deep breath before you open your eyes.

This visualisation alone has a powerful effect on our bodies. You are deeply relaxed, you have expanded your mind energy out into the universe and you have lifted your consciousness to a higher level. You should feel relaxed and calm. You will need to practise this many times. If you got fed up halfway through or felt you couldn't do it, keep persevering. Some people are naturals, but others find it a lot harder. The better you become at it, the more you reap the benefits.

Questions to ask yourself

1. Did you find it easy to visualise? If not, remember that it is just as important to get a sense or sound of the scene, even if you can't 'see' it clearly.
2. Did you find it easy to lift up into the sky? If you found it hard to rise up, then keep trying; you may feel nervous about letting go of being in control.

Exercise three: lift off

Imagine yourself walking through a field of daffodils. It is a spring afternoon and the sun is warm on your skin. But there is also a gentle breeze that makes you feel perfectly comfortable. You breathe in the light, sweet scent of the flowers and it makes you feel calm. There is no one else around. In the distance there is a boundary of beautiful trees and an attractive tall building of white stone. You walk towards it, seeing white marble steps that go up to an imposing door. You climb up the steps slowly feeling the marble beneath your feet. There are seven steps. One, take a deep breath, two, three, four, five, six and seven. As you get to the door, it swings open as if on command. Inside there is an ornate reception room and you look around at the winding staircase with engraved banister. The floor is covered in shining stone tiles that reflect the light. Then you stare at the walls of the building. You wonder what they are decorated with; and as you go nearer to look, you realise that they are studded with gems of all types, from rubies and sapphires to emeralds. In between there are tiny crystals. You are amazed by their iridescent colours. As you turn round you see an elevator. You feel drawn to walk over and press the button.

You notice there are eleven floors and you press the top floor, wanting to see the spectacular views from the roof. As you go into the lift, it wobbles a little and then you feel yourself rise to the next floor, one, two; you feel the lift gently move, three, four, and you feel yourself becoming lighter and lighter, five, six, seven; lighter still and very calm, eight, nine, ten and eleven. When you get to the top the doors open and you walk out on to the roof where there is a stunning panoramic view. You look down over the edge of a small wall and from this distance the field of daffodils becomes a golden glow. You seem much further away than you thought and the azure blue of the sky seems to surround you. You sit on the rooftop and feel at peace with the surrounding beauty. Take a minute to focus on the landscape.

You take three deep breaths before you enter the lift and slowly go back down the ten floors, ten, nine, eight, seven, six, five, four, three, two, one. You go back into the reception room and down the seven steps outside the front door: seven, six, five, four, three, two, one. You are now back in the field of daffodils. Feel yourself back in your body where you are lying in your room. You have once again expanded your mind energy and you should feel lighter and more relaxed.

Healing colours for your visual technique

Using colour in your visualisations is essential for strengthening your higher mind energy, so it is important to practise reproducing different colours in your mental scenarios. The more you can picture certain shades in your imaginary scenes, the more vividly realistic your visualisations will become. This means your receptive mind will get a full exercise work-out, as it were, and expand and strengthen more effectively. And of course, this will enhance your psychic abilities.

Colour is so essential to our imaginative exercises that you can also discover which hue you can use in your visualisations to change your present mood. Using your imagination in this way can have tremendous restorative effects to your sense of wellbeing. Different colours can have a peaceful or invigorating effect depending on the tone and how they're used. For example, red can stir up the emotions, while blue cools and calms us down.

Consequently, colour can give an essential boost to our health. Even hospitals have come to realise this, using shades of blue and green to create a peaceful environment or reds and oranges to cheer patients up. Some colours have even been proven to help reduce blood pressure by their calming effects.

Most of us are instinctively drawn to certain colours when we decorate our homes. Even when a shade is used because it seems to be merely fashionable, we still choose it because we like it on a psychological level. But it isn't always for the right reasons. Sometimes the colour is a reflection of our state of mind, which could be one of depression or anxiety. And while it mirrors how we are feeling, it can't actually help alter our mindset for the better.

When I moved into my house in Bath and all the previous occupant's furniture was removed, I was horrified to see that every room was painted a hideous shade of muddy brown, with a mix of khaki green thrown in for good measure. Somehow their plants and pictures had masked the surroundings before. I couldn't bear to live in the house until it was repainted. It made me feel quite ill. Fortunately, when contracts were exchanged I was still renting my old flat, so I immediately hired a decorator. Within three days he had completely transformed the walls and the feel of the house with the shades I had chosen. What a difference the sky blue of one of the spare bedrooms made when you walked in compared to its previous oppressive colour.

If this can happen by merely changing a shade in our physical life, then imagine how invigorating it can be for our mind energy if we picture certain colourful scenes. I know that when I feel stressed out, imagining a beautiful blue sky over a sparkling sapphire sea will help calm me down – even if it's pouring with rain outside. And if you want to be re-energised, or feel more optimistic, you know you can look at your own inner film show of a field of daffodils or a garden of brightly coloured flowers in pinks and yellows, even if you are forced to live with an unpleasant colour scheme.

Do remember that all colours used in your mental imagery will help strengthen and develop the right side of your mind. And the more and varied they are the better. Along with reproducing your senses, your mind will start working in 3-D technicolour and you will really start to fly far into the realms of the higher mind. So if you want to understand more about what each shade can do to produce beneficial effects on your mind and body when you visualise, then look at the colour chart in the box below.

Colour chart

Red	A colour to be careful with. Makes you feel energised, but can make you feel too aggressive. Helps the circulation.
Rose pink	Very good for using when you want to visualise loving energy. Around you or a partner or when you want to give compassion.
Orange	Stimulating and energising, particularly when you feel sluggish or poorly. Particularly good for enhancing your sexual energy.
Yellow	Very uplifting. Can help lift depression and feeling the

---

	lack of sunshine. Yellow concentrates the mind, particularly for studying.
Green	Calming, balancing and peaceful. Very good for healing, particularly areas of the heart. It is good for nurturing people.
Blue	Calming and cooling. Very good for when you want to communicate succinctly and clearly; and also for depression.
Brown	Can be very grounding if you feel light-headed, but too much can make you feel morose.
Purple	Gives a sense of spiritual power and increases leadership abilities.
Gold	Brings a sense of understanding as it enhances the higher mind.

See yourself as the artist of your internal pictures. With your mental paint pallet you can re-energise yourself if you are feeling sluggish or calm yourself down if you feel stressed or angry.

But if you associate a certain colour with a painful experience, it would be wise not to use it in your visualisations. Otherwise your mental link may undermine the benefits that you want to produce.

The history and science of colour healing

The effect of colour is nothing new. The ancient Egyptians were great believers in the powers of the mind and knew about the healing benefits of colour. In their sacred temples, such as at Karnak and Thebes, there were colour halls solely used for research into its use.

So why does colour have the power to influence us? Just as sound is made up of a vibrational wave, so is colour. Both have a frequency of vibration. But sound and coloured light are very different. Sound is a longitudinal compression wave that needs a material substance like the air or the wall of your house to be transmitted. Coloured light, however, is an electromagnetic wave that can exist even in a vacuum and its frequencies can travel anywhere, even into outer space. In simple terms, that means coloured light has no barriers to its effect upon us and it can be used in many ways.

It was a Hindu scientist, D.P. Ghadiali, who discovered the scientific principles of the therapeutic effects of coloured rays on people's health. After years of research, in 1933 Ghadiali published *The Spectro Chromemetry Encyclopaedia*, a masterwork on colour therapy, which has become the basis for chromotherapy (colour healing). He taught in the US, developing many types of coloured lamps. He showed that colours had different effects on various parts of the body. He found that if he directed the red ray of colour at a person it could actually stimulate their liver, while the violet ray stimulates the spleen. The green ray was found to be a balancer that could encourage the activity of the pituitary gland, known as the master gland, which could affect every part of the body.

Transform your mood with a colour meditation

In the last chapter we talked about the aura and how we pick up information psychically from these fields. The seven levels of our energy field also interlink and are connected to our physical body at our seven chakras located in the spine. Chakra is Sanskrit for 'wheel'. They are power centres, which look like whirling lotus petals or vortices.

Just like the levels of the aura, the chakras start with a base power centre, and end with the crown centre. Each one relates to the physical (first auric level) through to the higher mind (seventh auric level). Each of our chakras attracts a colour ray essential for our health (see box below). Too little or too much colour shows we are out of balance and the energy wheels do not spin correctly. But with the power of our minds we can give our chakras the colour they need to re-energise and keep them spinning effectively. The more balanced our chakras are, the healthier and more stable we feel on all levels, which again helps us to strengthen our intuitive powers.

Our chakra energy points

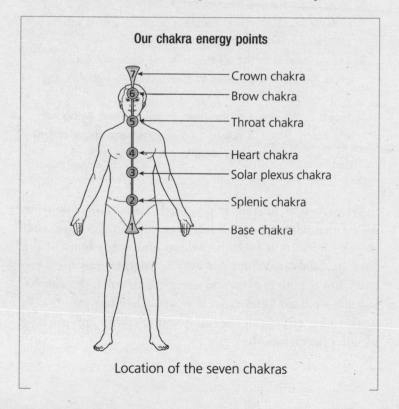

- Crown chakra
- Brow chakra
- Throat chakra
- Heart chakra
- Solar plexus chakra
- Splenic chakra
- Base chakra

Location of the seven chakras

1. **Red**: the lowest centre in the base of the spine. It relates to our physical body.
2. **Orange**: in the small of the back, to the left-hand side of the spine. It relates to our vitality and sexuality.
3. **Yellow**: in the middle of the back (solar plexus area). It relates to our emotions and lower mind.
4. **Green**: located between the shoulder blades in line with the heart. It governs the higher mind but also influences emotions such as compassion, unconditional love, sympathy and empathy.
5. **Blue**: located at the base of the skull (throat centre). It governs communication and speaking our truth, saying what we really feel as well as our intuitive instincts.
6. **Indigo**: located in the forehead, in the centre of your brow (third eye centre). It relates to clairvoyance, spiritual intuition and healing.
7. **Violet**: in the dome of the head (crown centre). Along with the indigo centre, it relates to the higher aspirations of the soul: spiritual truths and enlightenment.

When colour healing is practised, clairvoyant vision has shown that where the aura has been drooping or dull, after colour breathing it looks revitalised and the colours in the aura are brighter. When our aura is brighter, our life force flows through our chakras and energy fields and helps dissolve any stress-related blockages. This will allow our intuition to work more effectively because our chakras are working together harmoniously.

Meditation on colour breathing to rebalance your energy

The following meditation will help rebalance your energy and is based on the colours of the chakra points along the spine up to the dome of the head. It may help you to find those colours in the form of crayons or felt tips so you can memorise them better.

When you are relaxed begin by visualising the base chakra colour red. Think of a scarlet red for the right shade and imagine breathing this colour up through the soles of your feet and picture it moving through your body. Imagine it entering your knees, arms and chest and into your head. Hold your breath for a few seconds and then slowly breathe out, and the red colour is then exhaled.

Then visualise the colour orange. Think of the orange fruit for the right shade and again visualise breathing this through your feet and see it washing through your body, into your lower back, stomach and chest and into your head. Again, after a few seconds, slowly breathe out. Don't be concerned if you can't imagine any of these colours leaving your body when you breathe out. It may be that you need this colour for different areas of the body.

Next visualise the colour yellow. Imagine a bright yellow like the skin of a lemon. Breathe in through the soles of your feet and visualise the colour going through your body. Hold your breath for a few seconds and breathe out.

Then visualise the colour of a grass green. This time visualise breathing it from above your stomach (your solar plexus area). Breathe it into your stomach and then slowly imagine it going both ways, up into your chest and head and down into your legs. You may need to practise doing this a few times. Then slowly breathe out.

This time you need to breathe in the colour blue. Imagine this flowing down from above, entering your head and pouring down into your body. You feel it spreading into your arms, hands, fingers, and down though your legs. Then breathe out.

Next see the colour indigo; imagine a blue-black sky at night for this. Feel it enter from above your head and wash down through you. Finally visualise the colour violet. Again picture it entering from the top of your head and down into your chest and legs. Hold your breath for a few seconds and breathe out.

Lie quietly for a few minutes, feeling the effects that these colours have had on you. Then breathe in and visualise a clear beam of white light from above your head going down through your crown and flowing down the centre of your being and through your feet. This white light will help you to feel grounded again.

Find the colour you need right now

This is an exercise to find a colour that will help you to feel more balanced about a situation in your life. This colour will have the right vibration that you need at the moment. It may be that you are tired or stressed. Perhaps you have high levels of anxiety and find it hard to sleep at night. Obviously the more you are tired and stressed, the less able you will be to relax and tap in to your intuition. The more positive and relaxed you feel, the easier it will be.

With this visualisation I want you to focus on the problem you have in your mind and ask which colour will help you. Write down your question on a piece of paper and put it next to you. For example, I have split from my boyfriend and I'm heartbroken. Which colour will help me to feel better? Or I am tired and need more energy. Which colour will energise me?

There are seven colours that are helpful. Imagine them now: red, orange, yellow, green, blue, indigo and violet. Hold each colour in your mind, starting with the red; close your eyes and imagine it surrounding you. Get a sense of how you feel as the red floats across your chest and over your shoulders. It's as if the colour is wrapping itself around you until your body is immersed in it. Then move on to the orange colour and picture the same things. You are looking for a good feeling or sensation. Continue with yellow, green, blue, indigo and violet. Then start to bring in all the other shades, so you have seven floating and swirling around you. There will be one that you are most drawn to. Feel that colour stay with you. From this visualisation you will have discovered which colour you need to comfort and bring you into harmony with that particular problem. Keep imagining it washing over you for the next few minutes.

You could wear something in that colour. Even if it's a scarf or underwear! Other people don't have to see it for you to absorb its positive vibrations.

You have focused on making all your senses real with feeling, hearing and sight, and brought colour more vividly into your pictures. Your mind energy has really been doing some mental gymnastics. Now that you have expanded and awakened your higher mind using all aspects of these imaginary tools, you will start to feel the effects. You may feel different in some way, perhaps with a sense of lightness. But let me assure you, you will be recharged and on your way into the higher realms feeling relaxed and energised. If you don't feel like this, then you might be trying too hard. Go back to the beginning of this chapter and try again. Have fun this time. There is no point in moving on if you are uptight and tense. The exercises *will* work for you, if you enjoy the process. When you are relaxed you will be ready to learn how to focus.

4

Discover Mind-Focusing Techniques
and Arm Yourself with Psychic Protection

It's all right letting yourself go, as long as you can get yourself back.
Mick Jagger, 1943–, British rock musician

Now it is time to prepare the ground for the next stage of development. Imagine you are setting out on a new voyage. You want to make sure that you've got your compass, otherwise you won't be able to find the way to your destination, but you also want to arm yourself with some protective clothing and special ammunition in case you come across any unfriendly natives. Well, this journey is no different.

You are becoming an intrepid explorer of the higher realms and on these planes you may encounter distracting or annoying negative forces that you will want to ward off. Feeling protected is about how strong our boundaries are and how safe we feel within ourselves. If you feel safe and secure, then you will be. I have included some visualisations in this chapter that will give you all the ammunition you need.

But first I'm going to introduce the methods that will quieten your mind enough to allow your intuition to come through: a 'sneaky' navigation kit to give you a focus point. I say 'sneaky' because the mind is a very tricky customer. It needs discipline, otherwise it will take control by bombarding us with thoughts. Just like an unruly child that runs wild, if it thinks it has to behave you can guarantee it will do the opposite. So we need to capture its attention and make it interested enough to settle down and become a little more still. This is where the navigation kit will help it refocus.

Think of yourself as a mental magician. You will entertain your mind by giving it a diversion, and as you do so, your psychic powers – already enlivened by your visualisations – can start to do their work. When you are fully developed as a psychic with confidence in your abilities you do not need any 'tools' to be able to 'read' a person or a situation. Information will just flow. Some psychics or tarot readers, however, don't ever develop themselves enough and grow increasingly reliant on the tools they are using rather than their own capable intuition.

So what are these tools or 'mind distracters' as I like to think of them? What's important is to be aware that everything we touch carries with it the vibrations of who we are. When we concentrate on something, whether it be a piece of jewellery that someone has worn, a photograph or the powerful sound of a mantra, what we are doing is simply focusing our mind, slowing it down so that we can really listen to our intuitive feeling within.

And for anyone who thinks that these different methods are a waste of time, do remember that each technique I have given you is the equivalent of a mental keep-fit session at the gym. They will keep your mind flexible and open to exploration. By using these tools your intuitive powers will grow and you will be in a much stronger position to activate your psychic abilities in all aspects of your daily life.

Psychometry: the hidden history of objects

Psychometry is one of the quickest and easiest methods I know for any budding psychic to tap into their psychic powers. Most people get results this way and it will help to build your confidence and allow information to flow easily.

Psychometry means using an object to reveal information about the past, present and future, either about the person to whom the object belongs or the history of its previous owners. It could be an old family heirloom, such as a ring, a bracelet or a watch. All objects are porous. And every emotion or thought we have is energy that is absorbed by the object, leaving a lasting impression. The stronger the emotions and strength of character of the owner the stronger the impressions that are left. This can help establish a stronger link with the person by boosting our intuitive feedback.

Why houses tell us a story

We can also use psychometry in a building. That's often why so many of us can walk into a house and feel uneasy or just 'love it' straight away. The vibrations that we feel are the true 'history' of a property and we are picking up on the effects left by the previous occupants. This can have devastating consequences if there has been a past of problems to do with relationships or bad business luck. The sense of emotional loss, stress, anger or melancholy is not only felt in the building, but can end up affecting the new owners. The walls of houses really do have ears and by just standing in a room you can feel its energy.

I've heard several stories of people who have bought a house only to find their marriage has split up months later. It could have been a coincidence, but one newly divorced man told me that he was amazed when he discovered the previous two couples had ended their marriages while living in the house that he and his ex-wife had bought. He told me his ex-wife said to him a few times, 'If it wasn't for that house, I'm sure we would still be together.' It could be an easy excuse, but if there is a restless or 'angry' energy that has been absorbed into the walls by previous occupants, you could find that it breaks an already weak link.

I personally believe that when looking for a house on the market, it's wise to check out the emotional history of the place, if you can. It could end up being more important to your health and wellbeing than a structural survey!

How to practise psychometry

It is important to start with someone you don't know well, so that you have no assumptions about them. The more you can free your mind the better your intuition can work. An old heirloom could be a good item. But someone needs to know the previous owner's character to be able to tell you whether you are picking up accurately on their great-grandmother or aunt. Even if it is, for example, a watch someone wears all the time, try to make sure it has not been worn by anyone else since, otherwise you may get conflicting messages. If her great-aunt was a hard-nosed, irritable spinster, these stored emotions would spill over into the current owner's feelings. Especially if they are easy-going and relaxed, the stronger past emotion may override everything and you may give a reading for the dead person! The same thing would happen if the watch or jewellery were second-hand. You could possibly get conflicting information.

Initially just get a feel of the item in your hand. Feel the shape of it and get a sense of whether it is warm or cold. Does it feel heavy or light? Try to get a sense of the energy that is emanating from it. How is it making you feel? Are you feeling tired, irritable or happy? You may start seeing pictures, or get a sense about something. With experience you will soon start to know whether something relates to the present, the past or the future. Allow any information that comes into your head to flow without being self-critical. It could even be a sense of unhappiness or a feeling of neck pain. Often you pick up a pain in your body from the object if the person suffers from a bad back, for example. Keep practising and you will get better.

Scrying

Scrying is perceived as one of the oldest clichés of the typical clairvoyant gypsy woman as she peers into her crystal ball. It is the act of looking into a reflective surface, whether a mirror, a crystal ball or water, and seeing the images either on the shining surface or in your mind's eye. Some psychics like to make a big deal about their apparatus, making their altars and tables look mysterious. And, of course, in some cases objects can be made more powerful. If we place a sacred importance on the crystal ball or mirror, for example, we imbue it with energy. And that energy will be felt as a concentrated healing vibration for anyone who comes into contact with it. But it still won't do the clairvoyance for you; it can only help focus the mind more readily, as it acts as a subconscious anchor to relax your mind, so that intuition flows easily.

It's important to remember that anything we value highly and place a sacred significance on, such as a cross on a necklace, a ring, a statue of Buddha or other teacher, will hold that focused energy, and give off a higher vibration that can help us to lift our frequencies. The object can also change and charge the vibration of a room, which is helpful if you want to use a particular room for meditation or visualisations. The heightened vibration that the object gives off will quicken your own psychic awareness by raising your frequencies even more speedily.

How to practise scrying

Create the right environment by first lighting some candles and incense. Sit in front of a mirror and start to focus on the image of yourself. Look at your features and hair, and the clothes you are wearing and now close your eyes. Try to recreate yourself in your mind's eye. Ask yourself a question about a problem you might have and see if you can notice an image in the mirror or in your mind's eye. If it isn't reflected in the mirror it doesn't matter, the mirror is merely a focus point. Keep asking different questions and see what pictures appear. You can also try this same exercise with a bowl of water or a crystal ball. Keep looking at the reflective surface, focusing, but with a relaxed mind and see if images appear on the surface or in your mind's eye.

'Seeing' into photographs

I was once shown a picture of someone's boyfriend whom I'd never met and immediately knew that he was a chef and that he travelled a lot. Both were true. He worked as a chef in between his travels. There is the old saying that a camera steals your soul. Well, it's true in a sense. Even if the person is a stranger, their picture holds some of their energy, and you can discover as much information about them as if they were in the room.

How to read photographs

Start by focusing on the image and allow yourself to look around the outline of the person and into the background of the image. Don't get taken in by whether they look affluent or scruffy or whether they seem happy-go-lucky or sad. Assumptions get you nowhere in this life, especially on a psychic level. Get a sense of any light or dark areas that you might notice. The more you look at their face, the more you may see their expression change. What do you feel about them? It may be that you are picking up on how they felt at that time. But you can go beyond that to how they are feeling now. Ask yourself the question, 'How does this person feel?' Do you get a picture in your mind or a sense of something? Maybe you heard a word or a phrase. Relay what you sensed to the person who gave you the picture to see whether it's true. There's no point in picking up information about someone that no one can verify.

Crumpled paper

This is another one of the different ways we can tune in. Amazingly, if we ask someone to scrunch up a piece of plain paper, we can pick up information about them from it. Yes, you may think I'm mad, but it is true. Everything that someone touches holds their vibration and we can read images from the creases the paper has made.

When I first did this exercise, I thought it was nonsense. But when I was given the crumpled paper from my old pal Sandra, who I developed my skills with, I was sure from the shadowy creases that I saw her at a party. Somehow all the different folds seemed to create an impression that she was dressed up to the nines, wildly socialising with crowds of people. There was a particular person there whom she seemed to be keen on. When I told her, she said that she had been to a ball a few days ago and that she was with a new boyfriend. She was amazed and so was I. As I focused more, I got a feeling that he was going to propose to her. Three months later he did!

The different ways of focusing are all vehicles for your own intuition to come through. What you see are not the actual creased pictures themselves, but what your mind interprets and sees into them.

How to read crumpled paper

Get the person to scrunch up the paper for a few minutes keeping their mind blank. Then gently unfold the paper and look at the different creases and shadows that have been created.

Look into the different impressions. Can you see any images? It may be that something looks like a bird or a star, for example. If you can't work them out, give the person the information anyway. They may understand the significance. And ask yourself inwardly what those signs mean to you: they could be symbolic.

Now we shall move on to another way of focusing the mind and providing yourself with spiritual and psychic protection.

Mantras

A mantra is one of the most effective ways of quieting our mind and allowing us to feel spiritually protected. We all know how effective music can be in making us feel better.

Where would we be without it? There are times when I have been upset about something, and a certain melody is the only thing that will help me to feel calm.

Music is vibration and plays a very important role in healing. A mantra works in just the same way, but much more potently. The word mantra is derived from the sanskrit *man*, which means 'thought' and *tra*, indicating protection. And it does just that.

It is a way of stilling the mind and altering your state of being. By chanting a particular word or phrase, or humming, the sound resonates and makes a vibration, and this transforms negative energy into positive and awakens creative psychic powers. Even listening to chanting on a tape can alter our state of consciousness.

Jenny's story

Jenny, thirty-seven, was a prison officer. She chanted her own Buddhist mantra for half an hour every day. Even though she was new to it, she found that once she concentrated solely on the sounds she was saying, she became more aware of her inner self. She felt the pounding of her heartbeat and each breath as she breathed in and out. At times she also became aware of a subtler feeling underlying each breath and a sense of complete timelessness and of being totally in the 'now'. She began to feel an energy flow into her that literally seemed to wake her up inside. It was as if she felt on a high. It helped her mind to become clearer and she seemed suddenly to have a sixth sense about things; often she would be able to pick up on people's thoughts and at one time rang up a friend to ask if she was all right when coincidentally her friend had just heard the news that a relative had died. Jenny was able to give her some support when she needed it most. Previously she had been too tied up in her own problems to pick up on anything and would never have considered that she had a psychic bone in her body.

The other benefit she noticed was something she didn't expect. She lives in a particularly rough area of south-east London and often felt uneasy walking home at night. One wintry evening she went out for a takeaway, and was approached by a drunken tramp. But instead of her normal reaction of frozen fear that made her bristle, she suddenly sensed that her body was behaving differently. The typical increased pulse rate, pumping heartbeat and rush of adrenaline that she would normally feel if she was approached by someone on a dark night, was replaced by a serene inner confidence, and she felt completely unafraid. Because she was calmer, she noticed that the tramp was staggering along the road harmlessly, on a completely different planet and hadn't really registered her properly. He would do more harm to himself.

She came to realise that she had a tremendous feeling of empowerment and protection after her mantra sessions. It wasn't that she was blocking out danger signs, but more that she felt an aura of invincibility around her and that no one could harm her. And from the changes in her energy field that is exactly what happened.

When you chant, the vibration of the noise is picked up by the ear and is sent via the brain through the central nervous system. Through sound vibration a mantra can alter your state of being, give you a sense of psychic protection and take you beyond your mind to a deep stillness within. The sound that you chant is so powerful that it changes your auric field and brings you into an altered state of consciousness. It sends you into the orbit of your higher mind, ready to listen to your deeper intuitive self.

Jenny's story makes total sense even on a physiological level. Research has shown that vulnerable body language in the way we walk gives off a 'victim' vibe and is more likely to attract violence or harm. A mantra can centre you, meaning that you become composed and alert, so that you can take control of a situation rather than just reacting to it. And with a strong, vibrant spirit exuding power and inner strength how could someone even dare to approach you?

A mantra can produce a wonderful feeling, and it will be unique to you. You may feel energised, calm or have a feeling of being on a high. You may also feel weepy and emotional afterwards. But this is the effect of healing as you let go of any negative energies. A mantra can take you to deeper parts of yourself if you allow yourself to let go. I have at times had a strong sense of overflowing love in my heart chakra that can feel like a circular feeling of blissful loving energy. Then there is the exquisite aroma of what I can only describe as a divine heady scent of flowers like gardenias, or roses. It is the presence of higher energies. We can even experience the ultimate liberation and feel as if we are flying inside our own universe. It is this state of divine ecstasy that the great masters have talked about throughout the centuries. The simple message is always the same: that all the answers we need exist within us.

How to begin chanting mantras

Do not compare your experience to anyone else's. Do not worry that you don't feel anything afterwards. It will still help you. You may struggle to concentrate your mind at first, but you don't even have to chant in tune. It is the constant repetition of the word or sound that intensifies the vibration it creates. Even if you start with just ten minutes, you can always build up to more time with practice. The more you focus, the more you can become lost in the sound and reap the benefits.

Before you start make sure you are comfortable, take it

slowly and take three deep breaths. Do not push yourself if you get out of breath. There are many mantras to try; below I have listed some words and phrases to give you a start, but there may be others that you feel more comfortable with.

HU   is an ancient word for God. It will help to calm you and help you remain receptive. Start by chanting HUUU, pacing yourself and taking breaths in between. Try this for ten minutes at first.

I AM   is a very strong, powerful phrase that immediately helps to centre you.

OM   this tried and tested ancient sound is easy to chant.

The science of sound

Swiss scientist Dr Hans Jening investigated the powerful vibrations sound produces in his book, *Cymatics*, exploring the nature of sound frequency. Over the past ten years he discovered that when he placed fine grains of sand on to a metal plate and then sent an unbroken sound frequency through the plate, the sand would form specific patterns. When he changed the pitch and tone of the sound, he got a different pattern. Then when he repeated the first sound, he got the original pattern back again.

Dr Guy Manners, a British osteopath based in Worcestershire, teamed up with Dr Jening to try to create three-dimensional forms from sound. They found that when they tried five sound frequencies simultaneously, the fine grains of sand on the metal plate took on a three-dimensional form. Since then, after twenty years of research, Dr Manners has discovered how sound is instrumental in healing the body. He found that a certain sound-tone combination could help the function of each organ in the body. Each organ vibrates to its own frequency, which can be altered by the application of sound waves. He has invented a machine called the Cymatics Instrument to reproduce these sound frequencies in clinical practice. It involves a hand-held instrument, which produces sound vibration on to the part of the body needing treatment. This helps to bring about healing by altering the cells, organs or parts of the body on an energy level. The machine is now used all over the world.

Why protect yourself psychically?

If we are very open and sensitive in our everyday life, we are bound to be taken advantage of. The same is true of psychic levels. As we become more psychically sensitive we naturally fall prey to other energies and spirits. Nothing bad will happen to you. The way in which I teach psychic development incorporates higher energies that provide protection. But in the same way as you can hear a tramp calling out an obscenity or pestering you on the street, the same thing can happen with a spirit. It is important therefore to have strength of mind. If you feel weak-minded and find it hard to say no to people, then you will need to feel safer within yourself. If you are as definite as I am, and hear an occasional negative word or phrase from a spirit, you simply say 'Get lost' or if you're more polite a firm 'Go away' as you would to anyone who hassled you (if you've any sense) in the physical world.

A cautionary tale

Whenever you begin psychic work please ensure that you

never drink or take any drugs beforehand – that includes the now legally friendly marijuana. You do not need anything to help you relax. What you do need more than anything is clarity. When you begin working with the higher energies, if you are clouded or muddled with chemical substances you may attract negative energy to you.

To illustrate this here is the story of a pleasant lady in her forties I met at a psychic circle. I always sensed she was a little melancholy, but it was difficult to tell too much, because she was always sozzled. In fact she confessed that she would have three or four glasses of wine before attending just to help her unwind after work. And that was added on to a somewhat boozy lunch and then drinks before bedtime.

Her behaviour might sound excessive, but you might think that a few drinks to calm you down before developing yourself is a good idea. Perhaps you think it might help you on your way to releasing tension. **Wrong**. Nothing could be worse. Chemical substances do not mix well with developing your higher mind. Drugs, it is true, can open a doorway to the higher realms, but this is done through force when the person is not ready. And the results are often a little scary. Positive spiritual and psychic experiences happen when we have earned it, through proper development done in the right way.

This particular lady told me after several weeks that she was haunted by ugly gargoyle-type faces that kept coming to her at night, and often heard voices shouting swear words at her. She did worry about it, but only a little, because with several glasses of wine inside her, her own judgement and senses were impaired and it was hard for her to see sense. As she was numbing and sedating herself with alcohol, the weird visions could even have been self-induced. She could also have been attracting energy and 'spirits' of a lower level. We all exist on different levels and know when we have met someone who's a bit coarse or ignorant. It's the same in the spirit world. Remember the principle of like attracting like, and draw only positive clear mind energy to you. You want positive forces joining to help you, not unpleasant ones that will only hinder and upset you.

In fact, once you start to facilitate your psychic energy by visualising and focusing your mind, using mantras and other techniques, you will find you have a natural 'high' and feel energised and relaxed.

Visualisation for protection

Now you are going to do a visualisation that will help you feel more psychically protected. In this mental scene there will be steps down into a cave. This is a form of self-hypnosis, which will help you to relax and take you into your subconscious mind. You are totally in control at all times.

Visualise yourself walking through a forest. It is a warm summer evening and there is a wide, clear pathway through the many varieties of trees. You can hear the crunch of twigs under your feet, it smells a little damp, but the air is fresh and crisp. You walk through listening to the sounds of the birds and rustling of the leaves and branches of the trees. As you stroll along the path you see a squirrel eating some nuts by a tree. You notice its huge eyes and fluffy tail. It runs ahead and you follow as it leads you to a clearing.

You notice there are old stone steps going down and you feel curious as to where they lead. There are ten steps and as you walk down you feel the worn and rough stone underneath your feet. Start with ten, nine, taking each step slowly; eight, seven, six, you feel relaxed and calm; five, four, calmer and calmer; three, two, one. You step into a cave-like room that has a light shining down that illuminates strange etchings on the walls, which, as you move closer you can see are pictures of animals carved into the stone. As you study them in detail, you notice some of them are bears, wolves, tigers and deer. There are many more, even pictures of eagles. As you turn around you see a door with light pouring through it. You decide to open it and you can see the room beyond lit up as if bathed in light. You stand in this white light that makes you feel at ease and cleansed. Take a deep breath and relax. You notice another long winding corridor that as you follow it leads to another cave-like room.

You enter a room full of large crystals of different shapes, sizes and colours. Take a good look around you. Now visualise yourself shrinking and entering into the crystal that you feel most comfortable with. Feel yourself inside it looking out. What is the crystal shaped like? Does it have lots of facets and points or is it smooth? Is it clear or cloudy? Has it been polished and shiny or is it still in its natural state? Can you see any images through its walls that relate to you?

Get a sense of what you feel like inside there. Do you feel comfortable or hemmed in? Stay there for a few minutes while you adjust.

Then feel yourself outside the crystal again, feeling light and relaxed. As you walk towards the opening and back down the long winding corridor you return to the room filled with light and then into the cave with the walls of carved animals.

Begin to climb up the ten stairs, starting with one, feeling your feet firmly on the stone. Pause in between each number: two, three, four, pause a little longer and continue with five, feeling alert, six, seven, eight, nine and ten. As you get to the opening at the top of the stairs take a deep breath of fresh air and look around. Then you hear the sound of something moving in the trees, but you feel perfectly safe.

Just as you begin to make your way back along the winding path through the forest, an animal slowly walks up to you. You are not scared, it is friendly and you sense a kinship with it. Make a note of what this animal is. It could be small or large. Look at the expression on its face. Is it friendly or stern? However it appears, this is your power animal. And it walks with you until you reach the edge of the forest. It is an ancient shamanic symbol and its essence and strength will remain with you, even if you are not aware of it in the future, to help you feel protected and secure as you develop your psychic skills.

Know that you can call on your power animal for help at any time.

Questions to ask yourself

1. What was your animal, its size, colour and shape?
2. Did you feel comfortable with it? If not, don't worry. This animal is a powerful symbol from your subconscious that can help you accept your inner strength and boundaries. You may feel nervous about discovering another aspect of yourself. It may take time for you to get used to it.
3. How did you feel under the white light?
4. What was your crystal like, its colour, shape and spheres? Was it faceted and polished or in its natural state?

This crystal represents the development of your soul consciousness. The clearer and brighter it was, the more advanced your mind energy. The more unusually shaped, the more your mind thinks in unusual ways. Even if the crystal was still in its natural form, it is part of your advancement and is not judgemental. It could mean you have simplicity and directness. If there are any black or negative areas in the crystal make a note and get a sense of where they represent negative mental thoughts or repressed emotions that you carry. But do not judge yourself. This visualisation is a way of getting your subconscious mind to reveal more to you and to provide you with a sense of protection. You can try this exercise again at the end of this book and see if your crystal has changed.

Closing down

This short exercise can be very helpful if you are left light-headed after any psychic work. As you are working with higher vibrations, it can help you to feel more grounded.

Just visualise a white light going through the top of your head and imagine it flowing down the centre of your being, and down into the core of the earth. Then you can visualise that your feet have roots, like those of trees reaching deep into the ground. Afterwards picture a cloak of white light immersing you. This will make you feel grounded and protected.

The mirror and egg protection

Just as we often need to strengthen our immune system to help us resist any viruses or infection, we also at times need to strengthen our energy systems against any negative thoughts or feelings whether they are coming from an angry person or a bad atmosphere in a building. If you ever feel a little bit weak or overly sensitive, you might like to try these two alter native exercises whenever you need. They will strengthen your boundaries and make you feel stronger.

1. Visualise yourself surrounded by a reflective mirror. Any negative energy, like aggression, gossip or bad feelings, that you sense is being directed at you will simply bounce off and be reflected back at the person concerned.

2. Picture a solid egg. It has a door in it. When you are inside you notice the walls are padded and you are cosy and comfortable. You can then imagine the walls of the egg and the door becoming rock hard, so you feel completely safe. This is good for anyone who is in the caring professions. It will help you with any draining people who constantly hassle you with problems. Once you feel stronger in your everyday life, you will be stronger in your psychic work.

Positive intent is good enough protection

Do the protective exercises to feel better if you want to. But try not to get caught up in worrying too much about protection, otherwise you will block your psychic energy. The best protective device I know is intention. If our intentions are good before we 'read' for someone or for ourselves, that intention is positive energy that we are sending out – and it will naturally bounce back to us. As I lift my vibration up, I usually say, 'To my guides and helpers in spirit, please help me with love and protection to have access to all the information I need.'

Physical exercise will tone your psychic muscle

When I first started developing myself, my psychic awareness evolved quickly for many reasons. First I was open-minded, second I visualised as often as I could and third I practised using many of the navigator tools above regularly two evenings a week after work. During the readings on willing 'guinea-pigs', I mainly used psychometry to give me an extra boost as I sat in front of them. These were people I'd never previously met. They would simply reply yes or no to what I told them and I would receive feedback the next day on whether I was correct. Ninety-five per cent of the time I was accurate. When

I got home at night I would do fifteen to thirty minutes of visualisation.

Something else that helped me was a regular exercise routine that I did for an hour three times a week. I did aerobics but you might prefer swimming, yoga or a game of tennis. I was exercising both my higher mind and my body, a combination that can only increase your psychic powers. It certainly did mine. Although I was only just at the beginning of my studies, during this time of regularly exercising I could pick up on someone's thoughts as soon as I looked at them. I even discovered my healing powers. It became known at the Neurology Institute in central London that if someone had a headache I could walk over to them, and it would literally disappear.

One of the girls once said to me that she had been to the doctor with an aching shoulder. It was like a trapped nerve and she couldn't get rid of the pain. 'Give it a go, Sherron', she asked. I placed my hand on her shoulder and I still remember laughing as she said within a minute, 'I can't believe it. The pain is going, Shell.' As a rather impatient kind of person, I was happy. I like results to be fast – and there's no reason why they can't be.

As well as toning the physical body, exercise clears out a lot of the negativity and stress held in our bodies and minds, releasing the blockages and irritability that can keep our mind energy funnelled inwards, instead of outwards towards the universe. Exercise charges your aura and helps establish a strong mind–body connection. The combination of the two is a powerful mixture that will speed everything up.

*   *   *

Now you have come to the end of this chapter, you have learned the many different ways of focusing and slowing down the mind. Remember that these are all just vehicles for you to activate your sixth sense. On trying out some of these techniques you may have lots of questions about pictures, words or feelings that you are not sure of. Don't worry, in the next chapter all will be revealed when we look at how to interpret the intuitive language of the mind.

5

The Code-Breakers:
Your Inner Language Revealed

Do not assume the other fellow has intelligence to match yours.
He may have more.
Terry-Thomas, 1911–90, British comedian

At last: you've reached your destination. You are now ready to learn a new, yet very ancient language, one that you have known since you were first born. Soon you will realise that there has always been a direct communication from your deeper intuitive self to your conscious mind. This inner voice has been gently but firmly guiding you with all the knowledge you need for a fulfilling life. You just needed to listen and understand what it was saying. Now you can. The previous exercises and visualisations have paved the way and helped you connect with this wisdom by expanding and focusing your mind energy. You have already come a long way in your development. But discovering the language of your inner psyche is vital if you want access to information.

It's no good asking yourself if you'll get that great job, or if a house sale will come through, if all that flashes through your mind, for example, is a piece of apple pie, or a no parking sign. Just like hearing French or Italian for the first time, it will mean nothing if you don't understand the lingo. In the same way that our subconscious mind can provide the answers with a symbolic image in our dreams, these sometimes obscure pictures that form in our minds can help relay everything there is to know about the past, present and future. And your psychic vision comes from the same unconscious world that we experience in our sleep state. As in the language of dreams, it is relayed in signs and symbols as well as feelings, inspiration, insights and whispered words. Now you can read your own mind properly and learn how to break the symbolic codes if you want to know how to help yourself and others.

Sight, sound and feeling

First we need to look at the foundations of your new language; that means identifying your predominant senses and discovering whether you are naturally clairvoyant, clairaudient or clairsensient. These three words relate to whether we receive psychic information in the form of sight, sound or feeling. The most commonly known is clairvoyance (seeing what is not physically there) because it is the term often used for psychics 'seeing' into the future. Then there is clairaudience (hearing what is not physically there) and clairsentience (feeling or smelling what is not physically present). Everyone experiences all three, but our minds will show us information more predominantly in one of these forms. As your psychic powers are strengthened and knowledge flows, you will find that you will naturally start to link them together for clearer insight.

These sensory descriptions should already be ringing bells for you. Clairvoyance, clairaudience and clairsentience are alternative words for visual, auditory and kinesthetic thought processes. As you have discovered in chapter three on utilising your imaginative skills, you will now have an idea of how your mind predominantly works. But there are questions you can ask yourself to see whether you have managed to strengthen your weaker senses and therefore integrate your psychic perception.

Questions to ask yourself

1. Are you able to see pictures in your mind clearly? Can you see all the visualisations I have given you easily? A sunset, a beautiful beach or a field of golden flowers?
2. Can you feel emotion in your pictures? Can you picture yourself happy or sad? Can you get a sense of whether you are hot or cold? Can you imagine the taste of a piece of hot apple pie or a crisp piece of cold pizza?
3. How are your mental audio skills? Can you hear the sound of the sea, the rustle of the leaves on trees, or the sound of a choir singing?

If not, don't worry, keep practising the visualisations and do the best you can, but make a point of going back to chapter three and honing up your weaker skills.

Clairvoyance

A clairvoyant is a popular alternative name for a psychic, because of the potential ability to see into the future. It is to do with using our inner vision, utilising our sixth chakra, which is known as our third eye. Physically it is located in the centre of our brow. When you see something clairvoyantly, you are seeing situations and feelings represented in a mental picture.

The language of clairvoyance is the same as that used in our dream state. We can have symbolic dreams with a liberal sprinkling of archetypes, or literal (straightforward realistic) dreams. In the same way psychically we see pictures in our mind that are either presented symbolically, in archetypes or a literal reality. You get to know with practice how to interpret a literal picture. For example, images of someone doing something that is part of their everyday life or something that you discover is a reality, such as the person showing anger or happiness because of their present emotional state, seeing a wedding ring when the person is getting married, or seeing a picture of someone with their hands tied behind their back would mean they feel restricted. Their hands are literally tied.

When it comes to other aspects of imagery we have to learn how to decipher the meanings. Most of us have an innate knowledge of what Jung called archetypes (a universal meaning which we can all relate to). They are primordial images that originate from an inherited ancestral memory. This means that, just like the inheritance of physical characteristics, we also have access to images formed in our 'collective' psyche. For example, seeing the image of a messenger means a message from our unconscious, a witch or old wise woman is a symbol of ancient knowledge, the sign of the cross means a sacrifice, the devil can mean risky temptation, and the full moon represents the hidden side of ourselves. These archetypes are so often used that they are represented on many tarot cards and have a common theme.

But symbols are very different from archetypes and are unique to every individual. A symbol is a picture we see in our mind's eye that can represent anything you ask about whether it's a solution to a problem, someone's emotional state or even financial circumstances. Symbols are powerful because within a simple picture they often show us the heart of a situation or person much more truthfully than any rational viewpoint could. That is because they come from our unconscious source of knowledge and are not invented by our conscious mind.

Seeing an image of a plate of food to me can mean comfort and nourishment in our emotional and sexual life. I once saw a dinner plate full of bugs and worms when I tuned in to a married woman. That picture symbolised to me that whatever was happening in her emotional and sexual life was abhorrent to her and that she couldn't enjoy intimacy and affection in the way she should be able to. I also got a sense of sadness and frustration linked with it. She agreed totally and said that her love life with her husband was non-existent because he physically repelled her. She had married him out of loneliness and wanted to find someone else, but felt stuck in the situation. It still amazes me how a picture can sum a situation up so well. But if I tuned in to another person and got a plate of food, it might mean that they needed to eat a healthier diet, or they couldn't stop eating. Picturing flowers in my mind, for example, can represent a situation that is blossoming, but it could also mean optimism. These meanings have come from my own psychic dictionary, and that is the key.

Symbolic pictures are personal to each one of us and they are never fixed, which is why you have to trust your intuition to tell you what each image means. The same symbol could mean something different in answering a different question. It is important for accuracy that you must trust what that image means to you and not ask someone else. Your own sense of what it means will help to clarify any doubts.

To illustrate this, I remember doing a reading for a young Italian girl. She asked about her family and I saw a picture of her mother symbolically frozen in a block of ice, unable to move and looking scared. Her father looked angry (which was literal). The girl nodded to me that she understood and then told me that her mother was petrified of her father and felt trapped. My higher mind showed me symbolically that her mother was frozen with fear. But if I had asked someone else what being frozen in a block of ice meant, they might have said that it meant she was a cold person who couldn't show love. That's why you need to go with what it represents to you and how you feel.

Clairaudience

This is where you hear things psychically, or you see a word written in your mind's eye, or sometimes whispered in your ear. Words and phrases aren't usually heard in the form of someone's voice (although on occasion that can happen), but come into your mind quite separate from your own thoughts. They can come from your own higher self or from your spirit guides or be telepathically transmitted when you tune in to someone else's thoughts. They can be from people who have passed over and want to make contact or help you. This is part of mediumship and I will discuss that next in chapter six.

Real proof of clairaudience happens when you hear an unfamiliar word that sums up a situation or person and you have to look up the meaning in a dictionary. It is fascinating when you discover how appropriate it is to the situation and proves that it isn't coming from your conscious mind.

Sometimes you can hear telepathically what someone is thinking and that can be scary. When Diana, a thirty something exec based in London, had sent a business contact based in Brussels an e-mail, she was a little shocked at her clairaudient discovery. She told him that she could meet up with him as she had to fly over there on business. They had had a pleasant flirtation going on over several months, although she knew very little about him. But he had made it clear to her in several e-mails that he wanted to take things further.

As she was sitting at her computer the day after he had received her e-mail, she actually heard him thinking, 'My God, she is desperate. She is lonely.' She then heard the word 'terrified' from another source separate from him.

Because of this psychic input, she wasn't too surprised when she received an unpleasant e-mail the next day protesting that he didn't know what she was on about and denying he had ever met up with her. Her clairaudient ability had helped her discover why he was so worked up. It turned out that her psychic input was very accurate. Information from a colleague showed that he was married. While he enjoyed a flirtation from a distance, he was clearly frightened that she would be on his territory and word would get out to his wife. She had been relayed his real paranoid thoughts on the matter through clairaudience.

Words and phrases can also tell you volumes about someone's character. A word that I heard clairaudiently with one woman I was reading for was 'efficiency'. I felt strongly that that word summed up her personality. She liked everything in her life to be 'just so'. Sometimes information can be extremely blunt. On one occasion I heard the words 'emotionally retarded' when I was focusing on a woman's husband. I told her tactfully that he was a little immature and unable to communicate with her on a level she wanted. She agreed that was the problem in her marriage. They were more like mother and son.

Clairsentience and intuition

I remember only too clearly a friend's remarks after she had walked into an empty warehouse to store some clothes. 'The hairs on the back of my neck stood up and I felt a strange feeling in my stomach and I could smell this faint aroma of tobacco.' That gave a perfect description of what someone psychically experiences with clairsentience, as she picked up on the atmosphere in the room from the previous owners. This psychic sense comes in the form of 'a feeling'. It could be a sense of danger, excitement or inner warmth, a distinctive scent or an innate 'knowing'. It is the feeling you have when you meet someone or walk into a house and suddenly feel a chill or uneasiness.

Clairsentience was experienced by a colleague, Annie, thirty-three, who worked in the media and did not particularly believe that she had many intuitive faculties. But as she was watching television a handsome presenter appeared on screen. Suddenly she got an overwhelming scent of expensive aftershave that was so strong it was as if this man were actually in the room with her. It was almost as if her sixth sense had penetrated the barrier of television to connect straight to the person. She began to realise that these invisible powers were much more potent than she had at first thought.

A 'knowingness' can also alert and prepare us for any troubles ahead.

Denise lived in a flat in London and was going away for a long weekend. She put the key under the mat for her friends to come and feed the cat and suddenly had a nagging feeling about the taxi driver as he waited outside the house. This concern kept gnawing away at her, so she decided to retrieve the key from under the mat and to take the taxi to her friends' house and give it to them personally. She even made a point of saying to the taxi driver that her friends were going to stay in her flat to comfort herself that nothing could go wrong. However, her sense that something wasn't right wouldn't leave her and she rang her friends every day. She just knew that she was going to get burgled, but her friends reassured her and said, 'Don't worry, everything's fine.' Until the third night when they rang her and said exactly what she had dreaded hearing: 'I'm really sorry. Your door's been kicked in and they've stolen your television and stereo.' When Denise got home, her friends said, 'It's weird that you kept telling us "I'm being burgled," before it had even happened.' Her sense of knowing had prepared and warned her about something that seemed to be unavoidable despite her fears.

Why being blind doesn't affect your inner sight

Don Ford is a forty-seven-year-old psychic based in Devon who discovered he had psychic abilities when he was only a child. His abilities are unique in that he has been blind since birth. He was born with a twin sister three months prematurely. He was so small that he weighed only two pounds ten ounces and his parents didn't think the twins would live. He was given oxygen to keep him going, but a mistake occurred and an overdose of oxygen burned out the cord in the back of his eyes and he was blinded. Despite his physical blindness, Don has always been able to use his inner sight. Unlike people who can see, Don sees symbols that are presented in a way he can understand.

He says, 'Every time I talk to someone, that person is a blank page in front of me. But I receive information in the form of smells, feelings and sounds.' In other words Don is primarily clairsentient and clairaudient. He continues, 'I often see words written in my mind's eye, but I can actually hear a voice telling me about someone and I pass on the message. It could be anything. I remember one occasion a few years ago when I said to a friend who was hungry, "Don't eat any-thing, because your wife's got a chicken salad ready for you when you get home." He didn't believe me, until he arrived home and called me up in amazement. He really thought that his wife had phoned and told me beforehand.

'Sometimes I get colours that provide a focus to give me information on someone, but I don't see different shades in the way someone with vision can. I actually feel the vibra-tion of the colour and get a sense of "knowing" with it that leads me to more information. I also get smells around differ-ent situations. If there is a bad feeling there is a smell of fear, but sometimes I get a sweet scent of roses, which represents happiness.' Don also keeps a crystal ball next to him as a focus point to tell people about their health. 'If I touch the crystal ball and it feels warm, their health is okay; if it's cold, there is illness; if it's icy cold, there could be a bereavement.' Don is perfect proof that our intuitive faculties remain well equipped despite any physical handicap.

Why you need a sounding board

Before you continue, I need to make a point. Even if you don't ever want to do readings for anyone else and only want to use your abilities on yourself, you will still need to prac-tise on others for your own development. Before you ask why, think of it this way. How will you know you are getting accur-ate information for yourself until you have had confirmation of accuracy from others? It is much harder to be objective with yourself, so you need to prepare and build up your con-fidence. Trust and confidence increase psychic powers, simply because you start to accept what comes through, however odd it might seem.

Be objective

The tip in reading for yourself or anyone else is to be as objective as possible. It can be difficult when it's an emotional situation, but try to step back and ask yourself a specific question
that you want answered. Always go with the first picture or
symbol, feeling or words that come into your mind. Once
you keep practising you will get used to seeing symbols and
hearing phrases and words; your intuitive feelings will be the
glue that can piece together the full story.

As Carol, a twenty-seven-year-old secretary, was sitting in
a taxi on her way to a party in east London, she wanted to
know psychically how the evening would go with her new
boyfriend who she was going to meet there. As she focused
on the impending scenario, she went with the first impression she got in her mind when she saw the symbolic sign
of food sizzling in a pan. She felt that it meant it would be
hot between them at first, but then she saw a door slamming
shut. She got a sad feeling and heard the word 'fleeting'. Her
information proved to be simple but very accurate. At the
beginning of the evening, things did seem to 'sizzle'. He was
all over her and very affectionate, but five hours later they'd
had a row and the relationship was over before it had really
begun. A door symbolically had closed. It's a sad fact, but we
always know the truth within ourselves. We just need to pay
attention to the signs.

When you read for someone else, the key is never to pre-
sume. Assumptions are the worst thing for a psychic and throw
you off track. Just because someone looks affluent and well
educated doesn't mean that they come from that kind of background or are happy. Just because someone has a wedding
ring on, it doesn't mean they're married. I've read for people

with wedding rings on, only to discover that they got divorced years ago, but still choose to continue wearing the ring. How often have you met the life and soul of the party only to discover at a later date that they are secret alcoholics or depressives? There are people who seem placid and nice but deep down are seething with resentment that they are afraid to express.

True psychics are not reading body language, but are going by their higher sixth sense. It's important to trust the information you are given and not go by outward appearances.

Be confident

Trusting what you hear, feel and see is imperative in developing your skills. If you don't trust what you get, then you won't have the confidence to say it, or believe in yourself. Put aside what your logic says. The mind cannot be trusted to tell you the truth. Use it to weigh things up with your intuition. The quicker you accept and believe in what you get psychically, the faster your intuitive powers will flow.

Be positive

Do not predict car crashes, misfortune or death. This can be very negative and cause someone to worry unnecessarily, and they can actually set about creating what you have said thinking it's their fate. I have often heard people express terror at being a passenger in a car or walking home in the dark because they have been told they will have an accident or be mugged. Negative things will always prey on someone's mind. If you see danger, there are ways of putting it over productively. If I thought someone might be openly inviting an attack by walking home alone late through a park, I would tell them that they should be a little bit more aware about their personal safety. You don't have to embellish or be specific.

Seven years ago I was staying in Vancouver in Canada with my aunt. I was dating an Italian and while we were at his parents' house, his mother asked me to give her a psychic reading. I picked up that her husband was going to become immobilised through ill health and saw him lying on a settee. He would have to keep his movement to a minimum. But I also felt he wouldn't live for very much longer. I was naturally cautious as to what I said and told her that they had a strong partnership but he was run down and very soon he would need a lot of spoiling. He was already due to see a doctor about a heart problem, but within a week he was practically immobile because of his heart condition and spent his days lying bored on the settee, just as I had seen. Six months later he had died.

I have heard some psychics say that if they tell someone about misfortune, they can avoid it. But some things are tragically unavoidable. Someone knowing about a death isn't going to thank you if they spend the next few months or years brooding over it and wondering when it's going to happen. Obviously, you can use your own discretion. If someone is very accepting of death and knows that it is merely a transition to a new spiritual life, you can discuss the impending news, so that the person can prepare themselves or the relative you were sensing. But people who accept death in a positive way are still few and far between, so err on the side of caution.

When you use your psychic skills you take on a responsibility for your wisdom. So make sure that whatever you say to someone, they are left with a feeling of positive uplift.

*   *   *

Before you start practising using your sixth senses in any psychic work, it is a good idea to do a visualisation, which will help you become more aware of the symbolism the unconscious mind uses. The following exercise will also continue to expand your mind and help you to relax, releasing any tension so that you allow your intuition to flow.

Limber up your mind with a symbol exercise

See yourself walking along a path towards a house. Immediately take notice of where the house is. Is it in a town or the countryside and what does the house look like? Is the path to the door straight or winding? Is there a large front garden? As you approach the front door, make a note of the size and colour of the door. Is it tatty or smart? What are the windows like, large or small? You walk inside the house and start to explore all the rooms. Start downstairs. Is there a kitchen? Where is the front room and is there a dining room? How are these rooms decorated? Look at the colour schemes. Is the decor boring and stale or fresh and bright?

Is there an upstairs? If so climb up the stairs and look at the rooms there. How many bedrooms are there? Or perhaps there aren't any. Is there a bathroom? Again look at the colours. Are there any plants around and is it light, bright and airy or dark and cluttered? Before you go outside, you see a washing basket for clothes. As you take off the lid, you see an object underneath that sums up your own character. Take the object with you or remember it.

Then go outside and look around the back garden. How big is it? Are there any vegetables growing there, flowers and shrubs? Keep exploring the garden and see what different flowers there are. Is the garden well kept or messy?

You suddenly see a golden trowel on the ground and you pick it up and decide to dig deep down in a piece of earth. As you do so, you uncover a box. What colour is the box? Ask a question about a simple problem you have in your mind. For example, 'Will I sell my house?' 'Will I get back together with my boyfriend?' 'Will I get the new job I want?' Whatever question you have open the box. Inside there is a gift, a symbol in whatever guise that will provide the answer. If you are not sure what it represents, ask yourself, 'What does this mean?' It could be a symbolic item, a word, or a feeling. Take whatever it is with you, however big or small, and begin to walk back down the path.

Questions to ask yourself

The house represents the real you, so how you saw it in your mind's eye will give you an idea of how you see yourself. Remember how it was decorated. Does it compare with how you take care of yourself?

If your house was well looked after, then you take care of your own needs well. If your house was neglected and drab, then maybe you need to give yourself a bit of nurturing. Perhaps you run around after everyone else, but ignore yourself.

How were all the different rooms? If you saw a bright, comfortable kitchen and front room, but a drab bedroom, it would mean that you put more energy into your social life than into your personal private life. If there was no bedroom, you might feel uncomfortable about the sexual side of yourself or have closed a door on that part of your life for the moment. What was the bathroom like? That expresses your ability to eliminate stress and problems. If it was tatty or old-fashioned, then that speaks volumes about baggage that you are hanging on to.

A flourishing garden represents your creativity and ability to develop things in the outside world. If you had a lot of vegetables, flowers and plants growing there, that shows growth and fulfilment in your life. If it's been left overgrown, then you need to put some effort in.

Look at the two symbols that you found. What does the first one represent about your character? Hold the symbol in your mind if you are confused. However strange it might be, what are the qualities it represents? To give you an idea, when Susanna, a girl friend, did this visual exercise, she saw a brush nozzle that attaches to the end of a hoover. Sounds crazy, doesn't it? But when she examined what it meant she could see that it was an attachment that you add on to clean the more difficult parts of the house. Even I could see that it expressed her diligence about wanting to get things done properly. It was an accurate description. She is very much a perfectionist in many areas of her life.

Does your second symbol give you an answer to your problem? Again focus on it in your mind and if you are confused, get a feeling of what it means.

A quick frequency lift before you tune in

Once your mind has got used to being expanded and focused by different exercises it will respond more readily to instructions. You won't need to go into lengthy visualisations. This next quick visualisation is a fast and effective way of raising your frequencies just before you tune in to yourself or somebody else. And will only take you a few minutes.

Imagine your mind has grown wings and is flying out of your head through the roof of your house and up into the sky. Picture it as a bird if it helps. Feel it going higher and higher above the clouds. Then say the words, 'Please could you help me in the vibration of love and protection to discover information about the past, present and future.' You should feel a sudden lift in your consciousness. You may have to do it a few times to get the hang of it. But practice makes perfect.

Developing telepathic skills

Before you practise your clairvoyance, clairaudient and clairsentient awareness we are going to start with the subject of telepathy. Telepathic skills are where you literally 'read' someone's mind and it is a good starting point for a psychic exercise. The reason for this is that it's fairly simple to pick up on someone's thoughts. It has happened to most people from time to time: picking up the phone just as someone was about to call you is a common occurrence, or sensing that someone is thinking about you. The information will come in a mixed bag of clairvoyance (pictures), clairsentience (feelings) and clairaudience (phrases or words) as discussed at the beginning of the chapter.

But we also need to be aware of the impact of our thoughts and how they affect others telepathically often without them knowing. We transmit telepathic thoughts every day of our lives just by dwelling on someone or something. When it comes to potent thought energies there are no barriers to mind-to-mind communication. A person doesn't have to be in touch with their psychic powers or share any telepathic bond with us to feel the effects. Thoughts have wings and whatever we concentrate on, they will travel there instantaneously, faster than the speed of sound and across many thousands of miles. Even if someone is based in Siberia and thinks about a person based in Scotland, the effects will still be felt as potently as if they were standing next to them. Obviously, the stronger the emotion behind the thought the greater the impact it will have. A thought sent out fuelled by strong feelings such as love, hatred, passion and anger will act like an invisible force, making the recipient suddenly warm towards us, or feel melancholy and depressed.

Fleeting irrelevant thoughts have little effect and simply drift through us.

Sending out this thought energy is the basis of all relationships in every area of your life, whether you want to pass an exam or get the builders in to renovate your house. It is incredibly beneficial if you want to heal a rift or smooth communication in certain situations. If you've had a row with your partner, instead of seething silently, which will create more negative energy, you could consciously decide to send out loving thoughts to them. It will help if you focus on the positive feelings you have, like why you enjoy being with them and their good points. They will know on subtle levels that you are thinking positively, because they will suddenly feel a surge of uplift, adrenaline or excitement and in return think of you warmly. Often when we get a positive burst of energy like this from out of the blue, it is a result of someone thinking of us with goodwill, and I certainly notice how quickly my mood changes to a happier one.

Conscious productive thoughts are so important in our lives. We don't realise how much we send out unconscious thoughts all the time, which can bombard the recipient with negative energy if we are angry or upset. While we are silently brooding on something or plotting revenge, the person on our mind is receiving the effects of our angst, wherever they are. It might make them feel edgy, irritable, melancholy or nervous. And it will also make them think of you in an uncomfortable way. So it is far better to choose to think good, happy thoughts.

Unfortunately, there are some people who may deliberately send out nasty thoughts to try to create disruptive energy around someone, believing that they have the power to hurt. Be careful if you do this, as you could end up the loser by lowering your psychic vibration and exposing your-self to unpleasant energies.

At times, when you think about someone, you may also sense that they are thinking about you. This is a telepathic connection and you can feel an energy as your minds touch each other. Practise sending someone loving feelings at a cer-tain time of the day and ask them how they felt at that time. It is often a very pleasant feeling. If you feel, however, that you are receiving negative vibes from someone, which are unsettling you, refer back to chapter four and read up on the egg or mirror protection. This will make your psychic bound-aries feel stronger and you will be unaffected by the inter-ference, or the energy will simply bounce back to the sender.

Testing out your telepathic abilities with someone gives you a good opportunity to gain confidence in your sixth sense. The more constructive the feedback, the better you will feel and the more your intuition can flow unhindered by your own self-doubt. Telepathy also gives you a constructive reference point. You need to know the difference between reading someone's mind about the issues in their life and accessing information from their higher mind and discovering more about the person, such as why someone might have acted in certain ways, why things didn't work out according to that person's conscious understanding and possible future outcomes if they remain on their current path. This will not necessarily be part of someone's conscious mind but part of their expansive higher mind – which you can connect to. So now we will start an exercise to hone your telepathic communication skills.

Exercise in telepathic communication

First, it would be good if you could find some experimental

'guinea-pigs', unfamiliar people who don't mind being part of your project. It could be a friend of a friend or an acquaintance through work. Put the word out and you'll soon find many people who would love to be the focus for a psychic reading. Prepare yourself on that day by choosing one of the visualisations in the previous chapters and/or a mantra to focus your mind before they arrive.

Sit in front of the person in a quiet room where there are no distractions and ask them to relax with open body language. In my experience it makes you feel tense if someone is sitting defensively with their arms folded or perched on the edge of their seat in eagerness. It makes no difference whether their mind is blank or they are worrying about something. They do not have to do anything. Visualise your mind expanding and rising upwards into the clouds, using the quick frequency lift exercise. Then focus on the person with your eyes shut and see what images or feelings come into your mind. If it helps, use psychometry and ask if you can hold their car keys, a ring, watch or any other item of jewellery they might have on them (that no one else has worn).

Talk the person through whatever input you are receiving. Remember that you are picking up on their thoughts and their mind will work on various levels. Initially you may just pick up on recurring thoughts about a relationship or work problem that override all the others. Or you may get a physical sense of any discomfort they are having, like a back pain or headache, which is on their mind. You could feel a sudden ache or pain in your own body such as back or neck pain. If this happens when you are tuning in to them, it will undoubtedly be their physical problem you are feeling. You may also pick up on any other clutter that might have been in their day and see buses, cars or other physical situations, such as an office or house.

Describe everything and see if it makes sense to them. If the person isn't worried or thinking about much, you may get more of a blank feeling with just a sense of being happy or sad. Let one thought link you to another. Relay this information back to the person, but don't get discouraged if you are wrong. It is important that you remain relaxed and focused on that person if you want your intuition to flow.

Now we will move on to another exercise where you can see how thoughts affect someone else telepathically and influence their mood.

Experiment with the telepathic power of thought transference

In this exercise you are going to send out specific thougths to a person, visualising them in a certain predicament. In return they will simply need to relay the impact of how your thoughts make them feel. Have a pen and paper next to each of you and practise, taking it in turns. Don't tell them what you are thinking. Ask them to relax and then take a few minutes to visualise them in a simple scenario that might create extreme feelings, such as sunbathing under a hot sun, standing under freezing water, feeling trapped, flying in the sky or floating on water. After you have visualised them in this situation for a few minutes, simply ask them for a response on how they feel. Make sure that you keep to a very simple picture that will evoke feelings. If you imagine a person swimming with dolphins or eating an ice cream, that may not have much effect. Keep experimenting and you will be surprised at the power of thought transmission.

For example, many years ago I practised thought transference with a girl friend, Jenny. As she was sprawled on her settee in her flat, I visualised her lying on a beach under the rays of a boiling hot sun. I made the picture as realistic as possible in my mind, and imagined her being so hot that sweat was pouring down her face. I focused on her skin being clammy and her feeling more and more uncomfortable. Then I asked her to describe any sensation she had. She said she suddenly felt uncomfortable and warm and she couldn't sit still. When she had confirmed what I had visualised I tried another picture. This time I imagined her flying through clouds. I sensed weightlessness and ease in her movement. I focused on this for a few minutes and she said she felt light and floaty and a bit ungrounded. We both found it fascinating and it was very entertaining when she linked her feelings with my thoughts.

The different psychic levels: you can never fly too high, but you can sink too low

Now that you know about telepathy, bear in mind that when you are tuning in to yourself or anyone else it is important that you give proper guidance and clear information. Seeing psychically with clarity means rising above conscious thoughts to the higher mind.

For example, how many people see a psychic and are thrilled that they get accurate feedback about their life now, yet the reading provides no guidance as to any obstacles in the person's life, and the probable future predicted never occurs? All that does is elicit false hope. What a psychic is doing in this instance is using only telepathic skills, without ever rising above into the person's higher mind to discover the truth. In fact, many practising psychics remain on this 'mind-reading' level and never go beyond it.

If you do this, although it may thrill you to know that you are proving your psychic ability, the danger is that by remaining on this level all you are getting is feedback from the person's wants, fears and desires at that time. And all they are receiving is a reflection of what is already in their heads. Good psychic ability is about much more than 'mind reading'. You have to make sure that you use your telepathic skills but also rise above them to a higher plane, so that you can give clear guidance to help someone overcome any hurdles or difficult circumstances in their lives.

For example, one woman came to me for a reading saying she was madly in love with her acupuncturist. She was very attractive and felt sure he would finally see the light and they would be together. She was thinking about him all the time. If I picked up information only on a telepathic level, I would feed back exactly what she wanted to hear, because she was so wilful and definite. But because I made sure that I lifted my vibration above her conscious thoughts, I knew that she was deluding herself and that this man would never step beyond his professional relationship to ask her out. Time and again she would argue the point with me, coming back regularly for more readings to prove that she was right. I told her that by staying fixated on this man, she was putting her life on hold and not allowing herself to be open to anyone else. I always felt that she would meet a much older man whom she would begin a relationship with. Eighteen months later, she met an older man whom she got involved with and she finally got over her obsession with her 'fantasy' man.

Now you have learned how to pick up on someone's thoughts, you are going to use your psychic senses to reach into the energy of their higher mind.

Exercise to practise your clairvoyance, clairaudient and clairsentient abilities

First prepare yourself for this exercise with a notepad and pen. You will need to write information down at first until you get used to remembering everything. Then once again focus on your experimental guinea-pig sitting in front of you and tune in with the quick frequency lift. But this time say in your mind that you want to rise above your subject's conscious mind in order to know the past, present and future.

Then feel your own intention. Intention means your own inner desire to go beyond mind reading, to the boundless universal knowledge that can give you the whole truth. This means venturing behind the mask of this person's personality and into what's really going on behind the outward scenes of their lives. It's okay telling someone there is a problem that they know about. But why do they have it? And why are they creating it? Can things change for them? This time you must focus on the deeper questions that affect a person, such as 'Are they doing what their heart wants them to do?' This can be at the root of a great deal of instability and unhappiness. As you become more experienced and pick up more, you can focus on what they should be doing. A dead-end job, for example, results in a person who consciously feels bored, depressed and listless. They may be in a rut, but not realise it. Write down any information you get at this point before you say anything to them. Don't let them feed you clues to anything. A simple yes or no from them for these exercises is all you need.

Focus on the past; get a sense with your own energy of being -pulled into the past. Then draw your awareness to anything that has held them back that they are still holding on to. It could be a childhood issue of abandonment that is affecting their relationships or a sense of over-protectiveness that stopped them taking responsibility. It doesn't have to be negative; you could pick up on an idyllic childhood. Make a note of any pictures that spring into your mind, however bizarre. Are you hearing any words or phrases? Write them down, however fleeting or uncertain you might be about them. Do you get any vibes from the person? Is there a sense of any deeper emotion underlying their personality: sadness or perhaps a sense of defensiveness? Or do you get a feeling of calm? Look at their future goals: is there a sense of inertia about their life, or do they have a sense of adventure? Try not to ask any questions, except in your own mind. Gather as much information as you can and write it down.

When you have enough data, you can start to piece them together like a jigsaw puzzle and feed back it back to the person. Don't worry if they say you are wrong about some aspects. You might be wrong, but sometimes people are blind to themselves. If it feels right to you, try to reword it in a way that they might understand. Focus on the things you have got right. This is just a starting point, so don't be too hard on yourself. It takes time to switch off your logical mind and be receptive to what filters through. Your intuition eventually will flow and you just have to let it happen. Most importantly you need to build your confidence and learn to trust what you get.

Penetrating the armour

You may sometimes find when you do a reading for someone that they put up a wall. You will be conscious of this if they disagree with everything you say or if their body language is defensive. Some people are cynics and just want to put you to the test. Others are so closed to their own mind personality that they are unaware that they are putting up such iron barriers. A psychic reading is like having a conversation with someone. If you are not in rapport with someone or they are uncooperative, it will be hard to talk openly and comfortably. With some people you will get an intuitive input that will allow you to break the wall down.

Over the years I have said very simple things that I didn't

realise had so much power. For example to one woman I said, 'I am being told to tell you that you have a lot to give. And you are doing the best you can.' She burst into tears. That phrase of acknowledgement went like the sword of truth straight to her heart. With someone else I said, 'You seem to be carrying a lot of sadness that you are hiding. You don't have to pretend to be okay.' This businessman sat there and sobbed uncontrollably. It is a huge relief for someone to let down their guard and intuitive honest truth can penetrate and allow them to do just that. It gets to the core of who they are. If you get this information then it is right for them to hear. Just remain quiet until they have finished and be gentle with them. Crying in this situation is a release of tension and recognition of who they are. This truthful penetration of someone's armour can not only transform their lives but allow more intuition to flow through you to help them further.

Practise with everything

Now you have access to your special abilities, practise, practise, practise. That's the only way to become good at something. That means every time you go for a job interview, meet someone new or buy a house, use the quick frequency lift and see what pictures, words or feelings spring into your mind. Don't prejudge the situation with your mind, which tricks us and can lead us down the wrong path. Just test your intuitive abilities and see how things pan out. They will tell you the truth. Your insights can even help with buying clothes. I once spent hours trying to find the perfect dress for a function. I was with a girl friend walking around endless shops and about to give up when I saw a turquoise dress in my mind that I knew would be perfect. I told my friend and I felt drawn to go into a shop I wouldn't usually bother with. And within seconds of going in, there it was: a turquoise silk evening dress that was a perfect fit. It just goes to show that it's worth while asking your sixth sense for help even in the most practical of situations.

Practice also means offering readings to other people, so that you can test your levels of accuracy. As I've mentioned earlier, it's important to keep getting accurate, objective feedback from others. That will help you to trust your instincts when it comes to your own problems. You can ask your intuition about anything and even check out a prospective partner using your own skills so you don't waste precious time – as depicted in the following examples. One acquaintance asked about a new man and saw an automatic typewriter going across a page, but it never reached the other side; it always stopped halfway. She got a feeling with the picture that he was like that in his life. He was always half-hearted about things and couldn't make proper commitments. Her symbology turned out to be right: he would often make a date and then cancel and he could never make up his mind about doing anything seriously. Needless to say, they didn't stay in touch for long.

David, thirty-seven, a travel agent, was very keen on a woman he wanted to ask out. She had been flirting with him for over five weeks. But before he did, he asked psychically what she was like. He got a picture of a bee going from flower to flower, sucking the nectar out of it and then moving on. He chose not to pay attention to the signs and saw her for a few dates, only to discover that she was living with another man and was an outrageous flirt with no serious intention of starting any new relationship.

On a more practical note, your intuition can also help with money or your working life. Margaret, a forty-three-year-old divorcee, asked psychically how she could make some money, and she got an overwhelming feeling that she should go into town and put £100 into as many building societies as she could afford. She felt a sense of compulsion so she chose to put the money into five accounts that very day. Over the next few years, every one of those five building societies turned into banks, as a result paying out to their members, and she made around £5,000 as a pay-off from her original stake. Her intuition earned her some real cash.

Even getting bad news psychically can prepare you if you are forewarned. Josie, twenty-five, found that was what happened when she was working as a secretary and got an insight that she was going to be made redundant. It was as she was waiting for the Tube on her way to work one morning that she suddenly felt a strange 'scratchy' feeling in her stomach. She felt like something bad was going to happen and then saw a (literal) picture of the staff in the personnel office discussing her. She was getting a live transmission of her impending fate. When she got to work, she had to wait all day until she was finally called up to personnel. She wasn't surprised when she was told that she wasn't wanted any longer, as they were cutting back, and she hadn't been there long enough to secure any redundancy money. She was upset but not as much as she would have been had it been a complete bolt from the blue. She'd already prepared herself psychologically for the outcome.

As you have probably realised, having psychic knowledge isn't always wonderful. It can be difficult, believe me, when you get the opposite information to what you would like to hear. All your delusions and fantasies have to melt into oblivion when you start to see the truth in a situation. Especially when you pick up on what somebody really thinks of you. It's often a shock to take in and you don't always want to believe it. But at least you know. And on the positive front, you can discover answers that will keep you one step ahead in every aspect of your life. You can take advantage of important opportunities and find solutions to any problem. Soon you will be able to have the confidence to take notice of all the signs and intuitive feelings you get to help give a constructive outcome and not waste your time with things that are doomed to fail from the start.

The past, present and future link

Now let's look at how we can see into the future. One of the most important questions for anyone who has ever had a reading and for any budding psychic is the question, 'Is there such a thing as fate?' Can the future be predicted or do we have free will? To look at this closely, we need to see how a psychic can tune in to the thread that runs through our past, present and future.

This future business has always been a bone of contention. In my experience many people seem to want to abdicate responsibility for their lives and think everything that happens to them is out of their hands. Perhaps it makes someone feel better to know if they fall in love it was magically predestined, and if they mess up it's equally nothing to do with them.

Well, let me explain why a certain predictive future can never be certain. Imagine the future as a long cord, which represents a time continuum that extends out connecting past, present and future. The past and present are fixed and they don't change. When you tune in psychically to the past, you are seeing a snapshot in time. Every emotion and thought will remain and you can see not only how the situation was then, but how it affects the person now and whether a problem from the past is still holding them back.

When you look at the present time, you can see the probability of how that person might react and how that could affect their future. A psychic can indeed see the future as a picture in time, as yet unaffected by life. But here's why no future prediction can be guaranteed. Imagine this endlessly long cord that connects the fixed past and present extending into the future untethered, constantly changing with limitless variables affecting it as time moves forward. Every reaction from a person makes a difference to the future result. And we all have a choice. Even if something seems to be preordained – which I believe it can be – our reactions to any given situation can change an entire outcome to our lives.

When it comes to affairs of the heart, living our lives is a bit like unscripted actors playing their part in a romantic movie. Two people have met and fallen in love, but a variety of circumstances (such as ex-spouses, children or money) have meant it's hard for things to go smoothly. A psychic could 'see' a future of how their story should continue: the lovelorn lovers will finally be together. But that is at the start of the film, before each actor has played their part. There may be a high probability of something happening, but as with any live performance there is always the chance of one of the actors improvising their lines to create a different outcome or acting completely out of character.

Theresa's story

An old friend of mine, Theresa, recounted how this new chap in her life, Paul, told her that he loved her the instant he saw her. A psychic had told him two years before that they would meet and be together. But

Theresa didn't feel the same. Because of personal circumstances, she moved away and then dumped him for someone else, which didn't last, but Paul still held on to his belief that she was the one for him. Although she never found him particularly attractive, she still wanted to remain in contact with him and he was always there for her. Slowly she began to realise how reliable Paul was and then she started to feel a connection in her heart pulling her towards him. She finally understood that they were meant to be together.

But then something went awry. Her beau apparently thought he'd got her where he wanted her, and started heavy drinking sessions and acting indifferently. He had always been an addictive type of person. Instead of being loving and attentive, he now started criticising her and becoming increasingly moody. In the past Theresa would have put up with this and accepted it as her fate, grateful just to have a man around. But because she had now developed her confidence enough, she decided she didn't want to continue with the relationship as she felt it was repeating past mistakes she'd made with men. Therefore the psychic's impression of the future could have come true had Theresa stayed true to her past character. But fortunately for her she broke a negative pattern.

Often when we get a psychic reading at the beginning of a relationship we hear the idealistic version and the potential for something good to blossom. But if our weaknesses of personality are given full rein, a relationship can quickly turn sour. We get given our opportunities in life, but I would say that it is choice not a chance fate that dictates the end result.

In case you wish to argue the point, think of this. Wouldn't it let us all off the hook if everything that happened in our lives were nothing to do with us? We could stay stuck in our ruts, miserable, unhappy in failed relationships or careers and simply put it down to destiny, muttering the immortal words,

'I was meant to suffer'. But we are not victims of fate. Life is a creative force and should be responded to moment by moment. Otherwise expectations are built up and we are blinded by the outcome and forget the opportunities presented to us in the moment we are in right now.

On the other side of the coin, I have seen a lot of disappointed people who have very set, boring lives. They have a monotonous pattern of going to work and coming home with not much in between. They are stuck in a rut and afraid to make a change and step outside their routine. They want to be told that something exciting is going to happen to improve their life without any effort on their part. A young girl in her early twenties who I met is a prime example. She doesn't work, opts out of every college course but says, 'I'm waiting for something to happen to me.' And of course nothing ever does. And she's still patiently waiting – for the universe to deliver a great man and a fabulous job. Apparently she hopes they will arrive on her doorstep. The fact is that nothing will improve unless you make a change and start investing energy into your own life right now.

Keep a development diary and notice your transformation

As you continue to develop psychically lots of things will awaken within you on many levels. A development diary will help you to remember some profound insights that will come from the fount of all wisdom – your inner self.

This diary will help you to crystallise your experiences as you work through this book. Every evening make a point of focusing on how you feel for a few minutes. Have you become more positive? Do you feel more confident and creative? Have you noticed more coincidences? Are your dreams more vivid?

Whatever flashes of intuition you get, write them down together with any pictures, words and feelings and see how it all pans out. It could be a telepathic occurrence or a real-isation that struck a chord. You'll soon know if you were on the right track.

But not everything in the garden will seem rosy. You are now walking a path into expansion and you may even reach a crossroads where you think that what you have been doing or the way you have been living doesn't fulfil you any longer. You may feel emotional, perhaps even unworthy or restless.

If you do feel like this, don't worry. It will pass. The new surge of energy flowing through your body and consciousness brings healing and, just like toxins being released from the body, old negative thought patterns naturally rise to the sur-face to be released. But once they are gone, you will feel clearer, cleaner and more alive.

This first step into using your intuition is just the begin-ning, and you start to notice how unconscious you once were. You are no longer a sleepwalker, blindly wandering through life, lost in your thoughts. Now you have been woken up inside and the transformation can only continue. Remember that it is only by developing your intuitive self that you can really live the rewarding life you want – with your eyes wide open.

6

Exploring Mediumship and How it Can Enhance Your Intuition

Every exit is an entrance somewhere.
Tom Stoppard, 1937–, British playwright

Let's take stock of what you have done so far. You have taken huge steps forward in developing your powerful psychic potential. You have learned how to balance your yin and yang energies, developed your imaginative skills and expanded your consciousness with colourful visualisations. You've raised your frequencies and focused your mind in preparation for learning a universal vocabulary: the language of intuition. In the process you have accessed your inner voice and creativity. You have achieved a lot, but all of this is the groundwork for a much bigger picture.

Now that you have made yourself familiar with the higher planes of your mind, your exploration has just begun. In this chapter we'll look at how your expanded mind energy can link you into influences from the spirit world, which can only enhance your intuitive skills.

The reason this happens is that intuition and mediumship abilities are often intertwined. You will soon discover why this happens, how you know the difference between the two and why you need to employ diplomacy. But don't panic. Before you decide that listening to dead people is not for you – read on. It is not as weird as it might sound.

To explain further, when we develop ourselves psychically

we bridge the divide between the physical and the unseen world. Our mind energy has expanded and opened up a channel for communication, rather like the installation of an invisible telephone wire. This creates a possible opportunity, if you are receptive, for spirits who want to help you or the person you are tuning in to to communicate. When you pass on that information, you become the interpreter between two worlds, which is commonly known as a 'medium'.

So why does this happen? Well, think of your favourite radio station. Realistically it could be transmitted to anywhere in the world, but you need to find the right frequency to listen to it. Awakening your psychic awareness works in the same way. Every thought we have is sent out into the cosmos. Your heightened frequencies mean that you are more tuned in to the network of thought energies that are constantly being transmitted into the atmosphere. But we need to accept that a person's spirit is immortal and mind energy exists beyond the physical body. This means that thoughts transmitted out into the universe come from all spirits – in the physical and unseen worlds.

In simple terms, provided you are able to 'receive' communication through your increased awareness, your grandfather could easily link up for a chat about building up your confidence, or a relative could come through to tell you that they are happy, even though they died in a traumatic accident. If you are fortunate, a guide (an evolved spirit assigned to help you) may want to pass on important information about love, awareness and wisdom. It really is that straightforward.

Why spirits communicate and how you know you're experiencing mediumship

Think of it this way: spirits are the same as us, but without a body. We will all die one day and when we do, our souls will fly away, leaving our bodies behind. We can only speculate about what happens to us in the afterlife journey, but startling evidence from mediums over the years has proved that our minds, personality and opinions still exist. Once a spirit is free from the earthly plane, they will probably want to help the loved ones they have left behind by trying to make contact and prove that death isn't the end.

Mediums are psychically aware people who are able to be exactly that: a mediator between the spirit on a higher dimension passing information to someone on earth. A mediumistic link could happen to you naturally and it seems that some people do have a certain talent for it, in the same way that some people are born interpreters. You may already be connecting with a spirit and not realise it. But if you are, there is nothing to be nervous about. However, if you really don't want it to happen, it probably won't. Intention is everything and a spirit won't come through to someone who has a closed mind on the issue.

You will start to become aware with practice that a mediumistic link is different from psychic information for a variety of reasons. You may feel the presence of another person's energy or get an image of them in your mind's eye. They may be people you or the person you are tuning in to are familiar with. Often a spirit will present themselves mediumistically as they will have been remembered physically. So they will say certain expressions and 'wear' something that may be familiar to relatives. They want to help you to connect with them. Alternatively, the messages could be coming from a guide and they will come through with a message specifically to help you or the other person. (The difference between guides and spirits will be explained in the next chapter.) Sometimes you can hear a voice in your ear or a whisper; other times the information is just in your head, transmitted from them telepathically. Their thoughts and attitudes will usually be very different from yours. Occasionally, you can even smell aftershave or flowers, which are connected with the person who has passed over.

When I tune in to someone psychically, I can sometimes sense their relatives walk in with them. The spirits seem to know there is an opportunity for a chat. People who were good communicators on earth will come through loud and clear in spirit. Others who are quiet and withdrawn may show themselves as a picture in your mind or make their presence felt, but not have anything to say. But they all come through with their obvious character traits. Sometimes a spirit will start talking to you before the person even arrives. With other people the reading remains on a purely psychic level where you use your clairvoyance, clairsentience and clairaudience as discussed in the last chapter.

Picking up on a spirit usually happens very naturally, without any of the flashes of lightning or clouds of smoke that are usually depicted in the movies.

Gwen's story

Gwen, a forty-two-year-old aromatherapist started a relationship with Derek, a man a few years older than her. When they had been dating for six months, like many couples, they realised that they had a tele-pathic link with each other, which meant they could pick up on each other's thoughts. Just as Derek was about to speak, Gwen would chip in with, 'I know what you're going to say,' and tell him. She would often ring him when he'd just walked in the door after work even though it was at different times. He'd always say, 'How did you know that I'd just got in?'

Both of them were intrigued, as they had never thought of themselves as psychic. But once this channel had been opened between them Gwen got an increasing awareness about something else. She kept sensing the presence of her father around her. He had passed away four years previously but she felt intuitively that he was trying to guide her and help her in the direction her life was taking. She also noticed that Derek would often make comments that her father would have said. But it was just a feeling and she kept it to herself in case Derek thought she was a bit crazy. Then one evening, they were sitting close together on the settee in the front room having an animated discussion about life and death and what happens to your soul when you die. Gwen continues, 'I was just about to say to Derek that I felt my dad was trying to contact me through him, and before I could speak Derek blurted out, "I've been feeling that your dad is using me to try to communicate with you for months, but I didn't know how to tell you."' She was amazed and shouted, 'Oh my God, I can't believe you said that, you took the words out of my mouth!'

Once Gwen had proof from her partner that she really had felt her father around, she felt comforted knowing that her dad was there for her. She knew it was a natural and warm-hearted gesture from her father's spirit, born of a desire to help. The impact of this new discovery made her realise that she should pay much more attention to her intuition and trust her feelings, as they were likely to be correct.

The spirit levels and why tact is essential

Just like the vast population on the planet today, different spirits exist on different levels of consciouness. We all mix with people like this in our everyday lives. I'm sure you know someone who operates on a basic level of survival, getting drunk every night and thinking only of their own needs and desires. There are some who enjoy abusing and dominating others for their own power, people who live on automatic pilot only living to work and sleep. And then there are the minority who aspire to something higher, whether it be in their creativity or searching for a deeper meaning to existence. These different levels of consciousness exist in the spiritual realms in exactly the same way. Yes, I know what you're thinking: unfortunately limited and judgemental views can survive death.

This perhaps explains why it is important to be cautious about passing over advice to people from their relatives without first reminding the person that each spirit will still have their own opinions, as they did when they were in their physical body.

Relaying information in the right way is the foundation to all healthy relationships, whether it's with our boss at work, a lover, or a friend. Constructive communication means using tact, discrimination and consideration. Without those qualities, misunderstandings and conflict happen all too easily. It is no different when we give information on a psychic or mediumistic level. To avoid confusion and crossed wires, you need to make sure the feedback given is positive and diplomatic.

For example, a grouchy biased grandfather who disliked any prospective suitor for his adored granddaughter may still try to put her off any new man coming into her life. If the grandfather was rude about someone in her life, then it is your responsibility to relay it accurately, but in a way that isn't offensive. But of course, each spirit/person is different and some may have learned to understand more since their earthly transition. You must judge each situation separately. But you can easily tell whether a spirit has tunnel vision or an expansive mind energy by the comments they make and the 'feel' of how they are, just as you would notice the attitude of someone you meet in your day-to-day life.

To avoid disappointments, it really is so important to break through any 'Pollyanna' ideas associated with death. Many people assume that someone will become angelic once they reach the other side, even if the person was a real villain. It can be quite a shock to discover your cynical old aunt has the same caustic views as before. So do remember that just because someone leaves their body behind when they die, they do not become elevated to sainthood. They can retain their personality with all its strengths and weaknesses.

I remember a woman whose formidable Greek mother came through to speak to her. She became very upset when it was obvious her mother had the same opinion she had when she was alive. She kept saying, 'I wish my daughter could find a nice man. She doesn't know what she's doing with her life.' The daughter was particularly perturbed, as she had been a lesbian for years and thought in the afterlife her mother would be more open-minded about those issues. Unfortunately, things hadn't changed.

At times it can be quite comical to hear a spirit give their view. I heard one old man come through and ask me to tell his grandson, 'Tell the idiot to use a condom next time.' I didn't want to pass on disparaging remarks but asked the twenty-five-year-old if he used contraception. He then confessed that he should have done as he'd just got two girls pregnant! If a person was blunt when they were alive, they will remain so. Be prepared; some spirits say quite shocking things that would make your hair curl and you could never pass on. It is up to you as the intermediary to make sure that you relay something tactfully, in the same way that an interpreter would when translating from another language.

How mediumship evidence can reveal our history

It has always amazed me how mediums can relay such historic and fascinating insights into our ancestors. And I believe such evidence can provide a wealth of information about our past heritage as well as useful guidance. One such case occurred when I first visited a spiritualist church at the age of twenty-six. The medium was a fifty something woman who looked remarkably like the late sitcom actress Yootha Joyce.

I didn't know what to expect and at first didn't recognise the person whom she brought through. She told me that she had a grandmotherly figure called Rachel, who spoke in broken English with a foreign accent and had long blonde hair. This woman was concerned that when I made a cup of tea, at times I didn't check to see how fresh the milk was. Although it didn't curdle in the cup, it occasionally had gone slightly 'off' and yet I still drank the tea. I shuddered, recognising a memory from a few days before when my fridge hadn't been working properly.

Then the medium went on to relay that Rachel suggested that if this continued to happen I should tie some cheese-cloth around the taps and drip the sour milk through it, so that when it had drained it became cream cheese. None of this made any sense, as I knew very little about my ancestors, until I asked my mother. She said that my great-grandfather was Russian and he married Rachel, who was Austrian. One of my mother's childhood memories was that Rachel always had muslin wrapped around her kitchen taps with sour milk dripping through the cloth to make cream cheese. I was amazed that there was such evidence from my forebears, knowing full well the medium couldn't have picked up the information telepathically, as I knew nothing about it. It was perfect proof of life hereafter.

Other people have told me amazing stories of evidence that has given them great confidence in an afterlife. Ann, a thirty-eight-year-old university lecturer, told me that her mother never believed in life after death and once cynically remarked to her daughter, 'When I die, if it's true, I'll contact you as Mickey Mouse.' And, amazingly, several years after her mother died of cancer, she got a message from a medium in her local spiritualist church. The medium suddenly said, 'This doesn't make any sense, but I've got Mickey Mouse here for you,' and Ann immediately screeched, 'Oh my God, it's my mother!'

My first experience of mediumship

Although I heard many stories from other mediums who have brought through amazing evidence for relatives and friends, it was only seven years ago that I first experienced my own mediumship abilities. It was an event that I shall never forget, especially for the deceased man's humour and audacity. But more importantly it demonstrated how very natural and easy communication from a spirit could be.

I had just arrived back from a six-week vacation in Canada and a girl friend, Jenny, who practised a form of Japanese Buddhism, had been looking after my flat. The night I returned home I was invited to a ceremonial Daimoku (which is a special evening of chanting) as the brother of one of

Jenny's Buddhist friends had sadly been stabbed to death. His relatives were still in a state of shock and grief and felt it important to do anything they could to help. Apparently in this brand of Buddhism, the seventh, forty-ninth and hundredth days after death are significant stages in the soul passing into the afterlife. So that evening, on the forty-ninth day, in a terraced town house in south-east London, a small room was packed full of people chanting to support the deceased's soul on its journey.

The chanting of Nam-Myoho-Renge-Kyo was new to me, so I didn't join in; but amidst the glow of lighted candles with the scent of sweet incense in the air, I sat quietly looking around at some of the women in the room, wondering what relation they might have been to the dead man. As the resonant mantric sound filled the room, what should have been a solemn occasion changed when I heard a loud male voice in my ear. 'Come on then, you can do it, you can do it,' he kept urging me. I looked around and wondered if I had really heard something or whether my mind was playing tricks on me. There was a sense of this strong male presence. I knew instinctively that it was the man (who I later discovered was called Rob) who'd died and I pictured a big bruiser of a black man. If anyone could break the mystique of death, he certainly did. Instead of a brooding, melancholy figure upset at his unfortunate demise, Rob seemed very animated with a forceful character. 'Come on, come on,' he bellowed in my ear.

So I took the bait rather apprehensively and in my mind said, 'Okay, prove that I'm not crazy. You obviously want me to pass a message on, but if you do, you'd better give me some evidence first.'

Rob seemed very eager. 'Okay,' was his reply. 'Ask my

woman about the mole on her left thigh and the horse-riding accident when she was seven or eleven,' he said.

I was a little uncertain, but thought this would be a good opportunity to prove to myself that I had an authentic experience of talking to a spirit. After the chanting was finished I mingled with everyone, and asked if a wife or girlfriend was there. I was introduced to 'his woman', a statuesque beauty called Kelly with whom he had a son and said, 'I know this sounds strange, but have you got a mole on your left thigh?'

'Yes,' was the bemused reply.

'And did you ever have a horse-riding accident?' I continued, feeling more positive.

'Yes,' she said, 'I regularly went riding when I was a kid. I fell off when I was eleven and had a bad shock.'

I giggled. 'You won't believe this,' I continued, feeling like I'd just passed an exam. 'Rob came through to me tonight while everyone was chanting.'

Despite the revelation and not knowing how she'd react, she actually looked relieved. 'Thank God,' she said. 'I've been praying that he'd try and get in contact with me. And during the evening I couldn't stop looking at you. I just had a feeling that you were going to say something.'

The next day I agreed to go to Kelly's house and see if anything else came through. What interested me, though, is that before I left the Buddhist ceremony, I asked Rob in my mind what he thought of the mantra that had been chanted to help his soul move on.

'Yeah, yeah,' was the dismissive reply. 'It's really sweet of them.' But he certainly didn't appear to need the chanting for help in the afterlife!

I had a stronger communication with him when I arrived at Kelly's house, with an even more extraordinary occurrence.

Kelly lived in a two-bed terraced maisonette in south-east London. Once again, I felt a strong presence as soon as I walked in the door. The evening went on until about four a.m. It was literally like a three-way telephone conversation, with me relaying what he was saying and her confirming it and giving her comments, which he'd then respond to. Often the communication was very funny. He cracked a lot of jokes and often spoke in Jamaican patois – a language that I wasn't familiar with.

But the strangest thing happened when he asked if I minded if he took over my body. A little concerned at what might happen, I quickly said that I'd prefer it if he didn't. Obviously he chose to ignore me because suddenly I felt a powerful energy move inside me that seemed to expand my chest and arms. I felt quite composed, but this forceful energy completely encompassed me. I even felt my head being gently but forcibly moved to look at Kelly directly. At that exact moment I heard her say, 'Oh, my God, for a moment you had Rob's look in your eye.' Then, just as suddenly, I felt his energy leave. And amazingly I felt completely comfortable without any strange after-effects. I explained to Kelly what had just happened and addressed him mentally saying, 'That was a bit of a cheek.' I heard the word 'sorry'. But there was no harm done. He was great fun and hung around all evening. I didn't feel even slightly drained afterwards.

I admit, if I had no inkling of what mediumship was about, I would have read the above account and thought it was strange. But it did happen, it was very real and the evidence was unbelievably accurate. Above all, it showed me that when someone initially passes over they reveal their personality and life force in the same way as when they were alive. Despite his traumatic passing, Rob came over as a positive, fun-loving guy. And, in or out of a body, he was the same optimistic soul.

All the exercises throughout this book can trigger your mediumship abilities, as it often happens naturally. But to experiment yourself, you can now try out an exercise designed to hone your mediumship abilities.

First, find a comfortable place to sit and put a pen and your development diary beside you for any notes you may want to make later. As always, remember to relax and enjoy the experience.

Visualisation to exercise your mediumistic abilities

Imagine a beam of light, rather like a laser, shining down on you from above. It is shining down, whether it's day or night, from way up in the sky, through the roof of your house and radiating on to your face. Imagine it lighting up your face, as if you are in a spotlight. Then feel the light expanding so it immerses you in its illumination from head to toe. Then feel yourself becoming smaller and the light beginning to look more like a tunnel that you can travel through. It is creating a vacuum within it, with glowing walls of light either side. You suddenly feel yourself gently being pulled into it. There is no problem with gravity here, so although you are travelling up the tunnel into the sky, you can walk along it if you wish, or feel a gentle force pulling you along. You feel comfortable and safe and you continue to move along the tunnel.

In your own time, when you finally reach the end, you find yourself stepping out of the golden tunnel into a beautiful garden. There is someone there to meet you. Pay attention to who this person is and what feeling you have about them. They are acting as your guide so let them lead you around the garden. Focus on the garden, and smell the exquisite scent of flowers in the air. There are blossoms and trees everywhere with the most amazing colours. Follow your guide, unless they have disappeared, and walk through this garden, listening to the sounds of birds flying overhead. You feel completely calm and at peace with yourself and your surroundings.

At the end of the garden is a large waiting room. As you get closer, the door opens automatically and someone steps outside to meet you. Greet them and ask their name, but don't worry if you don't relate to the name or hear one. This person will be relevant to you, either a relative or a friend who has passed on. They could be a great-great-grandparent from way back in your family history, so you may not instantly recognise them. But rest assured they have come to you in the spirit of love and friendship. Focus on this person. What is their expression? What clothes are they wearing? Do they hug you or just look at you? Do you get a familiar feeling about them? If you haven't heard them speak, ask them a question about who they are and listen for the words, either through feelings or words in your head. If you don't hear anything or it doesn't make sense, don't worry, just hold on to any information you get. Ask them if they want to communicate more and go and sit with them in the garden. Is there anything you feel they want to tell you? It could be a very simple message. Spend as much time with them as you want, but don't just remain there and drift off to sleep.

You must always return the way you came, otherwise you will end up feeling very light-headed and ungrounded. When you are ready, your guide will appear and walk you back through the garden towards the entrance of the golden tunnel. Take your time and feel the gentle tug of the tunnel as you walk inside it. Feel it gently move you back down towards the earth. When you feel yourself come back through the tunnel, visualise the tunnel becoming once again just a ray of light and yourself returning to your normal size. Take a deep breath and then write down anything you remember in your development diary.

Questions to ask yourself

1. Did you get an image or feeling of a guide meeting you from the golden tunnel? And did they seem familiar to you? They could be one of your personal guides helping you with this exercise.

2. How did you feel in the garden? Was it sunny?

3. Did you feel any recognition towards the person you met who came out of the waiting room? Who do you think they were? Did they give you a name?

4. Did you hear words or phrases that are different from the ones you usually use?

5. Did you see a picture of a person that you could describe? What clothes were they wearing and what era did they seem to come from? Spirits will often present themselves in the way they dressed and behaved on earth, so you can relate to them.

If you have an experience of receiving communication with a spirit, then trust and have confidence in it. You will know if it 'feels right'. If you don't, then you may not have an aptitude for mediumship, as I've mentioned earlier. Or it may happen when you use your intuition another time. Do not worry. It is not an exam. The exercise will still have expanded your mind energy, strengthening the receptive side of your mind.

Keep practising

The best way to continue developing mediumship abilities is to practise on people you don't know well, just as you did with developing your intuition. You don't want to make any assumptions. Don't ask questions, and use the visualisation exercises to allow your mind to rise above and expand your mind energy. Ask for help when you have finished visualising by saying, 'Please allow a relative of this person to draw close to me so that I can relay strong evidence.' And don't be afraid to describe whatever images or words you get, however strange they may seem. You are learning and part of this lesson is to have the confidence to express whatever information you receive. It may seem strange to you, but in my experience it often makes complete sense to the other person.

Ask for evidence

If you are in any doubt if you are getting a mediumistic link, then ask for evidence in the same way as I did at the Buddhist ceremony. But if a spirit doesn't give you direct verbal evidence, as Rob did to me, there are other remarkable ways in which proof can be given.

. I was staying in Alaska with my mother and my Aunt Shirley. Their brother (my uncle) Derek had died only a few weeks before, and they asked me if I could pick up anything from him. I was happy to try and sat quietly going through my normal process, visualising (as mentioned in the previous chapters) my mind flying up into the clouds rising higher and higher to lift my vibration. I felt I had a connection and sensed his strong presence. Although you can't just summon up a spirit like a genie in a bottle, they can often be waiting to communicate and come close as soon as there is an opportunity to do so. I passed over some information, but as a beginner I wasn't confident as to whether it was coming from my unconscious or from 'my uncle's spirit'. He had a very strong, distinct personality, but as I knew him I wanted proof. I then heard the strange expression 'Yuletide in July'.

It was the month of July, but I didn't know what it meant

and neither did my aunt or mother – until the next morning. My mother came rushing into my bedroom excitedly clutching that day's newspaper saying, 'Something you said yesterday is a headline in today's paper.' As I opened the page, I saw 'Yuletide in July' in big black letters. I felt instantly relieved at the evidence. I knew then that I had a sign I was definitely on the right track, which gave me confidence in my newly developing skills.

Dismiss the baloney

There are a lot of myths about doing psychic and mediumistic readings. Some mediums and psychics say the person awaiting a message through you shouldn't sit with their legs crossed or their arms folded. This seems strange to me. I have never noticed any problem with tuning in to someone because of the way they position themselves. I have even been able to pick up information from somebody's name that I had written down myself on a piece of paper. They could have been doing handstands at the time for all I know.

The other myth is that you can't read for relatives or close friends. Once again this is total rubbish. Provided you are objective and don't make presumptions, this can work perfectly well. I have read regularly for close friends and members of my family, and apparently often given them accurate information about present and future problems. The only concern with reading for close relatives is if you get insight into bad news. Then of course, it could be a source of worry as, after all, it's your family.

Trance mediumship

Another rare aspect of mediumship is when the subject goes into a trance state (deep sleep) which allows a spirit to take them over completely. Their voice and mannerisms can be transformed by this new energy. Edgar Cayce must be one of the most famous examples of trance mediumship. He was able to put himself into a self-induced sleep state and respond with uncanny accuracy to any question that was put to him ranging from health, intuition, past lives and ancient civil-isations. Although he died in 1945 there are more than 300 books written about the different subjects he covered. It has to be stressed, however, that this type of mediumship is almost unique and I would be hard pressed to find someone whom everyone agrees is genuine.

Automatic writing as a vehicle for intuition or mediumship

There has often been speculation about whether automatic writing comes from a spirit guide or from our own intuitive self. The truth is, just like other communications, both occur. Automatic writing is one of the ways in which this book was written. It is where the author receives information, either through hearing a voice or through a sense of knowing, to convey knowledge. The writing is a vehicle and a focus for the mind, so that a higher energy can flow and take over the conscious mind.

You know it's automatic writing when it flows faster then normal conscious script. The words may be joined together and some of the spellings may be unusual to you. The way the letters are formed and the way they lean to the left or the right may also vary enormously from your normal style.

This information can be imparted in various ways. In my case, I believe I was, at times, in communication with my own higher mind. When I was trying too hard I got stuck in my logical conscious mind, and got writer's block and didn't know where to begin. But when I relaxed and allowed my words to flow my writing provided a tool to focus my mind, as in the case of psychometry, to allow words to filter through from my own higher knowledge. Some people say they experience mediumship when they write, where discarnate beings communicate with them and convey information. As the author writes unconsciously, they open up a communication with a highly evolved spirit guide who may be knowledgeable about a particular subject. Many books have been written and published like this, the most famous of which was called *Conversations with God*.

If you want to check that the information is from a guide or spirit, you can be assured that their personality and opinions will be quite different from yours. Be honest with yourself. If you know that many of the views are yours, then it is probably from the higher part of yourself. That does not diminish anything as long as what you are writing can help others or offer useful information. This book is about tapping into the highest teacher within. The knowledge within us comes from our soul energy and can be just as amazing, compassionate and wise as from any evolved guide or spirit.

Alan's story

Alan is a twenty-five-year-old who without any training has been able to write down information, guidance and premonitions, which often come true.

He says, 'I was nineteen when I discovered automatic writing. I was in bed at night and started writing down some thoughts on paper.

Suddenly the writing changed and I couldn't stop the pen from moving. I didn't have to think about what I was saying. When I got to the end and looked through it I was amazed. It was perfect punctuation and perfect structure, better than I could ever do myself. At the end of it, it was signed Solomon. As in King Solomon. It was a higher inspirational message saying, "God our father is with you always, even though you cannot see him, you can feel him. Stay connected with God and spread your love around the world, because right now the world needs it."'

Since then he has received other guidance from spirits and done lots of spiritual counselling for people who have depression. He believes he also uses automatic writing not only as a vehicle for spirits to talk but as a focus for his higher intuition to make many predictions for people. On one occasion he told a woman who was deeply depressed and taking constant medication to keep her going that she would soon meet a painter and decorator who was going to turn her life around. She was suicidal and needed a lifeline to get her through the many restless nights. Two weeks later she bumped into this man when he came round to her neighbour to price a decorating job, exactly as Alan had predicted. His automatic writing had helped give her hope that she would find someone who could help her start on a new and constructive path.

How to start automatic writing

This method of writing is another way of unlocking the unconscious mind, although you may well find that a guide comes through to give information. First find a large notepad and a pen and a quiet place to sit at a table. Let your mind drift as you hold the pen loosely in your hand. Start with anything that comes into your head and allow a flow of words to continue. As with any of the other exercises, relax and don't try too hard. If there isn't a flow of words that makes sense initially, practise one of the visualisations in the previous chapters and then write when you get the urge to do so. That 'urge' will be your intuition prompting you and you may get a valuable message.

Now that you are aware of a mediumship link, you know there is nothing to be concerned about. But you cannot force things to happen. If a spirit wants to contact you with a message, it will be when they decide. You can only develop your intuition, which will provide a channel for them to communicate through. Constructive communication from spirit is a privileged and cherished connection. They want to prove that their soul lives on and bring back messages to help those who are still grieving. And by doing so you can build on your psychic repertoire.

7

How Angels and Guides Can Influence Your Life

In the depth of your hopes and desires lies the silent knowledge of the beyond.
Kahlil Gibran, 1883–1931, philosopher

Now that you are aware of how mediumship works, as you continue to strengthen your higher mind you will see how other beneficial influences will gradually start to filter through. These influences come from spirit helpers, known to us as angels and guides, whose invisible presence surrounds us constantly. In this chapter I will explain what guides and angels are and the way they differ from each other and, more importantly, the roles they play in accelerating your psychic powers.

During your lifetime you may have seen an angelic vision or received inspiration through someone visiting you in your dreams and giving you guidance. If you have, then you will discover that it doesn't have to be a rare encounter. And for those of you who think you've never had such an experience, you may be in for a surprise. These beings don't always appear to us in a spectacular vision. We all experience the effects of angels and guides through our hunches, dreams and intuitive feelings. Ponder on this for a moment. Have you suddenly thought compassionately or positively about someone out of the blue? Where do you think that idea came from? Sudden inspired flashes like these are often the effects of an angelic influence prompting you to get in contact with the person.

Angels see our future possibilities and know when we need to connect up with someone and why. Guides exert their knowledge in the same way. When you wake up in the morning with an unexpected insight into a situation, it is often due to wise counselling that you received while you were asleep. Hence the well-known expression 'Sleep on it – things will seem better in the morning.'

If you wonder where angels and guides reside, believe it or not, their presence has always been around us. We have just been too busy to notice. Through the rough and the smooth times, they know every thought we have and see every action we take. But rest assured, despite seeing every side of our nature – good and bad – these beings are supremely compassionate and never judge us. They want to bring you uplift, strength and love in times of illness or trauma. They want to guide you back on to the right path when you lose your way. And they understand you, better than any friend ever could.

So, by developing your intuition you open up a channel for communication, just as I mentioned in the last chapter about mediumship. But guides and angels are on a much higher level than a spirit that is popping in for a chat. They know the game plan of your life in its most perfect form. And they are there for you. Anything you pick up with your sixth sense can be enhanced with their help. You will understand, through different exercises, exactly how you can amplify your awareness of them. Then, if you allow them, they will work with you every day to overcome the obstacles in your life and help you make wise decisions about everything from work, relationships, children and your future. The many and varied anecdotes will prove that their influence can not only change our lives but at times even rescue us from death.

What is a guide?

Guides are entities who have usually had a physical life on earth. This is where they differ from angels, who are pure spirit and have never been incarnated. One of your guides could be a relative, such as a wise grandmother who has passed over into the spirit world, helping give you support through an illness or tricky relationship. You could also have an evolved guide who has seen many incarnations and lived thousands of years ago who is helping you to find your true calling. Depending on the various stages of your life and level of your development, different guides will be allocated to come and help you. And you can have several at any one time.

For example, my father Larry had died of a heart attack nearly twenty years ago when he came through to a medium after I had joined a psychic development circle. The medium told me that my father still suffered with guilty feelings about leaving my mother when I was only a baby. Although he suffered with depression and alcoholism while he was alive, several decades in the afterlife had helped him to see the cause and effects of his actions, rather than the limited viewpoint he had had on the earth plane. He now wanted me to know that he was around to support me and was focused on helping me to develop my intuitive abilities. But although my father was around to help in that area, I also had other guides who were more evolved to assist me in making the right choices in my life.

Why do we need guides? Well, as we all know life can be a tricky and, at times, painful process, so fortunately for us humans it is part of our life plan to be given guidance and help. And in the same way that we have to go to school to learn different subjects, we are all given our spiritual lessons.

Guides are there to influence us to do our homework and remind us of our finer feelings. But of course we all have free will and we can choose to ignore their influences. The outcome of alcoholics, drug addicts, murderers and people who perpetuate violence shows how far we can fall when we choose the path of negativity. But as much as they can, guides will endeavour to protect you so that dangerous situations are avoided, to help you make decisions, to teach you lessons about love, healing and humility, and to aid you in finding your true pathway. What you learn about will largely be down to your own evolvement. They may communicate with you through your dreams, visions, mediumship or intuitive feelings. Some privileged people see their guides manifest in spirit form before them and then receive a message.

But there is an important point to note. Although it can be of passing interest to know who your guides are, don't get caught up in the detail. It's the message not the vessel that you should be focusing on. To explore how guides work in our lives, I want to expand on the many ways in which different people have received guidance and how it affects us all if we take time really to listen.

Guidance on your career

Guides have played a part in my life since I was very young. It has always felt natural to me to receive information and I've accepted it as normal. It was through a guide manifesting themselves to me that this book came to be written.

It was only recently that I was looking for a change of direction in my career and was thinking about what I should do before I went to sleep. I had stopped doing my psychic work since I had my daughter Isabel to look after as I was too busy working as a journalist. In the middle of the night I had an extraordinarily realistic vision of an elderly man in white robes. He sat on the edge of my bed and was very polite as he gently said, 'Think about bringing together all the things you have learned in your life, your healing and psychic abilities and use them again in a new way.' 'Do it – trust us', was the message he left me with. There was no command, it was more a case of gentle coaxing. But the encounter was so vivid, and the urge to remember so strong, that I immediately got up around three a.m. and wrote everything down.

A second dream happened several weeks later. This time I didn't see a guide, but I had strong telepathic guidance to write about psychic development and the word 'real' was written in front of me. When I woke up, I kept thinking it meant *Real* magazine which at that time had just established itself. It was only when I thought about getting case studies of people who have developed themselves psychically, to write an article, that I finally twigged. I needed to write a book on psychic development. Guides won't figure your life out for you. You are given suggestions, but it's up to your own free will whether you act on them. After several promptings from my spirit guides, the message to write a book had finally sunk in. Within the space of two months I had a publishing deal.

This shows how quickly things can happen when we listen to our higher influences. They know ahead of time the opportune moment to act productively to gain the best results, especially when other people will be helped by the outcome.

When guides are your spiritual schoolteachers

As you read different anecdotes, you will realise that guides often visit us in our dream state. This is when our defences are down and our subconscious is open to influence. This is what happened to Ingrid as you'll see.

Ingrid's story

Ingrid is a forty-year-old mother of two and a former schoolteacher. Several years ago she had been very ill with ME-type symptoms that seemed to come on for no reason. At times she felt so debilitated she had become bedridden. Whatever she did to help herself through diet and exercise, her health didn't improve. She then received guidance during her sleep. Every night when she went to bed, she felt as if she were being tutored intensively.

She didn't see a guide, but felt a strong male presence and heard an authoritative voice in the dream who said that her health would improve dramatically if she could learn to see things from three sides simultaneously. She saw the pages of a flip chart being turned over very quickly and each page had a triangle on it. The theme was about taking control of your emotions. One side of the triangle represented happiness, another side depression/anger and the third side was neutral, neither one nor the other. As Ingrid had always been passionate and intense, she knew that emotional control was one of the hardest things to achieve in life. She learned through her guide that it was about distancing yourself from a feeling rather like an actor. Ingrid says, 'It wasn't anything to do with suppressing an emotion, but more to do with feeling it and then stepping outside of yourself and being a witness to what you are feeling.' The guidance was showing her that we have to take responsibility for the effects we produce in our life and not become a victim of them.

As she went through several night-times of focused learning, she would wake up exhausted, but found she had been imparted information from the guide on 'earth breathing'. This was a special way of breathing, which would help bring a person into a deeply relaxed alpha state (which is when you are in harmonic resonance with the earth's

Schumann waves, as mentioned in chapter two). This particular way of breathing would bring many benefits, one of them balance to the emotions. She wasn't aware of any healing benefits to herself at the time, but from the moment she started to use this breathing technique to help others, her health improved enormously and she once again had huge energy reserves.

In my experience, from listening to many different people, an illness that occurs out of the blue and seemingly for no reason can come with a higher purpose. Perhaps there is something that you need to learn or maybe you need to change the path you are on. The illness slows you down from your normal routine, so that you can really pay attention and listen. Once we have taken on board the lesson from our guide and changed our path, we automatically recover.

Now you have read about some of the different ways in which guides can be there to help, you can discover how to improve your awareness of them. First, have a pen and your development diary ready to write down your experiences.

Exercise in learning to communicate with your guide

Getting in touch with your guides is simple. They are always with you, so when you want them to communicate with you, you just need to become more aware of their presence through heightened sensitivity. All your previous work on psychic development will have helped in awakening your senses. Now you are going to do an exercise that will enable you to forge a more conscious connection with them.

Find somewhere to sit comfortably and then take three deep breaths. Be aware of your energy field as it expands outwards from your body.

Feel around your body with your mind, around your head, shoulders and down towards your legs. Sense how far your energy reaches out into the room. To do this, simply imagine what it feels like if your energy is touching the walls of the room. Feel the sensation of what the wall is like. Whatever furniture is in the room, feel your energy touching the material, wood or metal and get a sense of it. Next visualise your energy touching the window in the room and sense how the glass feels. Is it cold and hard? This part of the exercise allows you to sense your own aura. Now visualise somebody whom you respect who embodies wisdom and compassion. It could be anybody from Mahatma Gandhi to one of your grandparents. It doesn't matter if they are alive or dead. You are using them as a focus point. Now ask in your mind for your guide to draw close to you. Sense a person who contains that knowledge and understanding. Visualise them standing behind you with their hands on your shoulders. Can you feel the presence of anyone? Can you feel any tingling sensations or hot or cold? If you feel a presence, does it seem male or female? In your mind ask their name, but don't worry if you don't hear one being given to you. Then form a question you need an answer to and direct it at your guide. Make sure it is worth answering and not anything ridiculous or trivial. Don't try to test them. If it is a silly question, then not only will you not get an answer, but you are wasting precious energy. See if any response comes into your mind. You may hear an answer in your head, or as a voice in your ear or written in your mind. You may just get a sense about it. If you can't feel anything yet, don't worry. It's early days. You may be trying too hard and not allowing yourself to relax and feel their presence. As you continue exercising your intuition, you will begin to feel their presence in your life and allow their wisdom to help you.

Other ways of accessing your guides can be done through dreams, which will be clarified in the next chapter.

When guides monitor our behaviour

Sometimes we are given guidance as a parent corrects a child. Suzy was only twenty-two when she got a telling-off for behaving badly. As a part-time barmaid she had started dating one of the rugby players who frequented the pub in south London. The rugby player turned out to be a womanising drunk and treated Suzy in a rather cavalier manner. To get her revenge on him, she decided early one morning to send round several mini-cabs to his house, at five-minute intervals, knowing they would continually get him up out of bed. And in the evening she sent round several pizza deliveries.

She was feeling pretty pleased with herself as she got ready for bed until she heard a loud voice that seemed to echo through her mind speaking in old-fashioned language ''Tis the most beautiful thing to be in this form and to have a relationship,' said the booming voice. 'But you must stop all this buffoonery!' Suzy was shocked and realised that what she was doing was ridiculous and she was being brought back into line. She thought she was getting away with her juvenile behaviour, assuming that no one would know about it. This voice proved that no action goes unobserved by the higher powers. Luckily, guides are always compassionate and objective. They are the ultimate perfect parents, allowing us to make our mistakes but pulling us into line when we need it.

Guidance for working relationships

Mark, twenty-nine, is a hospital maintenance fitter based in Yorkshire. He has had many experiences of guides, but one incident helped him out of a problem with work. Mark doesn't need to dream to see guides; he actually sees their presence and feels them around his house. His great-grandfather, Anthony, came through to give him guidance after dying in 1971, thirty years ago, before Mark was even born. At the time Mark was having problems with management at work and getting constantly harangued by one of his bosses. His boss was trying to put pressure on Mark and set his colleagues against each other with management wrangles, and there was a threat of his salary being cut. His boss would make comments like 'If anyone gets the chop, you'll be the first.'

One day at work Mark felt his great-grandfather's presence and saw an image of him behind the manager's shoulder saying, 'Don't trust him. But don't worry, I'll sort him out.' Within a few days, the manager stopped pressurising Mark and making sniping remarks and hasn't caused him any bother since. Mark knows that his great-grandfather came through to intervene in a difficult situation that seemed impossible. With spiritual guidance miracles can happen. Who knows how his great-grandfather stopped the problems recurring. It really doesn't matter. We just need to be grateful for the constructive intervention – on both sides.

Another way to improve your awareness of guides is through daydreams. Once again have your development diary and a pen to hand.

Use daydreams to contact your guide

First think of a goal that you want to achieve in life, something that you've always wanted to do. It could range from spiritual development to marriage and children or career. Write this goal down in your diary.

Now visualise an anonymous individual who embodies

great wisdom standing in a column of white light in your mind's eye. Picture a golden thread coming down from the sky connected to this person. Visualise wisdom, compassion and knowledge flowing along this golden link and connecting through this illuminated person and then to you. Ask the question in your mind: 'Please work with me and show me how to reach my goal.' This is an invitation to your guide to come forward. Now focus on a fountain of water, and see how the water shimmers and constantly flows. Watch all the water droplets and the shape the water makes. Allow your mind to wander freely. Think of yourself doing something enjoyable such as sunbathing, eating a nice meal, sitting in a green field or anything else that makes you feel good. See where you mind takes you. What other images float through your head? Allow these images to take on a life of their own, without consciously thinking about something. You may see something strange or it may not make sense.

But before you forget, write everything down in your development diary, whatever the images are and whatever feeling you got with them. If the pictures aren't coherent, gradually piece them together like a jigsaw. It may be that something will come to you gradually that may not make sense at the moment. Perhaps during this daydream your guide approached you, or maybe you got a sense of them being close to you. Do not be upset if you didn't get to see what they looked like or feel them close. Be aware that you have made another step towards becoming more conscious of your guides in your life and that they can help you understand the meaning of your daydream imagery.

Guidance on an unhappy marriage

When Jim was thinking about getting back with his wife of seven years he had an unexpected appearance from a guide. His wife had promised she was going to change from the unloving, bad-tempered woman she had been. She had caused him a lot of pain by lying constantly about her feelings and he didn't feel he could have an honest relationship with her. But after three weeks apart, he was feeling lonely and the thought of being in a destructive relationship seemed better than being on his own.

He had planned a reconciliation with her when he suddenly had a vision of a female guide with long hair as he was watching television. She stood behind him with her hands on his shoulders. He heard the information as if it were a voice in his head. 'I don't want to cause you any more pain,' said the guide, 'but you must know the truth. Your wife is deceiving you and she isn't going to change; don't go back. This chapter is closed now and there is a better life waiting for you.'

The vision and the message were so astounding to Jim, and made such an impact on him, that the very next day he told his wife their marriage was finally over. He knew the guide was answering his deepest concerns. He was frightened of being alone again, but now realises it was the best decision. Once he was detached from the emotional situation he could see objectively how damaging their relationship was and how he needed to start a new life without her. Guides see ahead of time what is waiting for us in the future and try to deter us from destructive situations and people who can only hold us back.

When guides protect us from harm

An experience I had four years ago shows how guides step in to pre-empt our behaviour and ensure our safety. It was the night before I was driving to Devon to see my brother, Maurice. I have always driven fast and in the early hours of the morning, in a semi-sleep state, I could see a group of people in my bedroom bathed in light. It looked as if there were about five beings radiating a golden aura who were huddled together having a serious and concerned debate about me. I felt that they were a mixture of guides and angels. I was half asleep but still aware of them and they must have been discussing my driving because in the end I woke up properly and said with irritation, 'All right, all right, I won't drive more than seventy miles an hour.' It was as if I were being politely told off and I only agreed to curb my speeding to shut them up.

The next day all I could think of was the light beings and why they were in my room. I felt compelled to keep to the speed limit. During the journey from Bath to Devon I could suddenly understand the concern. There was an unbelievably bad storm that went on for hours and I could hardly see where I was going because of the torrential rain hitting the windscreen. A tree had fallen and blocked my normal route, while water flooded the roads. When I finally drove through a small village near Totnes, I opened a window to ask directions from someone and rain poured in as if a hose had been turned on. By the time I arrived at my brother's house, I'd somehow lost a headlight. It quickly dawned on me that if I had driven at my normal pace it was likely I'd have had an accident.

Once again, guides know the probabilities of what may

happen. They often step in to help and protect us from ourselves and our own craziness as well as from natural disasters.

At this stage it is a good idea to point out to yourself the ways in which you are being given guidance. This will help to establish a stronger link with your guides as they become aware you are acknowledging them in your life. And it will also help you to pay attention to the help you are already receiving. The more you are aware, the more guidance you can take in – which will help smooth your pathway through life.

How to remain aware of guidance

- Focus on a problem before you go to sleep and then be aware of how you feel when you wake up in the morning. Make a note of any changes in your own attitude to the situation. Do you feel calmer, more resolute or with a sense of strength?
- Pay attention to any sudden hunches, inspiration or intuitive flashes that urge you to do something. If you are busy at the time, write down what the compelling feeling is and act on it as soon as you can – timing is often essential.
- Be alert to any tingling sensations, or feelings of heat or cold. Sometimes you can get a feeling of a sensation, rather like a niggling tickle in your ear. This often indicates that a guide is near you and wants to attract your attention or reassure you. Be open, sit quietly and listen to any thoughts or feelings that come into your mind.

Now we are moving on to the subject of angels. Just like guides they help us through our lives, filtering information in our dreams, hunches and intuition. But you will discover why they are very different entities.

What is an angel?

Each one of us has a guardian angel and they are always with us from our first spark of life. They are not spirits, like your late granny or uncle or any other souls of people who have passed on. Those relatives can become helpers or in some cases guides. Angels, however, are unique. They have never had a physical life here on earth, so they have never known negative emotions. They are simply pure beings of love.

Before we are born we all have the perfect blueprint of our true destiny, the constructive outcome that we can have if we follow our intuition, which is the voice of our higher selves. Unfortunately we can often fall prey to our negative influences, also known as deterrent forces, reacting to events in our lives with negativity, anger, arrogance, impatience and for some even violence. When this happens we lose sight of our true path, and amid the hurdles and stresses of modern-day life it is all too easy to forget to listen to our inner voice. (This is why we can never have an absolute destined path in life, because we all have the free will to decide which way we react to circumstances. An intuitive decision may create a different outcome to one born out of self-will which breeds arrogance or anger.) But within a moment we can just as easily find our way back. When we sit quietly and take time to listen, the angelic forces are always around and help us to make decisions, influencing us through our conscience, our intuition, hunches, dreams and even our inspirations and creativity. They are there to bring us love, protection and peace.

They have nothing to do with being Christian or any other religious beliefs. Whatever your views and even if you are an atheist, they will still intervene when danger is looming if it's not your time to die or if you have had a traumatic experience.

But in times of need they have to await direction from us. We have free will, so they cannot intervene without our request. But we don't always have to ask a direct question or pray to feel their influence. Often they respond to our intent or even our inner concerns of 'What do I do now?' Their mission is to do divine work, so they want to encourage us to ask for their help.

They all have different qualities of wisdom, compassion, endurance and hope; they influence us to stay on the right path and remind us that we are here to be of service to others.

When angels change your destiny

It seems that thousands of people have an inspiring tale to tell about the magical appearance of angels. These divine beings seem to appear in people's lives when they are suffering and need to find the strength to go forward. At times they appear when that person has a special service to provide for mankind, as a spiritual teacher or helper. Perhaps the most famous is angel expert and author of ten books on the subject, Diana Cooper, who had her first angelic experience over eighteen years ago.

She recalls the moment that changed her life, when she was slumped in an armchair in her living room. It was late in the evening as she sat in the darkness feeling utterly miserable. Recently divorced from her husband at the age of forty-two, with three young children, she held no hope for the future. Although she had no spiritual beliefs, in her depths of despair she suddenly asked for help.

'It was like a cry from my heart,' says Diana. 'I pleaded, "If there's anything out there – show me."' Suddenly she saw what she believed to be an angel standing in front of her, a six-foot-tall androgynous being radiating light. 'Then an amazing thing happened,' she continued. 'I felt as if I had left my body and went flying with the angel. I was taken to a hilltop and golden light was all around me. At one point I fell and landed in the light and yet I felt completely supported by it. I heard the words in my head: "We're here protecting you if you fall."

'I didn't feel at all frightened, despite the fact that I had never believed in angels or felt even remotely religious. Instead, there was an overwhelming sense of peaceful familiarity, like a feeling of coming home. I was then taken again by the angel to look down at the earth and saw a vision of a hall full of people listening to someone speak. The people in the audience all had rainbow auras around them. I asked the angel if I was one of the people in the audience and the being replied, "No, you're on the stage speaking." When I looked at the stage I could see someone standing there with transparent rays of light radiating from them. I completely understood from then on that I was to become a spiritual teacher.'

Whether it actually happened or whether it was just a mystical vision, Diana doesn't know. What she does remember is that the experience felt very real and when she opened her eyes and looked at the clock, she noticed it was exactly one hour later. 'Afterwards, I felt transformed. I was full of optimism about my life and that something kind and good really did exist. But initially I felt I couldn't share my experience with anyone. I immediately wrote everything down. I wanted to remember this amazing adventure that had taken place.

'After that experience, I knew I had to change my life.' Says Diana, 'I was miserable and had been a complete doormat to my domineering husband. He had consistently put me down and undermined my confidence for most of my twenty-year marriage and I had accepted my fate obediently, like many women of my era. After my divorce I realised that I had lost my identity and simply didn't see a future for myself as a single woman. Now after this astounding vision I knew with complete certainty that I had to rebuild myself; I still had to move house and find a job, but there was a difference. I was now being propelled forward by the inner knowledge that I had a destiny to fulfil.'

Diana went on to train as a healer and hypnotherapist, but she wasn't to see the angels again for another twelve years. While she was lying in the bath three angels appeared to tell her to write a book on healing. She wasn't keen at first until she heard the message: 'Who's doing your work – your ego or your higher self?' The result was her first book called *A Little Light on Angels*.

But could her vision have perhaps been a figment of her imagination? 'For me,' says Diana, 'it felt very real. But in truth it doesn't matter whether it was real or not. The impact helped me to turn my life around. Without the angel's intervention I would still have remained a deeply unhappy woman who was waiting for something to come along and make me feel fulfilled. Instead, I was prompted to create my own happiness by doing what my heart wanted me to do – which was helping others.'

Now, at the age of sixty-one, Diana is the quintessential expert on angels and has had numerous mystical visitations. And angels, it seems, are all around us, certainly if the response from the public was anything to go by when Diana Cooper appeared several years ago on ITV's *This Morning with Richard & Judy*. Photographs of her aura were taken on the show and there, above her right shoulder, the face of a golden angel could be seen. Viewers were stunned and the phone lines jammed with callers wanting to ask her questions and share their experiences. Diana was invited on the show again the following day to answer them. Only Tony Blair had ever been requested to appear again so soon.

When angels save your life

Susan, forty-three, is single and lives in Windsor, Berkshire. Her angelic experience forced her to change the self-destructive path she was on when she was working as an executive assistant to a rich Japanese businessman based in Tokyo. 'I was leading a shallow jet-set lifestyle where I lived for buying exclusive designer labels and frequenting the most expensive nightclubs,' she says. 'And that's when I got hooked on cocaine. I resigned from my job in Japan when I saw that my life seemed totally meaningless and returned home to England. I was burned out from the whirlwind society life and long working hours. And despite the fact that I was rich, successful and had my pick of suitors, I felt desperately unhappy. Once I was back in England, I blew thousands of pounds on cocaine, as a way, I suppose, of escaping my fear of the future. Drinking two bottles of tequila a day became normal, as did a cocktail of Valium and sleeping pills. I forgot to eat and consequently my body suffered as I got painfully thin. They were extreme measures, but all designed to shut out the utter agony of the emptiness I felt inside.

'One day as I was lying on my bed I had a horrific convulsion and died. I knew I had died, because suddenly I was out of my body and looking down at myself and could see with some surprise that I had turned dark blue. Then, suddenly, the whole room was filled with blue light and this angel appeared who seemed to be fifteen feet tall. He told me telepathically that his name was Michael and immediately I felt this immense peace and tremendous feeling of love. He continued to say that it wasn't my time to die and that my empty, meaningless life so far was my greatest teacher. This moment was always meant to bring me to this point of total despair so that I could fulfil my true destiny – which was to be a healer and to write a book on the subject that millions could identify with. I listened in complete awe.

'Just as suddenly I found myself back in my body, picking up the phone next to me and dialling a telephone number. I had no idea whose this number was until I heard a woman's voice answer. I realised then that it was one of my closest friends, Trisha, whom I had lost touch with three years before. She was a film producer who I thought was still working in America and I was amazed to discover that she was also back home. I didn't have her new phone number and she didn't have mine, but she was a devout Christian who totally believed in angels. Sceptics might say I was delirious from the drugs, but it is a mystery to me how that phone number magically appeared in my mind. Sobbing, I told her of my experience, while she listened patiently before saying that she understood what had happened. That same night, she came over to see that I was all right and cooked me a meal. I was so grateful for finding her again and that's when we both realised that we'd been divinely guided to reconnect.

'Over the course of the next seven years I turned my life around. I admitted myself into a drug rehabilitation clinic and learned how to cope with life without resorting to drugs. One of the angel's messages was that I should learn to help others by sharing my experiences, so I also trained to became a healer helping patients with everything from cancerous brain tumours to asthma, ME and depression – and of course drug addiction. My family supported me in my new-found belief that there really was a god. Although they were never religious, they couldn't fail to believe in divine intervention once they had seen how my life was transformed. I do believe the angel Michael is my special guardian. I always feel him around me and now I have supreme proof that something powerful and benevolent really does protect us. Prior to my angelic experience I had no spiritual values or conception of anything beyond my shallow materialistic life. I had never taken any time out from my hedonistic pursuits even to consider what I felt. Yet I now feel so immensely fulfilled to be doing what I believe I was meant to do. I sense not just one, but many angels' divine presences. I will always be eternally grateful. They literally rescued me from death.'

Now you know just how angels can help give you the support you need, regardless of whatever problem you are going through. This is a meditation to put you in contact with your guardian angel.

Meditation to contact your angel

You don't have to have a grand vision to know your angel is there for you. Feelings are just as valuable. The most important thing is that angels bring uplift and optimism.

To evoke your angel, all you have to do is find a quiet place and sit comfortably. Relax and then breathe deeply and exhale slowly. Do this three times. Close your eyes and get a sense of where you are in the room. Focus on how you are sitting and sense the atmosphere around you as if you could feel the air against your skin. Feel your heart beating and listen to the sound of silence or any other noises in the background. Concentrate again on your regular breathing pattern as you take a breath in and out. By doing this you are centring yourself.

Silently ask your guardian angel to come close to you and imagine feeling its gentle wings enfold you. Pay attention to any tingling feelings however subtle or a sense of warmth anywhere in your body. Do you sense any changes around you? Do you get a feeling of uplift or optimism? In your mind, ask your angel its name. If a name comes into your mind be happy, but don't worry if it doesn't. Become aware that your guardian angel as well as many other angelic presences fill the room with love and healing.

Now imagine if love was a colour, what it would be? How would it feel? Would it feel warm, reassuring and fulfilling? Imagine breathing in this loving coloured energy and picture it flowing into your heart making your chest expand. Breathe in this colour of love until you feel full.

When angels help you through ill health

Sue, forty-one, is divorced with a son Oliver, aged eleven, and a daughter Hannah aged twelve. Sue believes that angels helped her through breast cancer at the age of thirty-eight. She now runs her busy private health club and feels that her experience led her to helping others face their fears. She says, 'I dreaded my breast cancer returning after an operation to remove a tumorous growth. I was feeling terribly lonely and anxious the night before I went in to have the operation in Heatherwood Hospital in Ascot. As I was divorced and single my deepest fear was that after surgery I might never find anyone to love me again. I dreaded the idea of what I might end up looking like.

'That night, while my children were fast asleep in their rooms, I went to bed early with my thoughts churning over about the outcome. Then I suddenly opened my eyes and saw this dark grey swirl. I thought it was smoke coming from a fire, but when I sniffed I couldn't smell anything. But as I looked around, to my astonishment the whole room was completely filled with luminous angels. They were each around four inches high with perfect white feathered wings and each one was encircled with light. Logically I should have been surprised and yet there was this deep feeling of comfort and recognition. My immediate reaction was that I wanted to fetch the children and bring them in so that they could see this wonderful sight, but I couldn't move. It was as if I were glued to the spot. Then just as suddenly, it was the morning and I awoke not remembering how I went to sleep, but still filled with the same contentment.

'I felt so happy on the day of my operation that I literally leaped out of bed. The worry and anxiety about my future had simply melted away. My children couldn't believe the difference in my mood and I treated the hospital more like a holiday camp than the place I so long feared.

'I told my children about the angels when they said, "I hope you're going to be all right, Mummy." "I'll be fine," I replied, "because I saw the angels last night!" They didn't even question it, they just said, "Oh, that's all right then," without any surprise. It was as if they already knew. Ever since then, although I haven't seen the angels in the same way, I often feel their protective warm presence around me and I immediately feel reassured. Without that uplifting experience I would still be living in fear, feeling distressed and believing the worst. I would have exacerbated the cancerous condition, possibly causing a recurrence, instead of which I now count my blessings. It's important to know that we don't have to take everything on ourselves. I do believe that angels are everywhere for everyone and if we could only take some time to sit quietly, we would feel their presence when we ask for their help.'

When angels affect our behaviour

Don't expect angels always to appear in luminous light. And they don't always come in times of abject despair. Sometimes they come in subtler ways through our conscience and hunches to help us make choices which will result in a constructive outcome.

I had just such an experience after returning home from a holiday. I had let a friend stay in my flat while I was away in order to feed my cat. But when I had rung home a few times she'd had other friends staying who answered the phone and didn't seem to know who I was.

I felt livid and was getting ready to bawl her out on my return when I heard this faint voice saying, 'Don't be so hard-hearted. Look at someone's positive attributes. She's got good points.' As I listened to this quiet voice, I felt a wave of calm come over me. I decided I wouldn't argue with her. Instead I gave her the present I had got for her and never mentioned the friends staying. It turned out that she wanted to be a student on my new psychic development course and recommended many people to me for readings. Over time we became closer as friends. The angels had influenced me by cutting through my angry reaction to assist in a constructive outcome. If I had acted differently we would both have lost important opportunities.

When angels give healing

At other times, angels can come to us to bring healing. Alice remembered bumping into an ex-boyfriend, Angus, in the street. She had wanted to meet him for ages to try and resolve the way things had ended between them. Initially, she was grateful to be caught on a day when she was looking her best. He walked over to her with a huge grin on his face and they both started talking. The problems arose when she suggested meeting for a drink as friends. Suddenly he started shouting, 'I know what you're trying to do – all you women are the same,' and he glared at her wildly. For some reason, although Alice was fiery by nature, she didn't retaliate, but simply said, 'Okay,' and walked off. But when she got home she felt deflated and upset.

That night, when she was half asleep, she was gently woken by her name being called as if it were coming from a long way off. Then she felt as if different people were moving their hands along her body, touching her feet and stroking her aura. She felt very comforted and knew she was receiving healing. She woke up in the morning refreshed and without a trace of bitterness towards Angus and feeling very positive and optimistic about life. In fact for some reason she suddenly thought, I really love Angus, and that love felt unconditional. She knew then that she didn't always have to try and resolve a situation physically, that it could happen on another level by relinquishing any negative feelings. That last thought was her sense of closure.

This is just another aspect of how angels come to us to bring healing and uplift.

Healing with angels

When you want to receive healing from the angels, you can once again use your imagination to allow them to come close to you.

First ask for the angels of healing to draw near. Now visualise your heart as a flower. Picture yourself focusing on the
flower in your chest. What does it look like? Is it in full bloom
or just a tiny bud? What colour is it and does it look like it's
been well nurtured or neglected? Take this flower in whatever shape or form and ask your angel to hold it in loving
energy to give it healing. Now think of anyone you know with
whom you have unresolved conflicts or issues. Visualise the
flower in their heart and once again see what shape it is. Ask
your angel to give healing to their heart flower and visualise
both hearts in a golden healing glow in the angel's hands.
Then ask your angel to communicate with the guardian angel
of that person to bring harmony between you. Do not ask out
of desperation or emotional angst. Simply ask uncondition-
ally without any motive except the highest good. Visualise
yourself with the person surrounded by love. You don't need
to exert any willpower to create healing; just trust that your
angel will heal the rift. Many times angelic influences can
create miracles and resolve seemingly impossible situations.
They allow a door to open that has previously been closed.

You can ask the angels to come close to you at any time,
wherever you are. Every situation has its own special angel,
such as relationships, career and home. Simply say in your
mind, can the angel for relationships please come close and
bring healing, and within moments your angel will be there
to support you. Trust the angels; their mission is to bring
healing and love to everyone.

If you want to strengthen your connection with angelic
forces then it is important that you are aware when they
affect your life. Your awareness of their help means a channel
can be opened between your higher self and their influence,

and their beneficial healing and supportive effects will be felt more easily.

How to remain aware of angelic influences

- Notice any sudden mood changes. If you are angry, depressed or sad and feel emotionally reactive, notice if your feelings become quickly transformed into positive ones for no reason. We all know what a black cloud of depression feels like. Think of an angelic influence as being encompassed in a cloud of optimism and compassion. If this happens you will know angelic forces are at work to change your reactions. Equally, if you feel in a destructive and negative state of mind, you can ask the angels to help change your mood to a more positive and caring one.
- Notice if you suddenly feel a wave of calm or warmth around you or any tingling sensations. They can also help you to connect with the 'love' inside you by giving you a sense of completeness. Angels often come to bring us comfort in times of need.

Diana Cooper has the last word when she says, 'We go through so much as human beings but we don't realise that there is a fundamental wealth of help available to us. Angels come to us with love, reassurance and comfort. And all we have to do is ask.'

'And what of the sceptics?' I asked.

'Well,' says Diana, 'scepticism is very healthy. We have to question to discover the truth. But I would say, always have an open mind – because you never know when you might need it.'

*   *   *

Angels and guides want us to realise that we never need to feel alone. Through their influences our psychic perceptions are clearer and more accurate, and developing our intuition means they get to give their input more easily as they connect with us through our higher minds. Their destiny is to give us support in all our endeavours so that we can create the successful life we want.

8

How to Accelerate Your Intuitive Powers
with Psychic Dreaming

They tease me now, telling me it was only a dream. But does it matter
whether it was a dream or reality, if the dream made known to me the truth?
Fyodor Dostoevsky, 1821–81, Russian writer

So far, I have led you on a step-by-step journey to the many tools that will enable you to use your psychic skills. You are now ready to open another door into the reservoir of your intuitive power: through your dreams. The more you develop your psychic awareness, the stronger the connection between your spirit (inner voice) and your conscious mind, and therefore the clearer and more profound the messages your dreams will relay. Of course when we sleep, dreams allow our souls to be free to learn and explore other dimensions within the depths of our subconscious. But if the right side (yin) of our mind is undeveloped and clouded with cynicism, we never fully experience the truth of our dreams. The rational side of our mind (yang) will put up resistance and try to block the message the dream has for us. This is why our dreams may be cloaked in confusing symbolism or vague imagery that can be hard to interpret. Or we might find it difficult to remember our dreams at all.

But when our mind has been expanded and focused with psychic awareness exercises we are naturally more conscious in our dream state. We can experience a heightened sense of reality and our dreams are therefore clearer, vivid and more significant, which is why I have left the subject of dreaming until this stage of the book. You won't need to work them out. The messages they impart will be obvious because our inner voice can influence our dreams with no restrictions.

You can now receive constructive help from angels and guides. You can be inspired creatively, solve any problems, have premonitions of the future and communicate telepathically. Dreams show us, beyond all doubt, that the answers to everything we need to know are within ourselves.

First, let's look at the many functions that dreams have:

1. Dreams are necessary for our sanity. It has been proven by sleep deprivation studies that loss of REM (dream) sleep leads to temporary personality changes.
2. Dreams are often a source of creativity.
3. Dreams can reveal through imagery repressed feelings or unconscious desires and conflicts so that the person can confront them.
4. Dreams can help resolve problems and act as a catalyst for change in our lives.
5. Recurring dreams may be dramatisations of issues you are avoiding. They are showing us the reasons behind our feelings.
6. Dreams help heal our bodies and minds by presenting unresolved issues that may make us feel unstable or stressed.
7. Dreams are vehicles for higher beings, such as guides and angels, to provide us with healing and insight.
8. Dreams provide a basis for psychic connections, such as telepathy and premonitions.
9. Dreams can give us insight into our past.
10. Dreams can provide an opportunity for learning.
11. Dreams can be a projection of yourself, as the characters

in the drama act out parts of you. The dream is to reclaim your part in the drama.

12. Dreams can be a release of sexual energy.

There are many books written on the subject of dreaming, but I am going to focus on the dreams that can expand your intuitive awareness.

When do we start dreaming?

Amazingly, we spend one-third of our lives asleep. Sleep patterns can be divided between light sleep known as NREM and deep REM sleep. Dreaming starts during our REM sleep, any time from one hour to ninety minutes after first falling asleep. We then move in and out of REM and NREM sleep roughly every 80–100 minutes. Our dream time increases with each successive REM stage, the longest period occurring in the last cycle before you wake up. That means that the more you sleep, the more you dream. During REM sleep is when you have bursts of rapid eye movement seen under the eyelids and our respiration and heartbeat become irregular. Although our body is effectively paralysed during REM sleep, research on brain activity during our dreams shows it is at times more active then when we are awake.

Creating a dream diary

It is important before doing any of the exercises to keep a specific dream diary, separate from your psychic development diary. Treat this book as a precious document. Use an attractive binder or book to inspire you. It will help you subconsciously to remember your dreams. The first part of your dream may be confusing, so draft the outline on to rough paper and then write up the dream neatly when you have filled in the gaps. Try to write down your dreams every day, and give each dream a number to help you keep track. Allow space not just for your dream, but also for any insights you have on them, whether they are problem-solving, a creative inspiration, premonitions, or telepathy. However confusing a dream may be, the more you become aware of them the more you strengthen the connection to your intuitive self. Remember also to note the atmosphere of the dream, and your mood. It might be a cold, frosty day but your mood may be alert. Once you've written down something, however odd it seems, you may suddenly have a moment of clarity as you brainstorm the meaning of it. The more your awareness increases the clearer and more vivid your dreams will become. Soon the majority of your dreams will be straightforward communication with a clear message that you won't have to struggle with to find the answers. And you will be able to understand the pattern your life is taking.

Using one of my own dreams, I'll give an example of how to set up your dream diary.

Example for setting up a dream diary

Date: 9 March 2002
Dream: 1
Time: Some time just before 8 a.m.
The dream: Skiing down a hillside just for the fun of it. A woman was in the dream in a ski suit, showing me how to ski and saying

clearly, 'There's no reason for skiing. We do it for the fun of it.' I then try to ski and slide down the hill. I find it exhilarating and can see why people like it.

Atmosphere: Bright snow, frosty.

Mood: Learning to be light-hearted.

Signs and symbols: Skiing, woman in ski suit, snow, hillside.

Type of dream: Answering a question from the day before.

Any associations: Having an in-depth discussion with a girl friend the day before about men we were dating and whether there was any point to it all. The dream imparted to me that I should 'lighten up' and just enjoy a situation for what it was, without trying to look for a reason.

Tips on how to improve your recall of dreams

* Research has proved that it is easier to recall your dreams if you stand up or sit up straight immediately on awakening. This stops you from feeling sleepy again and losing conscious memory of your dream.

* Always keep your dream diary by your bed with a pen. It is important to remember as many details as possible, even if they seem trivial or ridiculous. Dreams are often associative, which means a small part of the detail can link you to additional scenes of the dream.

* We always dream every night. If you were asleep, then you have dreamed. So if you wake up thinking you haven't dreamed anything, it is always because you have forgotten. In these circumstances, focus on the first thought in your mind on waking. This thought should always remind you of the last part of your dream. When you focus on the details it should help you recall the rest of the dream.

* If you know you have urgent things to do in the morning,

always write down on a piece of paper what they are before you go to sleep. It could be phoning the bank, paying the milkman, or buying some bread. If you already have a list, you won't worry first thing about what you have to do and can fully concentrate on recalling your dream.

- Sometimes you can 'break' or recall a dream that you had forgotten by something seemingly trivial happening in the day. Keep a pad and pen with you, so that if anything does make you remember you can quickly write it down.
- Try not to overeat or drink too much alcohol before you go to sleep. It will disrupt your sleep pattern and make you feel groggy and drowsy in the morning, which will hinder you waking up properly and recalling your dream memory.

Dream premonitions in history

Since our primitive ancestry we have had the capacity to dream, reminding us that knowledge and wisdom exist within. Predictive dreams date back nearly 4,000 years. Some of the earliest dream writings were written on Egyptian papyrus dating from the twelfth dynasty around 2000–1790 BC. There were also recorded dream premonitions on cuneiform-script clay tablets by the ancient Assyrians and Babylonians, while dreams were an accepted means of prophecy in the Greek and Roman civilisations.

Sadly, many reported prophetic dreams often have a common theme: the prediction of a major disaster. Unfortunately these cataclysms are a part of life whether they are terrorist attacks, natural events such as severe flooding or the result of a madman going berserk. The damage is always far-reaching as they affect so many people and seem so out of our hands. The same questions are always raised. Did this have to happen? Could we change the course of history?

Statistics have shown that precognitive dreams usually come true within a few hours or at the most within forty-eight hours, and a higher percentage of women dream the future than men. But although these premonitions may not make the tragedy avoidable, surely the individuals concerned can stop themselves being led to a premature death.

The story of the famous unsinkable *Titanic* is well known. The huge cruise liner struck an iceberg in 1912 and sank in the North Atlantic, taking 1,500 lives. Some of the passengers who were due to go on the voyage cancelled their trip at the last minute because of a precognitive dream about the disaster. Second engineer Colin MacDonald declined his position on the *Titanic* because of a hunch that disaster lay ahead when he awoke in the morning from a dream. Others cancelled because they just 'felt strange about it'. Their predictive dreams were a warning that although this terrible event couldn't be prevented in the overall course of history, they could perhaps control their own fate as to whether they lived or died.

One of the best established and most reputed cases of predictive dreams came from the disastrous events that occurred on 21 October 1966 in the town of Aberfan in Wales. A large heap of coalmining waste collapsed and buried a small section of the town including twenty-eight adults and a primary school containing 116 children. This devastating catastrophe effectively killed an entire generation of children and affected every family in the town. But afterwards there were signs that perhaps this bleak day in history could have been avoided when many reports of dream premonitions flooded in from all over the country.

It seemed that many people shared a common warning that somewhere in their higher consciousness this destruction of a small town seemed unavoidable. One lady had a nightmare that she suffocated in 'deep blackness'. Another dreamed of a small child being buried by a large landslide. The mother of one of the deceased students reported that her ten-year-old daughter had foreseen the disaster, in which she was doomed to die, the night before. The child had said to her mother, 'I dreamed I went to school, but there was no school there. Something black had come down on it.' Another clear premonition was reported by a man in the north-west of England who claimed the night before the disaster that he had a dream which consisted only of the letters, A B E R F A N, being spelled out in dazzling light. At the time the dream had no meaning to him. Only hours later, as he listened to the news, did he finally understand its grim message.

Because of the large number of reported premonitions, London psychiatrist J.C. Barker felt there must be a way of intervening to stop the destruction and death of so many people. So Barker headed a study with three independent organisations, whose results concluded that there were over twenty-four separate precognitive dreams foretelling the traumatic events of Aberfan. The psychiatrist then formed the British Premonitions Bureau to use the power of predictive dreams to try to change the course of history. So far, however, the bureau has failed to stop any other tragedies taking place.

Premonitions in our everyday life

Fortunately, not all premonitions predict such horrific news stories. Less commonly reported but more frequent premonitions give us practical warnings of events ahead of time, involving day-to-day problems with work, family and friends. I had a premonition when I was twenty-one and working as a secretary in a firm of accountants in Covent Garden. I became good friends with a secretary called Angie who had recently started work. We had great fun together and often went out in the evenings. She was always telling me funny anecdotes about her life in her strong Welsh accent.

But when I went on holiday to Spain for a week I had a prophetic dream. I dreamed that Angie told me that she would have to say goodbye. We went for a drink together to wish each other well. I asked her why she was going and she said, 'I can't explain. I just have to leave.' That was the dream, plain and simple. It seemed strange, because everything seemed fine when I last saw her.

However, when I got back to work on my return, I walked into the office to find that Angie wasn't there. I asked if anyone knew where she was and my boss mentioned that they hadn't heard from her for the last few days. 'Hasn't anyone rung her to find out?' I questioned. It all seemed a little strange. I told the partners of the firm about my dream and that she'd said goodbye. I rang up her home and was told by a friend that she had been involved in a violent row with her husband and had immediately fled back to her parents in Wales. They said she would never return to work. That was the last I saw of her. But how amazing that when I looked back at the timing of my dream, it was several days before the row with her husband. The power of the mind always astonishes me. Despite being thousands of miles away and knowing nothing of her absence from work, the dream had not only predicted the future, but allowed us, on another level, to say goodbye.

Sometimes premonitions can be warnings to curb our behaviour. Alison, a thirty-three-year-old nursery nurse from

Reading had a premonition of a problem that could be caused if she sniped about her neighbours. She dreamed that her neighbours on one side overheard her gossiping about them and it caused a lot of upset between them. A week later, Alison had forgotten the dream and was agreeing with some other neighbours how annoying these particular people could be. They talked at length about how these people were a bit nosy and intrusively over-friendly. The animated conversation continued while they were standing in their front gardens leaning over the fence. But unfortunately, the victims of the gossip, a young couple, overheard the disparaging remarks, as they didn't have any double-glazing to muffle the noise. Just as Alison's dream had accurately prophesied the couple came round to see her a few days later and relayed how upset they were. It took a long time to smooth things over and Alison felt extremely embarrassed. She realised her premonition was a warning that she didn't heed!

Stephanie Williams, forty-eight, a cosmetic surgery adviser, had a premonition at the age of eleven that her family have never forgotten. Two nights before her parents were taking Stephanie and her two sisters to visit relatives in Yorkshire, Stephanie had a nightmare. She dreamed that something horrible was going to occur on the 100-mile journey from their home in Hertfordshire and she felt terrified. The feeling stayed with her and she told her parents over breakfast, 'I'm not going with you, because something bad is going to happen.' Her father was not amused and told her off, saying, 'You're just saying this to get out of coming with us.' But Stephanie was so persistent and scared about the journey that finally one of her friend's parents said she could stay the weekend with them.

It turned out that Stephanie's dream came true. On the

return journey her family had a terrible car accident where her father had to swerve to avoid an oncoming vehicle and her mother was thrown from the car. They arrived home looking bruised and battered. Her mother needed ten stitches in her arm and her father had whiplash. Her sisters fortunately escaped with only a few scrapes but were badly shocked. All Stephanie could say when she saw them all was, 'I told you something bad was going to happen.' Stephanie's dream has now gone down in history, as her father frequently told other relatives in their family, 'That girl's a witch.'

Programme your dreams to see the future

A good dream exercise for developing premonitions involves focusing on a future front page of a newspaper. Successful studies have been done of dream premonitions when volunteers were given a future date and asked to dream what the front page of a US tabloid would be on that day. The volunteers programmed their dreams by focusing on the specific publication date of the said newspaper before they went to sleep. Sometimes they wrote down the date on a piece of paper and put it under their pillow or asked a question like, 'What will be on the front page of this newspaper on this date?' When they awoke they immediately wrote down their dreams, which had to be submitted postmarked no later than the day before the publication.

The examples were inspiring. One woman dreamed that she was sitting on her husband's lap making some kind of graph. She says, 'When I awoke I couldn't remember anything specifically about the graph except I believe it looked like a line graph rather than a bar graph. When I finished the graph my husband was very proud of me.'

When the newspaper was published on 17 August 1995, the judges were impressed that there was a line graph at the bottom left-hand corner of the page. The graph depicted that women voted more than men did. The line representing women voters sat on top of the line depicting men, just as the dreamer was sitting on her husband's lap. The dream had given a perfect predictive illustration of one of the news items on the front page.

A second dream for the same day's published page was from a woman who said, 'I was driving in a car, the weather was bad and the water and mud were so deep I kept getting stuck.'

On that day there was a photograph of a car, which appeared to be stuck in muddy water.

Your own premonition experiment

Before you go to sleep, think of a future date of a national newspaper front page, perhaps a few days ahead. Write the date down on a piece of paper and put it under your pillow. In your mind ask to be given pictures and information about what will appear on the front page on that specific date, for example 15 November 2002. Drift off to sleep with this on your mind. Your longest REM dream will be the one just before you wake up. If you know you will have disturbances, such as children, the dog or your partner distracting you first thing in the morning, set the alarm for fifteen minutes before your usual morning call, so that you have time to remember as much of your dream as you can.

When you wake, mull over your last thoughts, then allow as much of the rest of the dream to come back to you. Write it down immediately in your dream diary, with as many unimportant or minor details as possible. If it doesn't make sense, read it over later when you have the time and see what comes to your mind. Then wait a few days and compare it with the newspaper on your chosen day. It is incredibly exciting when it works. If it doesn't work, keep experimenting – but stay relaxed for optimum effects – as you'll be encouraging your mind to focus on future results. You could also try the same thing with broadcast news. As your mind energy continues to reach out towards the future in your dreams you will become more receptive to receiving any premonitions your subconscious wants to give you.

Of course, you can always ask to see the future with any situation, but do bear in mind that the future is not written in stone when it comes to people in our close relationships. Events can change with our free will, so don't become obsessed by trying to dream future predictions. Equally, if you ask about someone close to you, you could receive upsetting information. So for your own sake keep it as objective as you can, using newspapers or television events for major news stories.

Dream telepathy

Telepathic communication in our dreams happens more often than we realise. We can pick up mind-to-mind contact in our dream state that, if we used it more regularly, could almost dispense with a phone call or e-mail. Many years ago I arranged to go out with a work colleague, Sarah, at the weekend, to visit an art exhibition. I then had a dream two nights before that Sarah came into my office at work and said, 'I can't make it this weekend, something's come up. Can we rearrange?'

The next day she came into my office and said, 'About the weekend,' and I jumped in ahead, with 'I know exactly what you're going to say.' We both thought it was uncanny that I had obviously picked up on her thoughts the night before.

Sisters Maria and Katy Campbell have many telepathic dreams, which is a common theme with twins. Katy, aged nineteen, said, 'I had a dream where Maria was wearing a pink and grey jumper with a pink skirt. The next day Maria came over for lunch wearing this exact same outfit, which was brand-new and I'd never seen before. I'd obviously tuned in to what she was thinking of buying at the time.'

Carolyn, a forty-two-year-old advertising executive was dreaming one night when suddenly another dream cut across it, as if she were getting a news flash. The dream depicted an empty desert with a crusader's tomb in the middle of it. On the outside of the tomb were very slender black bars. But it was as if she could see someone in there struggling to get out. 'I knew the instant I woke up that my ex-lover had died.' She says, 'The crusader's tomb was significant as my ex-lover was Armenian and a Christian, and he had been suffering with cancer for a while.

'I immediately drove to the hospital where he had been bedridden and when I got there he was no longer conscious. He was pronounced dead twenty-four hours later. When I looked at his eyes, his eyelashes were plastered down on his lower lids, and it was as if I were looking at his eyes through the slender bars of the tomb as I saw in my dream. I really felt that it was as if he were telepathically telling me that he was dying in my dream state.'

Experiment with dream telepathy

There have been many studies done on dream telepathy with productive results. We can pick up on someone's thoughts about us or a situation in our dreams, as well as arrange to meet someone in our night-time journeys.

Focus on meeting a friend you know well outside a venue at a certain date and time and visualise giving them a gift. Plan it in your mind and make sure you arrange the place and time properly as you would in real life. Write it down if it helps. Imagine giving your friend something unusual that would stand out, like a silver flute or a golden rose. Pick a friend who is good at remembering dreams and has a flexible lifestyle where they won't forget your experiment. Ask them to write down whatever dream they have on the same night as you plan to dream about meeting them, but don't tell them why.

Before you go to sleep remind yourself where you are to meet this particular friend and the gift you will give them. Visualise meeting them as you drift off to sleep. Then write down your dream as soon as you wake up. Compare notes the next day. You may need to practise this a few times but the results could amaze you.

Communication with guides and angels through dreams

What makes a guidance dream different from other types of dreams? When guides and angels visit us in our dream state the information is presented with complete clarity. It isn't your typical dream, which may be puzzling or obscure. The dream will be more like a vision and will provide the answer to a question either verbally or through a picture.

Before you go to sleep, write down a question or problem in your dream diary that you need answering and keep your diary and a pen by your bed to jot down any dreams you have first thing. The question could be about your career, relationships, children or finances. It could even be about your own spiritual development if you wish. Ask in your mind for your guide to help you find the answers in your dream state. This should be simple enough. In my experience you don't have to make a ritual of it. Just be clear about the question and focus on asking it. In most dreams when a guide visits you, their presence is strong enough to wake you up to remember the vision. If you don't always see the guide or angel in a dream, you may still hear or sense them around you. Sometimes the question is answered in the dream. Or you may suddenly have a sense of clarity about the situation. You don't need to see someone for it to be valid.

Exploring our creativity through dreams

Expressing our creativity is vital to our psychic development. Creating something, whether it is painting, writing, cooking or thinking up ideas and putting them into action, relays a real connection between our higher intuitive selves and our conscious minds. Dreams are a huge creative source. And higher divine beings often filter through inspirational ideas that can help us.

For instance, a dream gave me an idea about integrating our feminine yin and masculine yang energy. It was five years ago when I had finished teaching a psychic development class and one of the students said to me, 'You're very yang, aren't you?' When I asked her what she meant she continued, 'Well, you're very in touch with your masculine side, you seem quite assertive.'

That night I went to bed thinking about this yin yang energy, which hadn't even occurred to me before. In the middle of the night my dream was so vivid it woke me up. I saw a vision of an article already written in the newspaper about blending our feminine and masculine energies together, so we could become more balanced.

In the morning I felt so confident and excited about writing it that I rang up the editor who was in charge of a new section at a newspaper. I told him about my new feature idea. He hesitated and I could tell he wasn't too sure what I was on about, but within a few minutes he said, 'Okay, do it then.'

I did some research, but the idea came from my intuition. I did a quiz, which flowed, and the feature and case studies came together easily. It was published a few months later and there was even a front-page leader to the section saying, 'Are your yin and yang out of balance?'

My experience not only proved that my dreams provided me with an answer to my thoughts on what had been said to me, but also how an innovative idea that someone else doesn't understand can still work when it comes from a higher source.

Claire, a forty-four-year-old journalist and mother of three children, says, 'Whenever I got stuck at university with an essay in my English and American lit class, I would often keep thinking of what to do and then I'd dream the introduction to it. It would always be vivid enough to wake me up so I could remember it, until I got it written down. It happened many times, and the introductions and phrases I got in my dreams were far more imaginative and inspiring then anything I could have written during the day.'

Susanna, a thirty-three-year-old cosmetic surgery consultant, had a dream that she must set up a credit card facility for patients. She didn't remember the dream exactly, but the message remained foremost in her mind. When she woke up, she thought what a good idea it was and immediately felt the impetus to ring up and make an appointment with the business manager of her bank. On hearing her proposal, the manager said to Susanna, 'Well, if you're going to have a credit card facility, I'll have my nose done!' Susanna realised that her dream was obviously a good marketing ploy to expand her business.

Programme your dreams for creativity

All you have to do is think for a while before you go to sleep about what help you need. Focus on quite specific things that you want help with creatively. It might be song lyrics, a new design for a kitchen, a colour scheme for your house, or novel ideas for selling a product. Write down what you need on a piece of paper if it helps and try to let the subject be the last thing on your mind as you drift off to sleep. Although in some cases your dream may be stirring enough to wake you up don't then be tempted to go back to sleep immediately. Write it down on a piece of paper until the morning, so you don't forget. Your dreams during the next REM sleep period may be entirely different and focus on another subject. If your dream hasn't woken you in the night, write down exactly what you dreamed first thing in the morning.

Study at the night school of learning

Many of us can underestimate the amount of learning that our higher minds receive during our 'dream time'. We can learn about many subjects when we commune with the vast universal energies within. Anything we want to find out about we can programme our dreams to tell us.

I can remember a vividly realistic dream shortly after Lady Diana's death. I was up in a tree looking down on Charles and Camilla walking through Balmoral. As strange as it might seem, I actually felt my spirit was sitting on one of the branches of the trees in the grounds. I looked down and assessed the state of Prince Charles's aura and analysed his grief. I noted any dark areas, focusing on the impact of shock to his energy field and then found myself back in a building and marking up a chart on the wall to give my assessment. Obviously I cannot know his true feelings. But within my dream I had a sense that he felt stunned and was reeling not just from her death but the impact it had made on everyone else. He was overwhelmed and in need of support from Camilla who I felt was his rock.

On another occasion, I shared a dream with a girl friend I was staying with at the time, who worked as a healer. I saw both of us sitting cross-legged in a classroom in front of a teacher. And, rather bizarrely, she had been asked to analyse the energy around a sock that someone had been wearing and see what she could pick up from it. She was struggling to glean anything from it. I was watching her, as one of the students. When I woke in the morning I mentioned the dream and she described being in exactly the same situation, sitting in a classroom with me. We both knew that developing her psychic powers had always been hard work for her and perhaps in her dream studies she was being helped along. Unfortunately, she still had a block about it in the dream. But she seemed to have visited this dream classroom in other dreams. 'I've been there before,' she said. 'It's just like a normal university where you sit with other people and study different subjects.' It seems there is a wealth of information to be learned with the unconscious.

Helping you travel to the school of learning

It is easy to receive insights on a subject and programme your mind for inspiration. Before you drift off to sleep at night, close your eyes and think about something you really want to learn about. It could be the aura, dream travelling or even love and relationships. Think about this subject for several nights. Then imagine being given a catalogue with different topics written in alphabetical order. Hold the catalogue in your hands and flick through the pages until you come to the subject you are interested in. If you want to find out about the powers of crystal healing, look under the letter C and imagine seeing all the different kinds of classes described. Look at the time that yours is held during the night. A description of a crystal healing class might read:

C

The healing powers of crystals

Techniques for opening your awareness to the many facets of crystals for healing and focusing the mind. Exercises will help you discover the different vibrations of crystals and how to use them to enhance your health and psychic energy.

Then imagine an angelic figure standing before you, who will guide you to your class. To learn about this subject, simply feel your desire to be in the class and remind yourself before you go to sleep, 'My class is at 4 a.m.,' and trust that you will be there. In the morning write down any information that you dreamed about. Do bear in mind that initially you may not have any conscious recollection, but you may suddenly have more knowledge or awareness on the subject than previously. Although I have seen myself in a dream university you may see yourself somewhere entirely different. Remember that when we sleep our spirit is awake and ready to learn. This is the part of us that dreams – not our conscious minds. The dream is then relayed back to us through our minds. Obviously you can't glean everything there is to know about a subject, but you can get helpful hints and tips that may come back to you through flashes of insight.

Lucid dreaming

Lucid dreaming is about being a conscious dreamer. Instead of just experiencing your dreams, you can actively learn how to control what happens in them. You can become the director of the scenes in your dream movie.

In dreams the strangest things can happen. You can meet up with your boss, who just happens to look like an android with no face. Or you could see your mother in a suit of armour ready for battle. When you dream lucidly you suddenly know within the dream that you are dreaming. It might start with you realising that your boss is really human and not a robot. Once you have become consciously aware in your dream, you can change your boss into the actor George Clooney and have an interview with him, or transform your mother into a pussycat if you wish.

You can effectively use your imaginative skills in the dream world, in the same way as you did at the beginning of this book. If you dream you are being chased by a wild animal, you can materialise a flying carpet to whisk you away, become invisible or make the wild animal disappear in a puff of smoke.

I once dreamed of a wild wolf trying to get to me by clawing at my half-open bedroom window. I was absolutely petrified in my dream state, but suddenly became aware that I was dreaming, and in my dream got up and slammed the window down to stop the animal getting in.

Once you have practised the art of lucid dreaming you can take advantage of your creativity and ask your dream symbols what they mean or ask for advice on any problems you have. Your dreams can be used in any way for your creative imagination to gain more insight into yourself.

Experiment with lucid dreaming

Look at your hands

Research has shown that your mind processes the things that have happened during your day into your dream scenes. It stands to reason that repeated information will filter into our dream life. So during the day look consciously at your hands and ask yourself, 'Am I dreaming?' When you do this often enough you will eventually look at your hands in your dream. When you do so, you will become more aware that you are actually dreaming.

Retrace your steps

During the day, repeatedly ask yourself, 'How did I get here?' Then retrace your steps in your thoughts. For example, if you are eating some lunch, think of the last four things you did that led up to that. You might have put the kettle on and poured yourself a cup of coffee, made a sandwich and then carried everything to the table before you sat down. Do that several times during the day with the last few things you did before you say again, 'How did I get here?' If you do this often enough, you will eventually ask yourself this in your dreams. When you ask yourself that question in the dream, you will know again that you are dreaming.

Wake up early

Set your alarm clock for the middle of the night. When you wake up, read about lucid dreams for half an hour. When you go back to sleep, allow your mind to drift over the subject of lucid dreaming and think about remaining conscious in your dream state. With your consciousness full of the subject, you may well have a lucid dream.

Trigger foods

There are certain foods that can trigger lucid dreaming, although it hasn't been scientifically proven. It might be worth experimenting with to see if it works for you. Eating the food could work anyway by provoking a subconscious anchor to remind you to lucid-dream or giving you indigestion to make you stir slightly during the night. This of course would wake you enough to know you are dreaming.

Try one of these food types half an hour before going to sleep, but be sensible and don't try them all at once, as you won't be able to sleep at all!

Dairy products, i.e. cheese, milk or yoghurt
Pickles
Lettuce
Popcorn
Fish
Ice cream

*　　*　　*

Now you have looked at the different ways you can use your dreams, take time to explore them, and enjoy the process. As I've mentioned before, you have to make an effort but not try so hard that you get stressed out and block your intuition. A real adventure can take place as you let your dreams take you on a magic carpet ride within. As you recall your many mind adventures, your true self can start to lead the way and guide you in the right direction. Throughout this book, you've expanded your mind in many different ways in order to contact the higher realms of consciousness. Soon you can discover how to use your mind to create the life you really want.

9

Reprogramme Your Mind and Create Your Own Destiny

People are just as happy as they make up their minds to be.
Abraham Lincoln, 1809–65, former US President

In this chapter I want you to reprogramme your mind to create a positive vision of life. By this I mean allowing your subconscious to absorb new information that will change the way you think. If it sounds complicated – don't worry. You will discover how simple it is. Most importantly this process is essential to the increased development of your psychic powers as well as enabling you to have the successful life you want.

As you have already discovered, our intuitive abilities can only grow when we expand our mind energy. This is done through our imagination, which acts as a bridge to a higher consciousness. Visualisations allow your mind to reach out into the universe to link up with this higher energy. So let me remind you that positive thoughts, feelings and visions keep our minds wide open. When we think negatively or focus too much on ourselves, our mind energy funnels inwards, creating a pressure on our brain and its surrounding tissues that can lead to misery, depression and ill health. And I'm afraid it is this that makes us one of society's 'narrow-minded' people and blocks our intuition from flowing.

So stop for a minute and just imagine what life-long re-current thought patterns could do if they are continually negative. Entrenched oppressive and judgemental attitudes can be hard to change and will switch off your sixth sense. But by reprogramming your subconscious with positive visualisations and affirmations you will keep your mind expanding outwards from deep within your belief system. And your psychic abilities will grow in potency as you tap in to the powerful energy within. But the bonus is that by using specific visualisations you will also become the producer and director of the successful life you really want. You will see true magic taking place when you begin to manifest the visions you believe to be true – and see your life transformed.

But it's important to establish how you feel your life is now, before you bring about any changes. As you have developed and strengthened your intuitive mind throughout this book, the pattern of your life will start to unfold. You will see this more clearly now that you have woken up to your psychic self. As I mentioned at the end of chapter five, since this creative energy has been awakened any confusion will gradually disappear and you will have a new-found clarity into yourself as well as others. With this increased insight you can ask yourself some important questions: Do you like what you see? Do you have a fulfilling and exciting existence? Or is it filled with conflict and unnecessary drama? (The thought exercise on page 196 will also help you clarify the areas of your life that are working well or not.) Whatever the problem – if you are in a cycle of difficult relationships, a dissatisfying job, addictive behaviour, money problems or just feel that your life is empty and stale – know that you can change it. It all starts with a thought. And a thought can be changed. But not just any old conscious thought, which will only give you rational options, good and bad. I mean allowing those intuitive inspired thoughts that stem from your higher mind to flow into your consciousness. These thoughts originate from the real you, your inner voice and they tell you that anything is possible. Just think of the difference in logical limited attitudes from someone who says, 'I hate my life, it's a mess,' to someone with an expansive mind who says, 'What can I do to make it work?' Repetitive thoughts create an attitude and attitudes affect our reactions to circumstances. The negative left-brain statement (yang) closes the door to any opportunities, but the positive right-brained one (yin) opens up your existence to new options.

Sadly, our subconscious thinking pattern usually results from negative programming that we received as children. Although we started off with natural psychic gifts, the link with our inner voice became dimmed when we were continually criticised and told to think sensibly. Our young minds were like sponges absorbing all the information that would one day define our adult view of the world. It's hard to wake up and think differently when our thoughts represent our deeply ingrained beliefs about life. If we were repeatedly ignored when we had creative ideas or unusual dreams, or told we were useless or silly whenever we said something deemed as 'whacky', our subconscious – just like a computer – will have programmed those beliefs as facts. This means you can negate the inner instinct that tells you you can fulfil your wildest dreams, and end up creating the sensible but limited life your subconscious believes you want. Relying only on your conscious mind leads to stress, burn-out, anxiety and self-doubt as you have to make double the effort. But deep within, whatever you do, there is the niggling feeling that it doesn't have to be like this. That life can be an easy and enjoyable adventure, when we allow our intuition to help smooth our path and bring us the success we deserve.

Fortunately our imaginative powers can once again help us to transcend our entrenched thoughts and allow us to connect with our psychic self and let our inner voice filter through.

In this chapter, there are exercises for you to delve into the depths of your subconscious – shake away those old beliefs and give it a good spring clean. You can finally put that self-doubt, pain and fear into the universal rubbish bin that stops you living the life you want.

When you activate your intuition you take the pressure off trying too hard. You allow your life to flow harmoniously so that you get maximum results for minimum effort. Life should be easy, not a struggle. You can transform your life and achieve anything you want . . .

- Create better health for yourself by visualising your own vibrant image and break free of addictive habits, such as smoking or over-eating.
- Boost your energy and self-esteem.
- Create harmonious and loving relationships with friends, family and lovers.
- Make money easily from doing a job that you love.
- Find your dream house.
- Pass your driving test.

Whatever it is you want to do – know that you have the power to make it happen. The benefits are endless.

Your self-esteem will sky-rocket when you realise that you can wave your mental magic wand and create a new life.

To make a start you simply have to choose what you want in your life. Remember what I said in chapter five: there is no such thing as a preordained fate. That notion lets you remain a powerless victim of life. This existence is a creative process and *you* have the opportunity to connect with the powerful psychic potential within, and shape your own destiny.

Before you begin to reprogramme your mind and create what you want in your life, you need to discover the way your mind works.

Becoming aware of your thoughts

Positive beliefs and thoughts are an important part of the development of your intuitive mind. In order to keep your mind expanding outwards into the universe, you must keep your thoughts constructive. Intuitive thoughts stem from your higher mind and create more joy and fulfilment in your life.

The first step is to become aware of the way you think. The root cause behind any situation, creative venture, relationship, or job lies in a thought. I'm sure we've all experienced feeling bad when a relationship breaks up. One miserable thought as we sit alone licking our wounds can easily spiral into a domino effect of, why me, nobody will ever love me, things always go wrong for me . . . The list goes on, and before you know it you're depressed, lethargic and planning a life of seclusion – until you snap out of it again. You have the power to nip that debilitating thought in the bud and focus on a constructive approach. Imagine that process again with different thoughts: I am lovable, things can only get better . . . It can take effort at first to get out of that mental rut, but you have to start somewhere. So let's begin with an exercise focusing on the power of a single thought.

Thought exercise

Have some paper and a pen handy and write down two headings: *Positive* and *Negative*. Look at the areas of your life where you have recurrent problems; it could be dissatisfaction at work, an ongoing conflict in a relationship or even persistent road rage! However stressful the circumstances, you can exert a positive influence that can help turn things around. But you need to stop reacting on automatic and start responding with clarity. So, think back to your thought processes when you're in that situation. It might be, 'Typical, I knew that would happen', 'It's their fault', or 'Why me?' These are the old limited beliefs that became stored in your subconscious and, before you know it, these attitudes become your habitual state of mind.

Write down your negative expressions as you recall them. Do you keep blaming other people for how you feel? Are you often critical, complaining, irritable or miserable? Notice your body language in these situations. Do you slouch or tense up? Perhaps your negative responses are symptomatic of something else that is going on inside you. Thinking negatively won't help you get to the root of any problem and it's all too easy to let these thoughts talk yourself out of making a change in your life or destroy an important opportunity. But now you can start to alter the way you think in areas of your life where conflict or difficulties keep arising. So be aware of your thought patterns and don't let them create unhappy and miserable scenarios.

Now look at the areas that are positive. Are you successful at work or do you have a circle of supportive friends? Do you have a lucky streak and have good things happen to you out of the blue? Note how you think in these areas. You might notice you think things like 'I'm happy to help', 'I'm sure it will work', 'I'll give it a try'. You'll find that your thoughts are much more compassionate, respectful and persistently constructive in these circumstances. Write them down in your column.

This exercise will have illuminated the areas of your life that work well or that need to change. Now you have awareness of the way your mind works, whenever you're in circumstances where you have a tendency to think negatively be aware of your attitude and feelings and change the thought to a positive one. This will take vigilance, but persist and you'll notice the difference in how people respond to you, as well as how much better you feel in yourself.

Take note: you will know when you are expressing intuitive thoughts in your life, because you will think and therefore act with courage, respect, creativity, wisdom and love. Everything that is joyful, easy, good and happy in our lives has been created from this potent force within. Any communication that is negative, difficult and destructive in our lives is an example of when your thoughts are not coming from your higher mind but your limited beliefs.

To reach any goals successfully you have to be consistently positive, often in the face of other people's negativity. If I had listened to other people's opinions or had any self-doubt about becoming a writer, I would never have carved a career in journalism and this book would never have been written. Comments such as 'It's who you know', or 'There's too much competition' formed most of the feedback I received. Believing in those limitations would have stifled my creative and intuitive feelings. But I ignored them and decided to give it my best shot. What did I have to lose? When I did that, I opened up my mind and allowed my inner voice to be heard. Then my hunches and instincts led me to the right people and opportunities.

If you think positively you can move mountains, regardless of the obstacles life throws at you because optimistic happy thoughts open up your mind, allowing you to tap in to your own psychic force, which lets your intuition flow and creates opportunities. People will then be drawn to your re-vitalised aura and instinctively want to help you.

Re-educating your thoughts will help you to take responsibility for the effects you create in the world around you. When you take the next step of programming your subconscious with positive visions, you will really begin to see that you are the orchestrator of your own destiny.

The importance of reprogramming our subconscious minds

The information stored in our subconscious determines what experiences we expect to have in our lives and therefore the scenarios we attract to ourselves. If we don't change our negative beliefs and thoughts we end up making the same mistakes over and over again. You can often see this with certain people who seem repeatedly to attract the same type of relationships into their lives.

One friend of mine had lived with a selfish, dominating husband for years. He always wanted to control her completely and have his own way. But after she plucked up the courage finally to leave, she kept meeting the same type of men cloaked in different disguises. After a few weeks she would find herself back in the same old circumstances, where she was being walked over and bullied. She couldn't understand why it kept happening to her, but I could see the patterns only too clearly. She thought she was to blame, and unfortunately she was. Subconsciously she believed that was all she deserved. She was so used to being browbeaten, she unconsciously focused on men who would behave like that and they were drawn to her. Her mind computer was attracting people who reflected what she was used to accepting. Until she changes this destructive cycle, subconsciously, to attract a different type of man, she will remain stuck with the same recurring pattern.

If you want to avoid getting stuck in negative patterns, then you need to re-input positive information to create a better reality, just as you have to place an order if you want your goods to arrive.

How you can programme your subconscious

The best way to reprogramme our minds is through the use of self-hypnosis using visualisations and affirmations. This has the same relaxing effects of being under hypnosis, except that it is self-induced. This technique is a way of inducing the deeply relaxed alpha state within us (mentioned in chapter two). This alpha state is powerful and healing and registers the same brain wave rhythms as you do when you use your psychic powers. So you are deeply connected to your own inner voice as well as being able to instruct your subconscious.

The visualisations in the exercises that follow later in the chapter all involve going down steps or in a lift. The reason for this is that the sensation of moving downwards releases huge amounts of congested energy in the subconscious and allows the mind to expand. As a result you may feel light-headed and your subconscious will be more receptive to new information. The more relaxed you become, the heavier your body will feel. But if you have any concerns, don't worry, you will always remain completely in control. Once we are deeply relaxed, our subconscious mind will easily absorb any information we give it, and we can then begin to feed through instructions in the form of visualisations and affirmations. (Affirmations are simply repeated statements.) A positive combination of a visualisation and affirmation will have powerful results in creating a vision of what you want to achieve. But our subconscious mind computer must be pro-grammed with the correct data in order to work effectively. To achieve this there is something vitally important that you *must* remember. Our subconscious mind does not understand the past or future. It only understands the present. The mental picture must therefore be visualised as if it's happening *now*. Whatever affirmations we make must be said in the present tense. So visualise whatever you want in the future as if it is already happening and express it in this way in your affirm-ation. Examples could be, 'I am enjoying a loving relation-ship', 'I have passed my driving test', 'I am enjoying my promotion at work, money is pouring into my life' or 'I am healthy, fit and happy', all coupled with a corresponding visual image.

But be careful: the subconscious mind will respond to every phrase as a literal instruction, so watch how you word things. If you keep it in the future that's where it will stay, just out of your reach.

The miracle that will happen works on many different levels of your mind. Once you create a new belief – this is your new reality. And as I mentioned in chapter two on your aura, your thoughts, beliefs and feelings are all stored in the layers of your auric energy field and radiate energy. Remember how, by picking up information from someone's aura, we psychic-ally 'know' things about someone; we get a feeling about whether we like them or not as soon as they walk into a room. Similarly, people who can help us reach our visionary goal will unconsciously be affected by your new thought energy. And as you will soon discover, thoughts travel and people will sense and respond to them, even from a distance.

Psychically, positive beliefs also give you a sense of know-ingness and expectation, expanding your mind energy, releasing stored-up mental tension and plugging you into your deeper instincts. Your own sixth sense will be sharpened and intuitively lead you to the situations that you want. Instead of believing unconsciously that you will fail your driving test or never get on at work, you are now operating from your inner vision. You believe that you will succeed. And your new expectations, heightened intuition and energised aura will send out magnetic vibes bringing you the help to achieve what you really believe you want.

Using your subconscious mind to get what you want

So how do we create something in our lives? A good start is to identify what it is you want. After all, how can you get what you want until you know what it is? In some cases 'knowing' is all you need to bring something into your life, although more entrenched or difficult problems will need the programming techniques. The best way of clarifying what you want is to write it down. First draw up a rough draft and then write it up beautifully and treat it like a precious document. Then write up the specifics of your ideal job, partner, house or car. Be honest with yourself and say exactly what it is you want. But be aware that your limited beliefs may rise to the surface as you start to wonder, Is this possible? Refuse to settle for only what you think you can get and aim for your dream. Make it as detailed as you can. The more specifics you can give, the more your sub-conscious can reach out like a radar and point it out to you. As I explained earlier, once you focus with intent, your new thought energies will influence other like-minded people who will bend over backwards to help you achieve your dream.

To give you an example, I'll explain what happened to me. A few years ago I had to give notice on my rented flat as the owners were selling it. I only had a few months and I decided it was time to buy a house. But after looking at various properties I felt incredibly depressed at what was on the market. In fact it was the most stressful two weeks of my entire year. All the houses within my price range seemed seriously neglected or didn't have what I felt were the basic necessities for a home. What I wanted quickly seemed impossible.

I was so fed up one afternoon, in desperation I decided to write down what I really wanted. I wrote a detailed description in the present tense as if I were already living there. The words were: 'I am living in a beautiful three-bedroom house, with an additional office, double glazing, central heating, a central fireplace, a fitted kitchen, a decent bathroom with a powerful shower, parking space, beautiful views from the windows. Loads of space and light and facilities for storage.' I was even specific enough to say I wanted it to be built on a hill and slanting upwards to ensure different views from each side with a patio viewed through glass sliding doors. It had to be only a few miles from the centre of town, near shops and a nursery for my daughter and not on a main road. I finished it by saying, 'I am living there now.'

As I wrote my list, cynical doubts were coming into my mind and I was thinking, Who are you kidding? You're not going to get this in such a short time scale. But I decided to ignore them and thought, See what happens. Two days later I got a call from a friend who was a director of several estate agents in the Bath area. 'I bet you're fed up with what's on the market?' he said questioningly. 'I've been looking through the papers for you and what's on offer is horrendous.' Then he mentioned one of the houses on the property page in the local paper, which was through a small agency on the other side of Bath. I'd seen the picture of the house and vague description but dismissed it because I couldn't see the picture clearly in print. He urged me to go and look at it immediately, saying, 'I used to live a few doors away and it has beautiful views from that hill.'

I was due to go away that weekend but went early the next morning before my journey and it was love at first sight. It was a town house on three levels and the first thing I saw was a large office with storage space. Everything was in immaculate condition with eight-foot-long windows in every room and a wonderful view over Salisbury Hill. I was even more amazed when upstairs, as I walked into the dining room, there were glass sliding doors that led to a large patio with roses and jasmine entwined around long wooden trellises. Built on a hill, as I had asked, it could be entered from two different levels.

It had only just come on the market a few days before and I was the first person to view. With a sigh of relief I put in an offer within half an hour and went off on my weekend jaunt with a much lighter heart. It may not be everybody's dream house, but it was what I wanted and needed at the time.

When my estate agent friend came to see it on the second viewing he said I was lucky to have had my offer accepted so swiftly as it had been undervalued and I would have ended up in a bidding war had anyone else got a foot in the door. Weeks later I reread my list and saw how accurately the house fitted my specific description.

You can see exactly what happened on a psychic level. As my beliefs changed and I knew what I was looking for, my thought forms flew out into the universe. A friend was influenced by my new thought energy, held in my auric field, and told me where to go to find what I wanted. When I saw the house, my own intuition instantly recognised it as being what I wanted and I acted fast. Because my new expectations of having a house like this created such a positive belief, the couple who were selling bent over backwards to ensure that no one else looked at it, even though it had been on the market only a few days. They couldn't help but respond with confidence.

The code of conduct

Before we go on to to the visualisation exercises, it is important for you to understand the code of conduct in the world of psychic power. Whatever you visualise happening, you must do so with good intention and for the greater good of everyone concerned. Cause and effect are real and if you send out negative thoughts or try to manipulate a situation to suit your own self-centred interests, it will backfire on you. It either won't work or it won't last. As I mentioned in chapter six on mediumship there are people who exist on different levels of consciousness. When you focus on negative thoughts in this way you automatically lower your vibration, which weakens your psychic energy. Remember like energy attracts like, so you will automatically make yourself vulnerable to being the focus for unwanted attention – either from living people or the spirit world. So focus on what you want intently and from the heart.

You are going to begin some exercises that will start you on the journey into changing your entire belief system. So, now you know what you want, get ready for some intensive work in the depths of your subconscious mind.

Exercise for banishing old negative beliefs and boosting self-esteem

First we need to start afresh, so we are going to clear the decks. That means getting rid of any negative thoughts and working on your self-esteem. For optimum effects I suggest that you have someone else dictate this visualisation on to a tape for you, so you don't have to read through it. Visualisations work far more effectively, particularly with the subconscious, if your mind doesn't know what is coming next. This visualisation is perfect for anyone who's ever felt controlled by their addictions, whether food, cigarettes or alcohol, or for those who simply want to feel happier and more confident.

Visualise yourself on a tropical island. There are beautiful banana trees and lush vegetation. You walk along a path down to a blue lagoon surrounded by coconut palms. The light sparkles on the water. You pick up a pebble lying on the ground and throw it into the lagoon and watch how it creates ripples in the water. There are colourful exotic blooms everywhere and their heady aroma wafts through the air. You see the outline of white cliffs against the azure of the sky. As you walk towards them you see a cave entrance in the cliff and decide to go and explore. Walking to the back of the cave you see some old worn-out steps carved out of the rock. You feel drawn to climb down the stairs, and descend slowly, feeling the smooth rock surface underneath your feet. Count down slowly, ten, nine, eight, seven; you are becoming more and more relaxed, six, five, four; you feel calm and your breathing is becoming deeper and slower, three, two, one. As you reach the bottom of the stairs, the room is large and dimly lit and appears to be empty.

Then you notice a shiny lift in front of you, which can only go down. As you go into the lift you notice it is made of crystal, polished so much that it gleams and you can see through it. You can see the cave walls and notice many different engravings carved into the ancient rock. You see a gold button and press it and start to feel the movement of the lift as it descends. You will count down ten floors, ten, nine, eight, as it slowly goes down floor by floor. Feel yourself sinking effortlessly as you move downwards, seven, six; you feel yourself relaxing into a feeling of peacefulness, deeper and deeper. Five, four, three, deeper and deeper into relaxation, two and one. Slowly walk out of the lift. Although you are relaxed you are alert and ready to absorb any information.

As you step into a larger room in the cave, it is light enough for you to see clearly. As you walk through you can see some familiar snapshots covering one of the walls. You then notice that each of the pictures represents you at different ages throughout the stages of your life in various states of mind. Go up to the pictures and take a closer look. You are drawn to a particular one. Study it. What age are you in the picture? What does the picture tell you? Because you are healing a part of your past that is affecting your life now, your intuition will show you a picture that is linked to an ongoing debilitating pattern. This picture will show an experience that is the root cause of any unhappiness in your current situation. But don't worry if the answer doesn't spring to mind immediately – it will. Take that picture with you. You are going to heal this pattern. What words come to mind that associate the problems with that picture?

Now notice a door and walk through it along a corridor. You are going to the back room right at the end of the corridor. This is where all your rubbish gets dumped. There are only negative thoughts, memories and feelings stored here; repressed feelings of anger and hurt. There may also be some bags of self-hate, or destructive habits that you want to get rid of. All these old negative thoughts need to be discarded. Anything that is blocking your progress and stopping you from moving on with your life is here. So what does this room look like? Is it dirty and cluttered with piles of accumulated rubbish with cobwebs everywhere? Or is it clean and tidy? In the wall there is a rubbish chute. At the bottom of the rubbish chute is pure laser energy. When the rubbish hits the laser, it will instantly vaporise.

Look at the picture of yourself that you are carrying with you. Ask in your mind what this picture represents with regard to negative emotions that you are holding on to. Is it abandonment, fear, or anxiety to do with your parents that has been collecting in this room? Or something else? Look around and see the bag of accumulated pain that is associated with that time in the picture. Visualise yourself picking up the bag of pain and throwing it down the rubbish chute. The picture has now disappeared. Take a deep breath then clear up the rest of the room and throw out the rest of the rubbish, knowing that it will be turned to dust and absorbed back into the earth. Take some time putting all the rubbish down the chute. As you get rid of it, sense any parts of your body that you feel are getting lighter. Are there any other sensations? The room should be looking emptier and tidier. If you can't get rid of any rubbish, or something is stopping you, leave it for now. You may not be ready. Do as much as you can.

You are now ready to continue. You can leave this room but instead of walking back the way you came, you see another door and when you open it there is a long slide going down to a pool of crystal-clear water. Take off your clothes and step on to the slide and feel yourself slip into the comforting warm pool. Immediately you are in the water, you feel a sense of calmness and comfort. The room you are in is small and cosy. You feel deeply relaxed and safe. Your breathing is much slower and deeper now. Your subconscious is ready to be programmed.

As you sit in the pool, you can start to visualise the self you ideally want to be. Look at any aspect of yourself that will make you feel more fulfilled as an independent person. If you are stressed, shy or see yourself as a failure then change your thoughts. See yourself as radiating happiness and confidence. Imagine what that feels like and see yourself glowing and deeply contented. Visualise any emptiness inside yourself as being filled up with golden light. If you want to focus on your weight, see yourself as a healthy size, toned, happy and slim. Bad habits can also be knocked on the head; whether it is overeating, smoking or excessive drinking, you can make them disappear. Say the affirmation, 'I am positive, happy and healthy.' If you want to eat, drink or smoke less say the words, 'I am free from my addiction to food. I am eating healthy food that nourishes me.' Always use positive words. Repeat this affirmation as you visualise yourself being the healthy person you want to be. Say, 'I am free from my addiction to cigarettes.' Or 'I am free from my addiction to alcohol. I am healthy and happy.' Continue to visualise yourself looking radiantly healthy. Keep focusing on this visualisation and positive affirmations. If your mind wanders off, simply bring it back into focus.

When you feel ready, climb out of the pool of water. You will see a soft fluffy towel to dry yourself off and your clothes are miraculously clean and ready for you to wear. You do not need to worry about the slide. You will see the crystal lift on the other side of the small room. You walk inside and press the button to ascend ten floors. Slowly count each floor, and as you feel yourself rise you begin to feel a little more alert. One, two, three, four, five, six, seven, eight, nine, ten. Feel the lift ascending and yourself becoming more and more awake. As you leave the lift, notice the stairs ahead back up to the cave. Always leave the same way as you came in. And slowly count up again: one, two, three, four, five, six, seven, eight, nine, ten. When you reach the top of the stairs you feel alert, positive and very content. Take a deep breath and feel your awareness back into the room where you are sitting.

You need to continue doing this visualisation every day for the next week and it should only take up twenty minutes of your morning or evening. You can do this type of visualisation any time you want to reprogramme your mind or create something in your life. You can simply change the scenery if you wish. But, believe me, this form of mind programming really works. It will change the way you think, so that you can activate your willpower and achieve your goals. And it will release tension and expand your mind energy.

When I did this visualisation I focused on having a healthy body. Despite the fact that I hated exercising, within a week I was craving exercise with a vengeance. Strangely, I didn't tie it in with my visualisation at first. I just wanted to be active and I felt a real desire to eat healthily without having to prise myself away from packets of biscuits.

Use this visualisation any time you feel low and you will notice the difference in your confidence and self-control. You don't have to be a slave to your self-doubt or behaviour. You can feel free to be the healthy, confident, contented person you want to be. Now we are moving on to the next step of achieving your ultimate aims.

Exercise for creating a vision for the life you want

Whatever it is that you want to achieve, whether it's harmonious loving relationships, a job promotion or passing your driving test, this next visualisation exercise will help you to accomplish it.

See yourself in a large green field. The grass smells fresh and the fields seem to go on for miles. The sun is shining and you can see birds flying overhead in the blue sky. There are tiny houses dotted on the landscape, and you feel that you are the only person around. As you wander through the grass you suddenly see something in the distance. As you walk towards it, you can see it's an ancient well. Only this well is much bigger than normal and you can see when you look over the edge that it no longer has any water in it. In fact, as you look down you see steps carved into the walls, which lead to a large opening at the bottom. You feel drawn to explore and walk down the steps slowly counting down as you go, ten, nine, eight, seven; breathe deeply, six, five, four; feeling more and more relaxed, three, two, one.

When you get to the bottom, you look around the room, which is suprisingly very large, and notice a library full of books. You walk to the bookshelves and focus on all the titles. One in particular is relevant to you and what you want to create in your life. Pull the book out so that you can remember the title. Then walk along the corridor and see some more steps going down to another room. You see a golden light at the bottom and walk down them slowly towards it: ten, nine, eight, seven, six, five, four, three, two, one. When you are downstairs you see a magnificent room filled with big soft cushions and dimmed lighting. Lush satins and velvets cover the stone walls and give the room a cosy womb-like quality. Sit down and relax against the cushions, as you smell an exquisite aroma of lightly scented incense. This is another room within your mind where you can create.

Start by focusing on the picture of what you would like to happen. Whatever you want to create in your life, you will need to be able to picture it in your mind. For example, if you have a difficult relationship with a family member or friend, then simply change your mental image of the situation. Visualise yourself with them talking happily and feeling contented in each other's company. Picture it as if it is happening now. And make it as realistic as possible, using all your senses. The chapter on imagination will have helped you do this. Feel where you are sitting, perhaps at the kitchen table in your house, look at what are you both wearing. Can you smell anything, like coffee percolating? What is going

on around you? Can you hear the television or radio in the background? It may be difficult to keep visualising all these senses that
you have activated in your picture, but practice will help and the more
real you make the image the more effective it will be. Repeat an affirmation mentally as you visualise the picture. Perhaps something like 'My
relationship with (name of person) is relaxed and harmonious. We talk
easily together.'

Using pictures combined with an affirmation gives very
powerful results and you are effectively programming your
mind to create a potential future event. If the situation you
want to change doesn't improve after a week of visualising
keep trying, be patient and trust that it will be solved, but
don't stress yourself out, because stress is the opposing force
to the alpha state you need to be in to programme your subconscious.

To illustrate how far you can influence someone's behaviour, I'll tell you about Joanne.

Joanne's story

Joanne was a twenty-seven-year-old secretary and madly in love with
a guy called Lewis. He was thirty-three and a college lecturer, but uncom-
mitted to any kind of relationship with her. She spent a lot of time chasing
him, but he wouldn't even take her out to dinner. She was very upset
about why she wasn't being treated decently, and desperately wanted
him to wine and dine her. So every evening for half an hour over a
week, I told her to visualise herself and this man in a restaurant eating
and having fun together. What was important was that she made everything as real as possible so that the vision was almost palpable. She
needed to create the picture, bringing in all her senses of vision, hearing,
smell, taste and emotion.

She imagined herself wearing a dress that she loved and looking her
best. (Using clothes you already own will add to the reality.) She saw

them sitting opposite each other in a cosy restaurant near where he lived and imagined what they might be eating. As she tasted her pasta she smelled the aroma of the food. As she sipped her chilled wine, she got a sense of sitting on the wooden chair, and listened to the sound of music in the background amidst the chattering of other customers. She imagined Lewis leaning forward and talking to her intimately and smiling, while continuing to imagine the other sounds, the taste of her food and the atmosphere in the room. She imagined that they were both very happy and content in each other's company. Over the entire picture she visualised a pale pink glow which represents loving energy and said an affirmation in the present: 'Lewis and I are loving and secure together. Passion and love are flowing between us.'

After a week she stopped doing it, but phoned him and asked if they could meet up. He agreed rather nonchalantly but a few nights later she was getting ready when the phone rang. She ignored it, thinking it might be him trying to cancel. When she arrived at his house in Richmond, Surrey he smiled and said, 'I tried to ring you earlier to tell you not to eat anything. I thought we'd go out to dinner.' He took her out to a cosy restaurant, much to her surprise, and was loving and intimate all evening. The whole evening had unfolded in just the way she had imagined. In theory, the dinner date seemed to be his decision. But she had influenced his mind through her focusing positive thought energy. In effect she had transmitted a telepathic picture of how she'd wanted him to behave. Unfortunately, he didn't remain keen for long. After that night was over nothing much else happened.

This is an important point to make. Whatever you visualise, if the person concerned is not willing to make an effort too, you cannot make a situation permanent – and the cumulative effects won't last. You would have to keep visualising to make things continue, which ultimately would waste your energy and exhaust you by excessive use of your willpower.

Visualise with good intentions and for the good of everyone and then you can't go wrong. Similarly if you have outgrown each other, no amount of positive thinking can make it better, unless you are also willing really to work at it. But you can create and focus on harmony as an end result, which helps everyone and eases the stress of separation.

With belief and trust anything is possible

The visualisations, coupled with affirmations, that I have shown you, do have very powerful results. What's important with these visualisations is to focus on them only for the time you are doing them. You must let the outcome go and trust that it will happen. If you keep thinking about it, you will drain yourself mentally. Trust is a vitally important word. It is so intrinsically powerful when we put our trust in the universe taking care of us, that doing just that and nothing else can often create miracles. Trust is about taking belief to a much higher level: you are not just believing from your own confidence. To trust in this way you have to learn to surrender to a higher power and simply know that it will happen. The problem is that we often live with fear and worry, and fears can grow quickly without us even realising. When we fear something, whether it is intimacy, lack of money or more commonly simply not being good enough, trust flies out of the window. Fear blocks our intuition and our progress as we get caught up in the agony it causes. It is trust that creates true belief that a situation can become a reality.

Accept that your creative reality can come to you in many ways. The connection to what you visualise might come via a friend ringing to tell you about something, or you may be introduced to someone who leads you to whatever it is. You may suddenly be offered what you need right out of the blue via a strange coincidence or a dream may tell you the next step. Be open to the way the universe brings you what you want. And have the self-worth to accept it when you get it.

To explain how trust can work even in an everyday scenario I will tell you about Catherine.

Catherine's story

Catherine was only eighteen and lived in London. She really wanted to see her sister in Manchester who she missed and hadn't seen for ages. But living on a college grant, she couldn't afford the fare to go by coach or train and she didn't want to ask her sister for the money. So Catherine decided to do something a little strange. She decided to head towards Victoria Bus Station and trust that something would happen that would get her there, although she didn't know how. She already had an Underground pass so that part of the journey wasn't a problem.

When she was getting off the Tube a man she was standing next to asked her directions on how to get to the coach station. Catherine told him she was heading that way as she was travelling to Manchester. Animatedly he replied that he was also going that way. As they got into a conversation he mentioned that his car was parked near the coach station. He then offered her a lift all the way there. Catherine had no strange vibes from him, and felt that her trust in being taken care of would protect her. Just like Jenny's mantra in chapter four, trust in a higher energy will always give you a sense of protection that people unconsciously respond to. She accepted the invitation and arrived at her sister's hours earlier than she would have done if she'd got the bus. I'm not suggesting you accept lifts from strangers, but when you really trust that things will turn out you hand over your life to a higher plan. And remember that what you want can be given to you – but not always in the way that you expect.

Eight steps to creating your perfect life

1. Write a list of what you want, e.g. the qualities your perfect man has or the ideal house, job, friends, circumstances etc.

2. Write everything in the present tense. Your subconscious mind doesn't understand past or future. It only experiences life in the now.

3. Be aware that doubts may come up about what you write. Don't settle for what you think you can get; push away any negative thoughts and go for what you really want.

4. Read through your list and visualise yourself with the perfect partner, house or job as though it's already happened.

5. Practise your self-hypnosis exercise and visualise what you want with an affirmation every morning or evening for twenty minutes.

6. If you want to add extra power to your thoughts you can create a life map. On a large piece of paper or board, cut out pictures that represent what you want in your life. The ideal car, for example, could have low mileage but be in good condition with only one previous owner. The more specific you are, the more likely you are to get what you want. Cut out key words to emphasise what you want to say, like 'I am enjoying a loving relationship' or 'I love driving my new car.'

7. Most importantly, don't fret or worry about the outcome. It is essential to trust that this will happen. So let go, relax and know that it is coming.

8. And *keep trusting* that things will evolve the way they're meant to, once you get your heart's desire.

The magic of coincidences that show we're on the right path

Now you have learned about the power of your mind, you will realise that our thoughts are just forms of energy. Whoever we focus our thoughts on, the recipient will feel the impact and it will influence the way they then think about us. This is why it is so important for any budding psychic to understand how incredibly beneficial and influential the power of a single thought can be. Learning awareness of your thinking pattern and taking conscious control of your thoughts is one of the most useful, empowering skills that a psychic can develop. As I discussed earlier in the chapter, negative thoughts include our own inner doubts and beliefs as well as thinking unpleasant things about others. They will influence an outcome, so think constructively about everyone including yourself. When you have understood and mastered the effects of your thoughts, you can achieve immense success in any area of your life.

This leads us into another important aspect of our psychic potential: the power of coincidences. Coincidences are not just random happenings. The science behind coincidence lies in Albert Einstein's work in quantum physics, as discussed by historical author Jagdish Mehra in his book *Einstein, Physics and Reality*. What Einstein taught and proved with his dissection of the atom is that everything we see as physical is actually made up of patterns of energy. When this energy is looked at in its smallest form, he found that by just observing these molecules their components could change. In fact he noticed that these particles seemed to alter and respond to whatever the observer expected to see.

When we use thoughts to create what we want in our lives, our intention and our subconscious expectation send out a flow of energy that connects us more fully with our own higher minds and therefore the higher universal power.

Often the way the universal energy responds is to bring us into contact with people who can help us. If they resonate with our energy by being like-minded they will unconsciously respond from their higher mind and it will benefit both of you in some way. This happens in the form of coincidences that lead us to contacts, information and assistance.

The more we learn to use our minds intuitively and to create the lives we want, the more obvious these coincidences will become. You will see what an exciting adventure life is when you can get a direct response to a question or suddenly bump into someone who provides you with an important contact for a stage in your life. That's why it's often so common for someone to meet a lookalike lover or someone with the same star sign as a previous partner after a break-up: your thoughts are sending out messages of what is still in your mind and coincidentally they cross your path. Coincidences also show us a deeper pattern to our lives which enables us to see life as a magical interconnected chain of events that supports us in reaching our goals.

So from now on note that the more creative energy you invest in your life, by knowing and deciding what you want, the more the coincidences in your life will speed up and the quicker your life will change for the better.

When coincidences point us to the next step

Going back to the beginning of this book do you remember when I was seeking advice from a psychic? At that time becoming a writer was only in the back of my mind, but it was to become the next step that I would take in my career.

217

And what was the clairvoyant's other career? It so happened she was a journalist for car magazines. That could have meant nothing until I joined a psychic development course on her advice. Who should I meet, befriend and end up practising my psychic skills with? It was a freelance journalist, called Sandra. It was through Sandra that I got my word processor and landed on the first stepping stone of my new career. Just like me she had no university degrees in the subject of journalism or stepping stones from experience at local newspapers. Her only experience was from a short journalism course at City Lit that she went to two hours a week for a few months. She told me about the course teacher, Ken, who coincidentally appeared on a television documentary the next night. I got in touch with him and although I went to his course just twice, he proved invaluable in some of the basic tips he gave me using his experiences as a writer. It was only when I looked back that I could see how coincidences were pointing me in the right direction.

When coincidences respond to our thoughts

My friend Kate told me many years ago how she was comforting a friend who had split up with a boyfriend. This friend was heartbroken and couldn't come to terms with the loss. Her thoughts were going round in circles as to how she should deal with the situation. To help her sort through her feelings Kate took her for a drink in a local pub and suddenly a tramp bumped into them and shouted out, 'You've got to live in the moment and forget about the past. You can't turn the clock back.' It was a strange coincidence that this unlikely person should tell Kate's friend exactly what it was she needed to hear.

Some time ago a peculiar coincidence happened to me. I spent the weekend with a girl friend in the seaside town of Brighton in West Sussex.

My friend said that I should have more confidence in myself and be more positive in my own achievements. Suddenly, as we were crossing the road, a man rushed up to me and kissed me, wrapping his arms around me as I was very literally bowled over by his embrace, and proclaimed, 'I think you're wonderful, I think you're fantastic', before he rushed off. My friend Charlotte and I were totally shocked and stared at each other. As I turned round he was standing on the other side of the road smiling and waving at me. It could seem like he'd had a little too much of the old vino, but nothing in life is ever accidental. Everything is a response to thought forms. And I believe it was a direct message from the universe which gave an immediate response to our conversation!

When coincidences show us a pattern in our lives

Lucy was in her twenties when she experienced a chain of coincidences. She had been working as a holiday rep for the summer season in Spain. When she got back to England she got a part-time job in a bar in south-east London. On her first night in the bar, a guy suddenly said, 'You look familiar. Haven't you just got back from Spain?' It turned out he had been a guest in the hotel where she'd been working and had coincidentally happened to come to that bar. It wasn't even his regular haunt. When she went to work in Athens for a short while at a later date, her next-door neighbours were in the airport, frantically waving at her. She had a rota and just happened to be on airport duty at 5 a.m. that morning. The same night a close girl friend who she'd drifted apart from came up to her to ask directions, not realising who it was. At the time Lucy felt a bit lost as to where her life was going. But these coincidences made her feel that her life had a pattern and that she was where she needed to be at the time.

Sometimes coincidences highlight a pattern in our lives that shows how events can be inextricably linked together. When Sally met a boyfriend, Steve, he was living at door number 106, in London, while she was living at door number 107 in Bath. She didn't realise it until after their relationship ended. She always felt that they were meant to meet, and this door number sequence seemed to amplify the connection. When she planned to buy another house, it was door number 108, which seemed as if it was a sign for the next step in her life. She had a daughter who was four years old and was looking for schools for when she was five. The couple whose house she was buying had a baby and had already prepared a list of the best schools in the area. They didn't need it as they were emigrating to Australia. She was relieved to know she had a list to consider, without having to spend weeks discovering all the local schools.

It's fascinating to note the way coincidences happen in our lives and how they illuminate a chain of events as well as help provide support and guidance that we have often requested in our minds. From now on make a note of your coincidences in your psychic development diary. You may not be aware of them until after they have happened, but look back and see if there is any chain of events or response to your thoughts.

Thoughts have wings, and whatever we think about either blocks our progress or creates an opportunity. They are the building blocks of our life so the thoughts we have today create our future circumstances. Let your thoughts stem from your higher intuitive self that always wants a win-win situation. Make a point of consciously choosing your thoughts and, with time and practice, the work you do throughout this book will reflect a new way of living your life, one that involves endless connections, opportunities and potential.

10

Work, Passion and Psychic Energy: Finding the Business Success You've Always Wanted

When your work speaks for itself, don't interrupt.
Henry J. Kaiser, 1882–1967, entrepreneur

You have now reached a unique landmark in this book. In these next two chapters, whatever your circumstances, you will be able to go beyond your everyday horizons and turn your wildest dreams into reality. But before I continue I want you to sit quietly for a moment and realise the impact of the power that now lies in your hands. This is your opportunity to use all the skills learned from previous chapters to design your life the way you want it. By pulling all your psychic powers together you can achieve the ultimate goals that we all aspire to as human beings and find the career you've always wanted or enjoy a fulfilling relationship with your ideal partner.

First, we will focus on using your psychic powers to create great success in the work area of your life. This is of primary importance. After all we spend most of our time there.

To do this effectively, I want you to think big and smash through your limitations. A job is about so much more than earning a living or a cross you have to bear in order to pay the bills. I'm not just talking about a career that merely provides a high income or kudos. Or becoming successful or famous. There are plenty of stressed-out, affluent executives who feel utterly miserable with their lives. And there are plenty of depressed celebrities who are paranoid and miserable with living in a goldfish bowl. This is about finding your true calling – and making a profitable living from it. So from now on leave behind the sensible rational voice of your mind that puts up blocks and tells you the reasons why you can't do something, and make a pact to let your inner voice steer you in the right direction. You have exercised your higher mind, so to make the right progress towards your ideal career you only need to ask the right questions and pay attention to the answers your inner dialogue reveals. That intuitive wisdom will guide you so you can pre-empt problems and recognise opportunities. Your dreams can help give you the pointers you need. You will use clearer judgement in decisions and the right people will be drawn to you once you understand your goals (see chapter nine).

By using these magical qualities you are developing a passionate love affair with yourself by seeing your strengths, inspiration, talents and ideas made real. I use the word passion because that is the instinctive feeling you have of being 'fired up' about something. It is when this joyful flame is ignited in your heart that it tells you something really feels right. You have a sense of excitement and feel compelled to act on it. This is what gives you a sense of purpose. That's why our true vocation in life – what our intuitive self feels drawn to do – nourishes our deepest heartfelt ambition: to discover our true path.

Without this direction we drift aimlessly, wondering what it is we could do that makes us feel like useful human beings and fill up the emptiness inside. As I'm sure we've all experienced at some point, if you are in the wrong job – however short term – it is soul-destroying. However much you cloak your feelings it will cause boredom and inner frustration. In some long-term cases, lethargy, depression and illness set in as a sense of aimlessness takes over.

So before you step forward into your expansive new life and a career you love, you need to look clearly at where you are now. But first promise that you will be brutally honest with yourself. Putting on a brave face or deluding yourself cannot open the doors to the successful life you want. So let me ask you a crucial question. How do you feel about your work? Do you spend your time daydreaming or clock-watching until you can rush out of the door? Perhaps you're in a comfortable rut where you don't love your job, but you don't hate it either. Or is your career so demanding and pressurised that you live your life mentally exhausted by stress and wondering when you can actually have a real existence? If you feel this way, then you can absolutely guarantee it wasn't your sixth sense that put you there. Instead, you did what you felt you should do in the eyes of your peers, or accepted what came along.

But just maybe you are one of a small fortunate minority who feel passionate, challenged and stimulated by what they do. These people have a sparkle in their eyes and an inner glow that shows that they have found their true purpose and are generating success from it. But what makes those select individuals different from the norm? They didn't necessarily have the perfect childhood or know the right people. Some of these lucky few may have drawn the short straw, initially, with deprived or abused backgrounds, but had to rely on their own instinct for survival to push themselves forward. That natural instinct is what many describe as 'living on your wits'. But in truth, they tapped into their own inner resources, because they realised they had to. In doing so these people – whether they knew it or not – were led by their innate psychic instincts. They followed their dreams and their hunches and single-mindedly believed in their own vision of success. And their lives blossom as they create their own lucky opportunities.

Look at the famous chat show host Oprah Winfrey who overcame an abused childhood, weight problems and the prejudice of being black. She maintains that although those painful experiences wounded her deeply, they gave her an inner resilience to turn her life around. Often described as a visionary, without doubt she overcame her troubled life with persistent positive thinking. This belief in herself expanded her mind energy, and connected her with her own intuitive voice. She is a great believer in the power of the mind and her ongoing success in every venture, from television, film, production companies, beauty and health, shows how much her psychic senses lead her life. She has become a force to be reckoned with and there is no stopping her. As I mentioned in chapter nine anyone who expresses courage, wisdom, creativity and compassion is thinking intuitively. Anyone who has great success and creativity in their lives is strongly connected to their sixth sense. When life is joyful, good and happy it flows from this inner knowingness within. Oprah is a perfect example of how nothing from her past hindered her progress when she listened to what her inner voice told her to do. Despite a difficult beginning she has become known throughout the world and a millionairess to boot. Rest assured it's never too late to start with your dream career.

Think of Debbie Harry who found big success with her band Blondie in her thirties after years of struggling. She wasn't seen as too old, even though society might say she was over the hill as a pop star. Instead she was the pouting, peroxide vision of sex appeal that made her band so successful.

Yes, she was persistent. But look at the creative force, the passion, and the instinct for making the right contacts. And you've got to admire a woman who made a comeback and had a hit record in her fifties in a music industry obsessed with youth. That in itself shows her limited logic was shoved out of the way and her inner instinct took over. It wouldn't have been possible otherwise.

So don't let your self-limiting beliefs from your childhood, bad luck, age, race or difficult circumstances stop you from realising that a fantastic, satisfying career is in your hands. You've discovered a powerhouse of resources to draw on now that will give you all the ammunition you need.

But remember what I said back in chapter two. Balance is essential. So don't throw logic out of the window. We need to integrate the (intuitive) yin and (pragmatic) yang aspects of our minds. It's the nagging voice of your limited thinking that you don't want, the voice that tells you the reasons why you can't do something. But combining your intuition with your logic means that you are able to see your hunches, ideas and instincts become a reality. Hard graft and persistence are important but intuition gives you a smoother easier ride where you avoid problems and missed opportunities. By using your dreams, intuition, higher guidance and subconscious beliefs you can create a career that you'll love without the hassle. However, you may discover that your mind has a set idea about what will make you happy, yet your intuition may tell a radically different story. Listen to what that inner voice tells you. It knows what you really want.

Do you have life block? Become aware
and allow change into your life

You may be thinking: How can I have the job I love, if I just can't change? That's understandable. Change can be difficult and at times hard to contemplate. You may have become entrenched in set routines and find comfort in old habits. I call this 'life block'. When you have life block you are stuck in a deep rut that you cannot shift yourself from. You have let the left side of your brain take over and shut yourself off from the instinctive power of your higher mind. Some people call it the comfort zone or in other cases plain laziness. But I can tell you what it really is. Behind that mask of 'I can't be bothered', or 'it's easier where I am', is plain old-fashioned fear. You have allowed your mind energy to funnel inwards and forgotten to be inspired and trust that anything is possible (see chapter nine). Let's face it. It's scary to give up what you know and fulfil your dreams. What if you fail? What if you're not good enough? What about the poor job market? Or do you have beliefs that tell you that you can't earn good money doing what you really want to do?

But what's the alternative to not hearing your inner voice and being brave enough to go for your ultimate ambition? Boredom and resentment that you've missed the boat or wasted your life. Be completely honest with yourself. Do you want to spend your time on this planet with wasted talents and unfulfilled potential? Inside there's something nagging at you, because you know deep down that you have unique talents to offer the world – whether your brilliant ideas, compassion, humour, or patience. You might daydream of being that great inventor, high-powered executive or great actor. Well, keep doing that – dreams and ideas are great. Everything in our lives came from an individual with a dream or an idea. But you've got to let that fantasy become a reality if you want to change your life. No excuses; you're a valuable asset and the universe needs you to make your input right now.

I've devised a practical and simple exercise that you can do every day which will help wake up your intuitive fire within and push your limits out of the way. It's based on shifting your perceptions in order to create change. This will expand and open up your mind, and as your mind energy reaches out you will start to discover new opportunities. Start now. Unblock your life and tap into that resourceful and powerful mind of yours to bring what you and the world truly deserve.

How to increase awareness and let in change

Changing your perceptions is a key tool in awakening your higher mind and finding your dream job. Perceptions are just thoughts and shifting them is easier then you think. Change involves overcoming limited, bored and fearful thought patterns and creating an optimistic and alert open mind. This is how your mind expands and continues to awaken your psychic abilities. And the only way to create an open mind is to change the way you think and see things.

One way of shifting your perceptions is to become aware of the routines and rituals in your life. Routines allow us to switch off from our surroundings and we do things on automatic pilot. When this happens we become one of the 'walking dead'. We are virtually unconscious and not paying any attention to the present. And unconsciousness is lethal. This isn't positive daydreaming that releases tension and expands your mind, but a sleepy trance that dulls you to your environment and to yourself as your mind energy funnels inwards. It does this whenever you draw into yourself. You are miles away from your intuition, creativity and inner power while you remain in this state. When we drift off into no-man's-land, we don't really listen to what anyone says, we have endless accidents, make constant mistakes and life literally passes us by. How often do you put your household or car keys down and forget where they are? How much wasted time do you spend looking for them? How many times have you noticed yourself sliding into a semi-comatose state in a meeting or when you're walking along the road? How bad is your memory, because you can't remember what someone just said to you, since you were somewhere else? What's more, by not being entirely present, we close ourselves off from an awareness of life's new opportunities.

So start today by looking at the things you do repetitively that make you unconscious, and open up your higher mind. Ask yourself some essential questions. Do you always take the same route home every day? If so, then change it. Take a bus instead of a train. Or go home an alternative way. Walk to your house from a different direction. If you always sit in the same armchair when you relax in the evening, sit somewhere else. I bet you'll find things that you hardly ever noticed in your front room by simply seeing the room from another perspective. If you always eat at a certain time, alter it by an hour either side. If you always do your washing on a Sunday, change the day. You'll be amazed at how you see things from a different angle.

By trying other options and routes you will slowly allow your consciousness to accept change and you will begin to wake yourself up. When you change your routine, you will naturally be more consciously aware of your surroundings and notice things you never have before. Your mind will be focused on the present moment instead of in a daze and as a consequence your energy will start expanding outwards instead of closing in. As it reaches out, you will release masses of mental tension, which, as it lifts, will raise your consciousness and enable you to hear your intuitive voice more clearly. When you are more in tune with your intuition, you are more in touch with your creativity. When you are more creative, you feel more optimistic and inspired. You are put back in touch with your psychic wisdom that knows the true pathway to take in your life. And that's when you can begin the first step to realising a dream. Try it out and switch your awareness back on.

After changing your perceptions you'll now be ready to let in the changes necessary for finding the job of your dreams. Stephanie's story, below, illustrates perfectly what can happen when we use our intuition to create the career change that we want.

Stephanie's story

Stephanie had an innate feeling that she needed to change direction more than ten years ago. At that time she worked as a senior manager for a well-known department store. Despite earning a huge salary and having a lot of responsibility, she had a strong sense that she needed to do something different. She felt her life was slipping away in her twenty-four-hour role of exhausting travel and trouble-shooting. One afternoon the intuitive thought suddenly came to her that there was a better quality of life to be had working for herself and using her own natural flair. Her idea was inspired by a plastic surgeon she had met at a party the night before. Once she knew what she wanted to do, there was no stopping her. She immediately began researching and set up the London Cavendish, an advisory service of the best plastic surgeons that proved to be an instant hit. Before the month was out she had her own company. It happened fast because she listened to her inner voice and had the confidence to follow up on this insight.

'When it came to doing the research and building up my company I always went with my strong intuitive sense of direction,' she says. 'Any time I have a problem, I concentrate my mind, so it becomes still and try to listen to my feelings. That's why people say I'm so creative as I have hundreds of innovative ideas. But I do believe in dreams and if I am not sure about my hunches, I focus on the problem before I go to bed and when I've slept on it, it's like a puzzle that seems to get mentally slotted into place. Then I know that I'm being guided in the right decisions.'

Now, ten years on, her business is still thriving and Stephanie loves her job, knowing that she is in control of every aspect of her life. She proves that once you actually know what you want to do, it is only a matter of relying on intuitive decisions to put the plan into action.

I'm now going to suggest several techniques by which you can harness your psychic resources to discover a career that you'll love.

Visualisation to lead you to the right career

Keep your psychic development diary and a pen next to you. I'm now going to lead you into a visualisation that will help your heart lead you to the right career.

Take three deep breaths and focus on the centre of your chest where your heart chakra is. Focus on your ideal working scenario and imagine there is a door on your heart. What does the door look like? Is it made of iron, wood, or is it just a small gate? Whatever the door looks like, see or feel it opening up. Then visualise a pure white light in your chest and breathe in deeply. As you breathe in, imagine the white

Be Your Own Psychic

luminous colour filling up and expanding in your chest and throughout your body. Visualise the light pouring into your arms, legs and back. Then slowly breathe out. Feel the light calming and relaxing you. Visualise the light filling up your body so much that you can see a shimmering glow through your skin, which creates a white aura all around you. This light will help open up and activate your heart. Then feel a glowing stream of energy in your chest stretch out and gently pull you forward.

In your mind visualise yourself walking along a long path tugged by the stream of energy. Ask from your heart for your guide to come and help bring you knowledge. Feel the presence of your guide standing with you. Does the path look straight or is it winding? As you walk along it, you see something that represents your talent on the side of the path. It could be a symbol, a word or a feeling. Stop and pick it up. If you don't understand what it means, carry it with you. Then you come across a box in front of you. Inside is something that symbolises one of your strengths. Pick it up and take it with you. Keep walking along the path. Feel a sense of certainty. Know that at the end of your path you will find the work you love, even if you are not completely conscious of it. If the end of the path seems a long way off, don't worry. You are on your way. If you have reached the end, note if you can see, feel or hear anything that gives you information. Take this information with you. Whatever you find, you are on the way to your end result.

Questions to ask yourself

1. What did the door to your heart look like? If it was a heavy door that needed to be prised open, this shows how much you have closed off from your heart. But with awareness it only takes moments to allow your heart to speak to you. If it opens easily, then your heart is already open to leading you forward. Take time to open up your heart regularly and fill it with light. Our heart is

232

where our unconditional love comes from. It is through our hearts that we know which career we can rejoice in.

2. What was your path like? Was it winding or straight? Did it veer off? Was it hard to keep to? The straighter your path, the more direct you feel about reaching your goal at the moment. What were your talents and strengths? Look at what they mean practically. One girl I know who did this exercise saw a nutcracker to symbolise her strengths, which to her meant looking inside to get to the kernel of truth. And then she saw a sword, which to her meant the sword of truth. It was pretty accurate, as she actually became a counsellor. Truth and getting underneath what was going on was the basis of her new work.

An intuitive quiz to help you discover your true vocation

I have now devised a quiz that you need to answer with your intuitive self and not with your logical mind. It is so easy to think of work in terms of a pragmatic, sensible approach, because that's what we're used to. Some of these questions might seem straightforward and simple – and they are meant to be just that. It is our logical mind that likes to make things complicated. Our sixth sense simply points out what we always knew deep down. To ensure that you are answering from the yin side of your mind, sit quietly and do the quick frequency lift, described on page 100. Then answer these ten questions quickly with the first thoughts that flash into your head. Don't analyse what they're for. You want your psychic self to answer before your logic gets a look-in.

1. What is your dream job?
   a) How close do you feel to fulfilling that dream?
   b) Does it seem a long way off? Note what this dream job

is now and see if you feel the same when you reach the end of this chapter. It may change radically.

2. What are you passionate about? It could be anything: food, music, culture. These passions tell you what you are instinctively drawn to.

3. What are your hobbies? (By hobbies I mean the things you really love to do, not something you do just to pass the time.) They tell you what you enjoy.

4. What job did you want to do when you were a child? Think back to what you dreamed of doing. Remember why it interested you. If it was something like a pop star, astronaut or dancer, think about why you loved those things. Our childlike aspirations come pretty close to what our hearts wanted us to do.

5. What do people tell you you're good at? This could range from interior decorating, cooking, listening, or even talking for England! If in doubt, ask a few of your friends to be candid about what they think you do well.

6. What are your talents? Be honest and brazen with yourself. Talents are things you know you can do well. It could be writing, organising, or just being a harmonious influence.

7. What are your three best qualities? (Do *not* name a physical attribute. I'm after characteristics such as honesty, determination, courage or kindness.)

8. Which actor or actress inspires you? Who do you love to

watch? Ask yourself why they interest you so much. We are often attracted by qualities that we have within ourselves.

9. What type of books inspire you? Books tell you a lot about who you are. Someone who reads adrenaline-producing horror stories may be turned on by something very different to someone who enjoys a light romance.

10. What's your wildest work ambition? Think about what you would really like to do if you were granted a wish. Don't just focus on what will make money. Ask yourself why you'd want to do that. If it's something strange like being in the circus, then maybe you like taking risks, or something that involves performing.

The answers you have given should proven enlightening. These are the pieces of a larger picture that you can put together. It is our passions, interests, inspirations and child-hood ambitions that show us what stimulates and motivates us. You knew all this already, but you needed to bring it to the surface. And doing what you enjoy is what makes a career worth having and fires your enthusiasm. Keep a note of your responses and look through them again at the end of this chapter. They are the pointers that reveal the vision of where you want to be.

Your action plan

Now it's time to be specific about what you want. As you did in chapter nine, write a detailed description of what you want to achieve, describing your ideal dream job in the present tense, as if it is already happening. You can refer back to see why this technique will help (see page 201). If you don't yet know then say, 'I am fulfilled and successful in a job I love.' If you do know what you want then you could start with, 'I am enjoying my job in (advertising, journalism, catering).' Look at everything from the location to your status in the company, or whether you are running your own business. Think about everything in detail. The hours you are working, the salary you are earning. How many contracts are coming your way. Be realistic but aim high. Even focus on the temperament of your ideal work colleagues. Remember to add that you are coping with everything calmly and diligently and that money flows in to the company easily. The more information you put in, the better your awareness and focus will become.

Programme your subconscious to deliver the goods

Now it's time to programme your belief system to create your reality. This visualisation will take you into the deeply relaxed alpha state that allows your subconscious to be receptive to new data. It will expand your mind and send out the new thought energy into the universe. People who are able to help with your goal will respond. Your aura radiates and holds the energy of your new beliefs; in doing so magic happens and you will attract the support that you need from the right co-incidences and people.

Refer back to chapter nine and, using the tropical island visualisation on page 205, or the well on page 209, either descend to the room where there is a warm pool or the room filled with cushions, whichever you prefer. Once you are deeply relaxed and in the right room in your mind, begin to picture yourself where you'd like to be. If you still don't know what it is you'd like to do, see yourself happy and fulfilled in a job that you love. Focus on how you feel and say the affirmation again; 'I am fulfilled and successful in a job that I love.' If you know what you want to do, then you can start to bring all your senses into being. Visualise yourself doing the job well and focus on making every sense alive. How do you feel? What circumstances are you in? Are you working from home as your own boss? Or in a busy office? How many staff do you have? Think big and successful. Have you been promoted? If so, where are you sitting, at home or in the office? What does the background noise sound like? Focus on everyone feeling happy and busy. You could use the affirmation 'I am enjoying working in my own thriving business', for example.

While you are in this deeply relaxed alpha state, you can programme anything else you want. But remember to keep it simple. Perhaps you love your current job, but you have a difficult relationship with your boss who seems to make unreasonable demands. If you want to get on better with them, then use this time to change your mental image of the situation. Visualise yourself talking with your boss (or whoever else), perhaps in the office where you work, chatting happily and getting on well. Once again, picture it as if it is happening now. And make it as realistic as possible, using all your senses. Focus on what you and your boss are wearing. Can you smell anything, like aftershave or perfume? What is going on around you? Can you hear the chatter of people talking on the phone outside the office and are there other phones ringing? It may be difficult to keep visualising all these senses that you have activated in your picture, but practice will help (see chapter three on how to strengthen the senses), and the more real you make the image, the more effective it will be. Repeat an affirmation mentally as you visualise the picture. Perhaps something like 'My relationship with my boss is happy and productive. We talk calmly together about work.' Then let go of the outcome. This is important. (See the section on trust below.)

Notice your boss's behaviour as time goes on. If it doesn't change after a week of visualising (either in the morning or evening for around twenty minutes) keep trying, be patient and trust that it will be sorted out. But don't stress yourself out.

Programme your dreams to take the next step

Now you have focused your mind to achieve your vision, this is a good time to ask your dreams for help. As I mentioned in chapter eight there are amazing solutions to be found in programming your dreams. This technique will help inspire thoughts on what you'd like to do with your career.

Before you go to sleep write down the questions you want answers to. If you want more success, ask for help in how to get it. If you want a new career that you love, ask for guidance and support in taking the next step. Phrase it as a question: 'What should I do to find my ideal job?' or 'What should I do to build on my success?' And always write down your dreams as soon as you wake up. If you are prone to forgetting them quickly, then be diligent. Set your alarm for fifteen minutes earlier than usual and take your time in writing down everything you remember. If you don't remember the dream, write down the immediate feelings you have on waking.

You'll get a stronger clarity of the next step to take in your working life as your intuition becomes more awakened.

The follow-up

Trust that it will happen

Now focus on all the work that you have done throughout

this chapter. You have woken yourself up out of your daze by changing your routines and altering your perceptions. You have visualised your heart leading the way to the right career. You have illuminated what you really knew all along from the quiz. You have programmed your subconscious and your dreams to create a vision and bring you closer to your goal. You have focused your mind on what you want to achieve.

You now need to let go of the outcome and effort you have put in and trust that what you want will happen. It's important that you do this so that you don't get stressed or obsessive about it, as this will set up opposing forces to the receptive mind and can cause obstructions to what you want to create. Magic happens when our higher mind is leading the way and we allow everything to work as it should. If it's more success you're after, trust in the outcome, but pay attention to any intuitive thoughts that tell you to take action. It's also very important to trust in the higher intuitive minds of other people at work, whether your boss, work colleagues or clients. However they think, trusting in a successful communication or outcome will enable them to respond to you from their higher mind in the constructive way that you need. Trust really can work miracles and people can respond positively quite unconsciously if you just know absolutely that they will. Whatever you do, trust that the answer will come or you'll be put in contact with the right people who can provide the answers.

Evoke your angel

As mentioned in chapter seven, you can also evoke an angel to help you with work matters. Simply refer back to the chapter, sit quietly and say in your mind, 'Can the angel who helps with work-related issues, please step forward.' Be aware and sense whether there is anyone with you. If you can't feel anything, don't worry. Simply ask again: 'Please help success to unfold with the career of my choice.' If you want to ask specifically about other career issues or problems, then you can do so. Once again trust that they will help and their energy will help to smooth your pathway. Be prepared for the unexpected. Their divine and loving energy works in mysterious ways and things can occur out of the blue to support you in your endeavours.

Timing

If you get an intuitive hunch or an instinct to act on something – do it. Don't waste time procrastinating or talking it through with people. The visions and goals that you are focusing on will coincidentally lead you to the right opportunities. But you then have to act to make it happen. Getting that sense of timing is all-important in walking through the next door or making the right contact. You don't have to risk everything. But have the confidence to move forward and ask the right question or pick up the phone when you feel the intuitive urge to do so. It usually means your higher wiser self knows that it's the perfect strategy and wants to take you on the next step to reach your goal.

Have integrity

It is very important if you want things to work well for you that you behave with honesty and integrity in all your dealings. You don't need to lie or pretend to be successful or manipulate to make someone an ally. You don't need to step over anyone to get to where you want to be. This is when our limited fearful mind is in control. Acting in this way only makes you feel bad and nervous inside and ultimately trips you up. You create enemies and gain an unpleasant reputation.

Remember like attracts like. There is a great truth in the saying, You reap what you sow. Intuitive thoughts are respectful, courageous and caring. When you allow this higher power to guide you, you *will* be supported and helped.

Coincidences

As you set the wheels of your powerful mind in motion, be aware of the coincidences that happen in your life. You may not notice them at first, but you soon will. Write down any connections that link you to other people, places or events. Take notice even if someone rings up out of the blue and note any places, contacts or ideas that flash through your mind. This is your intuition speaking to you and coincidences will happen with more regularity as you proceed.

I used this in my work all the time. At one point I wanted to find a woman who was addicted to telephone tarot lines for a magazine article. I thought about it before I went to sleep and I wrote down the age range of the subject I needed. I requested that they spent a lot of money on their addiction and that they would be happy to be photographed. I decided to trust that it would happen. When the phone rang the next morning, it was a girl to talk about something entirely different. But when I asked her if she'd ever used tarot lines, she said she'd spent a fortune on them. She was thrilled to give her viewpoint and be photographed. I had my instant case study for a feature without any hard slog. And the miracle is that after making my request – she came to me!

At other times if I was looking for a case study, I would get a name in my mind that I recognised. I might not have spoken to this person for years, but when I rang them, they usually knew someone who was exactly what I was looking for.

Feleny's story

Feleny Georghiou's inspiring story is a perfect illustration of how someone can create success through using their intuitive skills. Aged thirty-nine, she is the successful owner of a business called Connect Hair Systems in north London. The company specialises in real hair extensions, and for the last fifteen years she has had streams of people, including celebrity clients, pouring through her doors. Her non-stop work often means that she has to fly overseas to attend to Arab princesses or create new identities on a film set. It's a thriving, well-established business, but it became successful because Feleny was a natural at using her psychic abilities to make her dreams come true.

Her path changed back in 1986 when she was managing a nightclub, but she felt unfulfilled with what she was doing. She was in a dilemma, as she didn't know which direction to take. Then things suddenly changed. Her job involved a glamorous existence where she had to look good and part of her beauty routine was having hair extensions. But she hated the artificial hair and the way it was attached. Then one night as she was lying in bed relaxing, it suddenly flashed into her mind that there was a gap in the market for something better than the normal hair extensions. But she didn't know where to go to find out more. Fifteen years ago, nobody in England was using real hair in the beauty business and the synthetic method was still very new. Feleny had always been a big believer in visualisations and intuition and once the idea came to her, she would lie in bed thinking pleasant thoughts of owning her own salon. She would see herself talking to numerous clients with the phone ringing constantly in the background. Her visions became a belief and, within a short time, the pattern of her life started to create her desire.

Within a few weeks an important coincidence took place which was to launch her new business. A young girl with beautiful long glossy hair came into the nightclub to book a party. And when Feleny commented on the condition of her hair she was amazed to hear that the girl was wearing real hair extensions, which she'd had done in the States. Feleny knew instantly that this girl had provided the answer to her problem and took advantage of the opportunity. The very next day she booked a flight to California and paid the specialist salon for some in-house training. She stayed a month and returned with newly acquired skills ready to start up on her own.

The next step was getting a bank loan for £15,000. She already had £15,000 of her own savings and continued to visualise her business as flourishing. Consequently, her bank manager handed over the money without any quibbles. 'Of course,' says Feleny, 'there were times when doubts would come into my mind and I'd think what if it doesn't take off and I lose everything. But I knew that if I wanted to keep my vision alive, I had to take those negative thoughts out of my mind and keep thinking constructively. If I wanted help I would programme my dreams by asking for solutions and would wake up not always remembering my visions, but just being clear about the next step. My new business became the first British company to produce real hair extensions.' So from a combination of dreams, coincidences, subconscious beliefs, intuition and trust everything blossomed for Feleny.

But her success wasn't just about sitting back and tuning in. There was a lot of discipline and hard work and at times she was working from 9 a.m. to midnight. She also had a lot of competitors. As Feleny continues. 'There was a chap who started a rival company within my first year who had got a half-a-million-pound backing. He started advertising furiously, and every new treatment we brought out he copied. But I learned not to compete, because that's when you fall flat on your face. Within two years he'd gone bust but, remarkably, it helped my company. All the response to his advertising for real hair extensions came to us when he went bankrupt. He spent so much time trying to find out what we were doing that he forgot to focus on his own profits. Now fifteen years later we've done the hard work and we don't need to advertise at all.

'I would say that when problems arise, don't panic, go with your hunches or intuition and act quickly when the time is right. If you get an instinct to do something, there can be a tendency to keep talking it through with different people. The more you discuss it, it takes on a negative force and you literally talk it out the window and lose the moment for action.'

When your vision becomes real and things are in the early stages, anything can happen. The key is not to panic, maintain your trust, follow your hunches and keep going with your vision.

Eight steps to achieving your perfect career

1. Programme your dreams and listen to your intuition and note the answers to what it is you really want to do.
2. Make a game plan. The first step is to be clear about what you want and write it down as if it's already happening. For real success, focus on what your heart wants you to do by listening to your intuition. Throw out any limited beliefs that you cannot make money from doing what you love.
3. Programme it into your subconscious using the exercises in chapter nine to take you into the deeply relaxed alpha state. This will expand your mind energy and you can begin to create your psychic vision.
4. Work towards the goal but forget the outcome.
5. Don't get sidetracked into competing with other businesses or people. Just calmly follow your own vision of success. Keep a positive view of what you want to achieve and brush aside negative doubts or self-pity. If you have any negative

thoughts, dismiss them from your mind unless you have a gut feeling that something is wrong.

6. Be prepared to put the graft in, but know when to stop and relax.

7. Follow your instincts and act quickly when something feels right. Your gut feelings tell you when the timing is right. Otherwise you lose the opportunity. Never panic – be calm. Fear and panic block intuition.

8. Don't be afraid of the future – look forward to it.

Everything starts with the germ of an idea (a thought). Although important, hard work isn't enough. You need judgement, integrity, trust and intuition to guide you in the right directions and to make the right decisions.

Exercise for making the right decisions

If you want to prepare something important relating to your career – a speech, a document, or even if you need to talk to your bank manager – then it will make life a lot easier if you work from your intuition. We are all sensitive to our sur-roundings and can easily end up feeling melancholy, anxious or irritable, states of mind that merely create stress and worry. But they are easy to remedy. A good way to get back into harmony and contentment before you start any communication or project is to do a ten-minute breathing exercise, which will harmonise all your chakras (energy points). This will help you to make the right decisions and act from your heart. The following visualisation exercise is to do with breathing into your chakra energy points. Our chakras can end up as dumping grounds blocked with negative emotions and thoughts from ourselves or others. If any chakra points ache as you go through the exercise, or feel hard to breathe into, then this energy point may be blocked. Just take several deep breaths into that chakra, until you feel it is easier to breathe into.

Imagine breathing first of all into the crown of your head, which is your seventh chakra. Take a deep breath and imagine feeling your head expand with energy and then slowly breathe out. Visualise the area as if it's a lung and you are breathing into it. The key here is to 'feel'. You must feel or imagine that you are feeling your head expand when you breathe in and contract when you breathe out. Then do the same, this time imagining your lungs are behind your forehead. Imagine breathing in and visualise your forehead expanding with air and then breathe out. You will do the same all the way down your chakras. The next is the throat chakra. Visualise this neck area alone being filled up and see it expanding in your mind. Then focus on your upper chest for the heart chakra where your lungs actually are, taking a deep breath in and feeling the area expand and then breathe out slowly. Then focus on the stomach, imagining there is a lung there. Now breathe into your lower abdomen between your belly button and public bone. It may help if you put your hand there to locate the area. Then once again breathe in and feel the area expand and then breathe out slowly as you feel it contract. Notice if any areas ache or hurt. If so, the energy is blocked here, but the breathing exercise will help clear it. Lastly breathe into the area located around the tip of your spine. This is your base chakra. Feel your pelvic area expand and contract.

The end result is not a dramatic turnaround of emotion. But you will find it exhilarating as the new energy pours into your chakra points. Our energies are subtle and you will notice that you feel energised, contented and calm. Feel your energy centres working together as one. Your chakras will now be spinning effectively and when you speak, write or act in connection with an important decision, this exercise will ensure that you do it with real intuitive intelligence and harmony.

This is a good time to reflect on the answers you gave to the intuitive quiz on page 233 and see whether they provide further insight.

Now that you've discovered the journey to your dream career, I hope you are inspired. The world is waiting for you to carve your own niche in it, one in which you can feel proud and justified with who you are and what you are doing. You are discovering that by listening to your inner voice, with wise judgements and instinctive hunches that may seem like a gamble, this innate instinct will bring you transformational results. You can be one step ahead in the game of life using all your psychic skills to chart your course. This is your life and you can make it what you want it to be with your own specific agenda. Once you know where your potential lies you can act upon it, with coincidences lending you a helping hand. Keep tuning in to your higher mind for your visions to become reality and enjoy the rewards.

11

Love, Sex and Psychic Energy:
Finding the Relationship You've Always Wanted

Love can sometimes be magic. But magic can sometimes be just an illusion
Javan, 1946–, American poet

Now that you have transformed one area of your life, you can use your psychic powers to improve the quality of your intimate relationships. If you are single, you can find your perfect partner; if you're already in a relationship you can become aware of whether it's really fulfilling your needs. You might be in a convenient but boring rut, or at the other end of the spectrum in a hopeless battlefield, or perhaps you're just waiting for your ideal partner. But maybe you're one of the lucky ones who has already found the love of their life. If so, then you can strengthen and develop your relationship on all levels.

So why will developing your intuition help you to find true long-lasting love? More then anything else in our lives, we need our psychic powers to be working well for us when it comes to affairs of the heart. When we meet someone, it's easy for our natural instincts to become clouded once hormones, emotions, negative beliefs and low self-esteem are thrown into the mix. Chemistry and attractions can be misleading as we can often veer towards familiar types. As I mentioned in chapter nine, at times it can seem as if we keep meeting the same type of person with similar characteristics, cloaked in different disguises. This is where we can become trapped in our programmed beliefs, creating destructive relationships, because that's what we consciously expect to happen.

Look back and note how many times your conscious limited thinking has brought you the wrong results. To make wise decisions in our love lives, it's essential that we allow our higher minds to steer us to the right person. That means letting go of your plans on how to attain happiness and trust that your intuition will naturally lead you to your goal. The first step is identifying what you want in a partner. Then you can combine all the exercises in this chapter to propel you towards the loving relationship you deserve.

Let me congratulate you in advance. You are now on a glorious adventure into a new life. And I ask only one thing of you. Give yourself a real chance to find love by putting your conscious mind to one side and becoming a student ready to learn. From hereon in you will:

- Know whether you are ready for love by understanding your own needs.
- Rid yourself of emotional baggage that blocks your sixth sense.
- Open up your heart to recognise the right partner.
- Become more acutely discerning when you meet someone.
- Stop giving knee-jerk reactions to the people in your life and start responding empathetically once you see beneath their veneer.
- Use your dreams to help you solve problems and lead you to new opportunities.
- Programme your subconscious mind to create positive visions that enable you to attract the looks, personality and qualities of the kind of person you really want.

You'll know if you are responding from your higher mind when communication in your relationships is joyful, flowing and harmonious. Arguments, jealousy, anger, controlling behaviour, infidelity and misery show that you are definitely on the wrong track. This chapter will also allow you to make another important discovery vital to expanding your intuitive intelligence. You will learn how to accelerate your psychic powers by awakening a source of sacred Kundalini energy. This will help you to understand how your sexuality is directly linked to your psychic abilities and how you can enhance this vital force. If you manage your sexual energy correctly, you can potentially explore a heightened awareness which can establish a telepathic connection and deeper bond with a current partner; and if you are single, it will enable you to become more connected with your creative and intuitive power. This brings clarity and a deeper understanding of what you want in a relationship.

What are you looking for and are you really ready for love?

Before you read any further, I want you to answer the following ten questions to discover if you are really ready for your dream partner. This is meant to be fun and not an exam. The answers you get will help you discover any blocks that are obstructing your path to happiness and find out your true needs. So to do this exercise properly, I want you to go through the questions twice. First sit quietly and do the quick frequency lift in chapter five (see page 100). Then look at the questions, allowing your intuition to answer each one. Let your head be clear of thoughts and allow your responses to come from your higher source. Next answer the questions again, but this time thinking logically and analytically. You may well be surprised at the different answers you get and how the two sides of your mind approach things. Now you know the difference, it will help to remind you that your higher mind wants only your happiness. The conscious mind is pre-set by your beliefs and limitations and likes to control everything including the outcome. Surrender to your intuition by letting go of the outcome and you can have what you want.

1. Name all the reasons why you haven't got the relationship you really want.

2. What are the different personal qualities (do not name a physical attribute) that would help you achieve this relationship?

3. Who would be your dream celebrity partner, if you could have anyone you wanted with no limits? What are the qualities you like in this person, leaving aside their looks? (For example, actor Antonio Banderas could be your idea of perfection because he seems to be passionate and hard-working but also a loyal family man. Or for the male reader, actress Angelina Jolie, because she is adventurous and exciting.)

4. If you could cherry-pick the qualities in your friends' partners that you admire, what would they be?

5. What is your primary motivation to be in a relationship? Is it loneliness, regular sex, social acceptance, boredom, financial problems, sharing mutual interests or acting instinctively on an attraction?

6. If you were granted a wish, what would you consider to be the two most important assets in a potential partner: money

and status, appearance, sex drive, decent character, spirituality or work ethic?

7. Do you have any anger or resentment towards any ex-lover or family member? Think of who it is and whether you believe the conflict is your fault.

8. If you look back on past relationships, was there anyone who could have been your dream partner? If so, what were the reasons why this relationship ended?

9. Are there any things about yourself that you feel stop you having the relationship you want, e.g. being overweight, bad skin, too tall, too short, too unattractive?

10. On a scale of 1–10, how close do you feel you are at the moment from being with your dream partner?

This exercise is important in letting you know how ready you are to find love. Some of the answers from your conscious and intuitive mind may be the same. But some may be quite different. We think that our conscious mind rules with its logical views and that we don't have anything else to learn. Our higher minds, however, show us the truth beyond the surface of things. You will know if your higher mind has answered a question properly, rather than your conscious mind, because it will have a ring of truth about it. You may be surprised or feel a sense of illumination. Our higher minds want the best outcome for us that will benefit everyone, whereas the conscious mind judges everything including ourselves. It thinks it knows it all.

Being ready for love comes from the openness within you

to attract love. Low self-esteem and negative beliefs, anger towards someone in the past, and not knowing what you want will all stop you from finding the happiness you deserve. So keep a note of your responses. As you read through this chapter, you will gain valuable insights into your own attitudes and what you really want from someone. You can use your own inner magic to transform your life.

Your emotional detox programme

Before you embark on finding a good relationship, you need to get rid of any emotional and psychological rubbish that might have accumulated which blocks you from being open to love. Otherwise this negative baggage will stifle your intuition and you will only be able to respond on a limited conscious level. Our minds want to control. But our inner voice tells us that there is another way of communicating. We need to be in touch with our inner selves, which promotes loving, positive feelings and actions if we want relationships to succeed. But first you need to be honest with yourself. Consider the following:

* Do you feel like a victim of fate or are you still angry at the way someone treated you?
* Look at the pattern of how your relationships have been. Are you so desperate to be in one that you will put up with a miserable existence rather than being alone?
* Do you keep picking the wrong person and wondering why you missed the important signs that told you to steer clear?
* Or did you wonder how something that had such a promising start went so badly wrong?
* Perhaps your current or past relationships seemed

compatible from the outside, but you were bored and shared no honest communication.

All these different cycles in your emotional life will have left their mark in emotional debris. Look at the consequences if you don't get rid of these stored-up feelings.

How can you nurture a new relationship or invest positively in a current one if you are still stewing over and reacting to old issues? You could unconsciously put your new love in the role of counsellor where they try and solve your problems. But when would your partner get to be listened to? Or you could end up distrusting someone new as you subconsciously expect them to behave in the same way as someone who hurt you in the past. You may overreact to what someone says to you because of old wounds.

One woman in her forties who I worked with has not been in a relationship that has lasted beyond a few weeks for the last fifteen years. She has never forgiven an old lover for leaving her for another woman and forcing her to have an abortion. She felt so betrayed and angry about him that she now treats every man with contempt. A lot of her thoughts focus on nursing old wounds, looking for ways of exacting revenge and pre-empting every new relationship by rejecting the man first. Any signs of a problem and she instantly terminates the liaison. She seems unable to move on and her emotional state is showing in her hard and bitter expression. She is a perfect example of someone who is out of touch with her own psychic power. Real development of your intuitive powers awakens you on your deepest levels and puts you in touch with your inner voice and heart feelings. That part of you knows only how to love, cherish and honour others. It doesn't understand anger. She is unable to see men as they really are, because they all represent something unpleasant to her.

Holding on to negative or vengeful thoughts and grudges to do with a past lover, friend or family member will hinder your progress. These thoughts show up in your energy field and body language and people can instinctively sense them. Remember what I said at the beginning of the book on how energy works? Like-minded people attract others. If you want someone positive, generous and in touch with their own intuition, you must develop it in yourself. Otherwise how can you draw them to you?

We've all been hurt. That is part of life, and clearing out the toxic emotional waste must be an ongoing process to allow us to keep our hearts open and free to move on.

Break free of emotional baggage and be ready to attract real love

This is an exercise that can help clear out the psychological junk, whatever your circumstances. One of the simplest methods that I learned many years ago, which worked well, is to visualise the situation in your past that caused you pain. It is a simple method that our intuitive inner self responds to without our logical mind and defences getting in the way.

Close your eyes and think about a particularly upsetting scenario. If it was a partner who was unfaithful, for example, then visualise the situation. Allow yourself to feel the emotion and simply say, 'Thank you,' in your mind to the person and the circumstances that caused the painful feelings, and really mean it. You say 'thank you' instead of 'I forgive' simply because there are some experiences that are so horrendous or painful that you simply can't forgive. But saying 'thank you' means you don't have to forgive, yet you accept the experience and recognise the lesson that you have learned from it, thereby releasing the emotional effects that you are holding on to.

It may be difficult to do at first. At times it is hard to stop blaming someone, particularly if what they did seems unforgivable. The more long-standing or traumatic the event, the harder it will be. But persevere; it will work when you are sincere about it. Once you do that, you release the old toxic thought. Old resentments and betrayals create blocks that show in our energy fields and repress our natural vitality. It takes a lot of energy to hold on to all those festering images. You will know when you have released these pent-up emotions because you will feel different. As you release masses of dammed-up energy that has been repressed through negative emotion, you will start to feel energy flowing back into your body. This may resemble a tingling sensation in different parts of the body. You may also feel lighter, happier or simply more at peace.

I did this process with someone I had an ongoing conflict with and at first I found it very difficult. But I persevered and kept remembering events that upset me and 'thanked' the person and the circumstances as I was reliving them. You can go through many scenarios of anyone who has hurt you and continue the process. I felt a huge amount of energy flowing back in to my legs and arms. You can do this with anything in your life, even if you feel lonely or angry. Thank the feeling with as much sincerity as you can muster. There is never a total end result. We continually collect negative thoughts that make us ill or depressed. But this exercise will teach you to become more aware of your thoughts and help you consciously to choose to think more positively. You will feel more energised and happier about your life, which will help you to attract the right person into your life.

I'm now going to take you through a visualisation that will enable you to feel more connected with your heart. Of course, I am not talking about your real heart, but your heart chakra, located in the centre of your upper chest, which connects you with your intuitive feelings of unconditional love. When this heart chakra is activated it tells you when a person or a relationship feels right because you will 'know' without reason. You may even feel a heat or energy in your heart centre. When you allow your heart to lead the way, you give up controlling and manipulating to get what you want and make room for genuine communication. This will help you to recognise and attract the right person into your life by acting on the intuitive thoughts and feelings that surface.

Visualisation to open your heart

Once again keep your psychic development diary and a pen next to you as you are about to embark on an exercise that will help your heart lead you to the right partner.

Take three deep breaths and focus on your heart chakra in the centre of your upper chest. Think about the kind of relationship you want and then visualise a door on your heart and see yourself opening it. Note what the door looks like, whether it is heavy or light to open. Then see yourself stepping outside your body and walking through the door of your own heart. There are seven steps going down. I want you to visualise walking down these steps, slowly counting down. Seven, six, five, four, three, two, one. As you go down the steps you are heading towards the core of who you are. This is the fount of all compassion and knowledge.

You find yourself in a room that is filled with light. Breathe this light into your heart and focus on the subject of relationships. Ask yourself the question, 'What do I need to let go of from the past to attract the right person?' Take note of whatever comes into your mind. You could be in for a surprise. Now see yourself sitting in the light inside your heart and say, 'I am ready and open to enjoy a loving relation-ship.' Imagine yourself walking down a diving board and leaping into a pool of light inside your heart that seems to be endless. Feel safe and immersed in this energy. Feel a sense of surrender and then sit within your heart again. Remain in this place and take three deep breaths, feeling a sense of expectancy. You don't need to climb back up the stairs of your heart, simply draw attention to where you are in the room and slowly open your eyes.

Questions to ask yourself

1. What did the door to your heart look like when you focused on relationships? If it was a heavy door that needed to be prised open, this shows how much you have closed off from a loving relation-ship. If it opens easily, then your heart is open and ready to con-nect on a deeper level. Whenever a problem or conflict occurs in a relationship or old negative emotions rise to the surface, then practise filling your heart up with light.

2. What was the answer you heard when you asked about what you needed to let go of? It may not be what you expected. This is what your heart knows is the real truth. It may be spite towards a former mate, low self-esteem or unrealistic expectations. Once your heart tells you how to let go, by jumping into the pool of light, you can begin to surrender to a higher power and attract someone who will relate to you on a deeper, more honest level.

Create a blueprint to attract the relationship you want

This is where you need to focus on what you want in your ideal mate to create a blueprint in your subconscious mind. Remember that expansion of your mind energy depends on regular positive visions and thoughts. By programming your subconscious you will blast through your negative beliefs and create positive expansive thoughts that will heighten your extrasensory perception. You can then break out of old negative cycles of attracting destructive relationships. Be aware of the people you may normally attract and the qualities you don't want. That is what your subconscious kept homing in on, possibly because of low expectations or familiar characters from your childhood.

Now you are going to reprogramme your mind to meet your deepest needs. If you keep meeting people who are unfaithful, controlling or stingy then you will want to make sure you are now attracting someone who is loyal, accommodating and generous. Write down your description of the person you want to attract, as if it is happening *now* and you are already in the relationship. For example, 'I am enjoying a loving relationship with a loving, loyal . . .' Initially you can write it as a rough draft, but treat it like an important document and then write or type it up neatly.

Be specific; the more detailed you are the more your subconscious mind can locate the person and coincidences will lead you to them. Don't settle for what you think you can have. Think about everything you really want in a partner, from the way they dress and look, as well as their age and height. Focus on the qualities you feel they will need to make a good relationship work, whether it's honesty, generosity or high morals. You decide what works for you. You can even be specific about the type of job or industry they work in that would be compatible with you. If looks, height or age don't matter to you, then focus just on their qualities, but be aware that your higher mind will pick out a wider cross-section. Your subconscious mind takes things literally, so don't forget to mention that you also want them to be single and sane. You can keep adding to your blueprint as you remember other qualities you want in a partner. Do this from your heart and be sincere, otherwise you will attract someone who may seem to be what you want, but turn out to be just an illusion.

Programme your subconscious

Now programme your mind to lead you to your perfect mate. Once again refer back to the visualisations in chapter nine to go back to your preferred room in your mind: the tropical island on page 205 or the cushioned room at the bottom of the well on page 209.

Once you have gone down all the steps and are deeply relaxed, begin to picture yourself with your ideal partner. Focus on how you feel and say the affirmation, 'I am enjoying a loving relationship. We are happy and secure together.' Keep repeating this throughout your image. Visualise both of you in whatever scenario you decide on, whether in a park, on a beach, having dinner together or relaxing at home. Focus on how contented you feel. If there is music in the background, make it relaxed and calm. Focus on what they are wearing and how you would like them to look and then focus on what you are wearing. How do they smell? Of expensive aftershave/perfume? What conversation are you having? Is there candlelight, dimmed lighting, or a sunset? Notice where you are sitting; feel the sense of sitting on a carpet, settee, sand or grass. Or are you in front of a roaring fire?

This is your creative reality not just a fantasy, so you want to make the mental picture as closely based on your life as possible. So if you *don't* have an open fire, visualise what you *do* have, even if it's an old-fashioned two-bar electric one. Similarly, if you are on a beach or in a park, make sure it's one that you know of that's easily accessible, and wear your own clothes.

It's entirely up to you to make this scene exactly as you would like it. Forget about the outcome and soon your subconscious will lead you to the right person. You will feel a mutual attraction. As I mentioned in the last chapter, you can also use this time to visualise other mind pictures and strengthen a current relationship or bring healing energy to conflicts you and your partner might be having. In this case, you can simply visualise yourself with your partner and focus on doing something you enjoy together. Once again make everything as tangibly real as you can in your mind picture and incorporate all your senses. Think of an affirmation to go with the image. It could be something like, 'We are enjoying a loving, fun relationship. We bring out the best in each other.' Once again, picture it as if it is happening now.

You can use this to inject positive energy into any relationship whether it's with your parents or a friendship. Quite un consciously you will be affected as your body language and behaviour are transformed by your subconscious positive thoughts. You may not notice any changes, but you will be generating loving energy and the object of your energy will respond without realising. Our minds and other people's minds respond to what they believe to be the truth. Your truth is your perceptions. Keep practising these visualisations every day for twenty minutes over several weeks and see the difference. Thoughts and visions are energy. Where you focus your mind, that energy will flow. When you hold a vision and make an affirmation about what you want in your life, that becomes your new reality.

If you want some inspiration from someone who tried this and found it really worked, read on.

Wendy's story

A few years ago Wendy decided to do some creative visualisation to find the perfect man. Everything in her life was going really well. She was a TV presenter and had lots of work and was therefore earning good money. She had great friends and was just about to move into a spacious new apartment in the City. But she was single and wanted to think more positively about relationships. She says, 'I was tired of going out with grown men who behaved like boys. With my current move it seemed the perfect time to make a new start.

'I didn't feel I need to have a man, but if I was going to have a relationship I wanted a constructive one. I learned about visualisation from an empowerment workshop on a weekend course. The first day was spent talking about how we felt about our lives now. It was very emotional and revealing, especially when we discussed among us recurring scenarios with relationships or work that were making us unhappy. I had a history of meeting a certain type of man who never had any money and I was always the nurturer in the relationships. These men never seemed to know what they wanted and I was always left feeling frustrated and needing more than I was getting. I seemed stuck in a cycle destined to keep attracting these lame ducks. The second day was focusing on what we actually wanted in our lives now.

'I had to write a very specific description of my ideal man. Being focused helps to build up the picture in your mind and make it a reality. It was only when I was put on the spot that I realised I really did want to be with a man – but the right man.

'I made a list, which filled a side of A4, in the present tense. I am enjoying a relationship with a man who is sporty, spiritual, in touch with his feminine side, intelligent, with good earning ability, vegetarian and a good cook. A good sense of humour was imperative and he had to be spontaneous, open-minded, adventurous and creative. Physically, I wasn't specific about what I was looking for, except I wanted him to be very fit. His nationality and height weren't important. It was the qualities I wanted.

'We then had to sit still and visualise what we'd asked for as if it were happening in the present.

'But intention was important. What we wanted had to come from the heart and not hurt anyone else. If I was complacent about it, it wouldn't be as potent and I wouldn't necessarily attract what I wanted. Once we'd done that we had to let go of the outcome and know that it was coming.

'After the course ended I forgot about it. I was caught up in the stress of where to put all my furniture. It wasn't until I spoke to the woman who ran the course two months later that she mentioned everyone on the course had got what they wanted and had I? I told her I hadn't. I did wonder about whether it was going to happen or not, but I decided to trust that it would.

'A month later I met the man I'd asked for. I was presenting a show for Channel 4 and we were filming in Chamonix in the mountains of France and I became friendly with one of the cameramen. I thought he was attractive but nothing else entered my head. But one of the things that really struck me about him was his ability to hug. When we left he gave me a huge hug in a very open way. I thought this is a really lovely man and I'd like us to stay friends. It was only when we both returned to England that things developed. We shared a cab from Heathrow air-port and for some reason ended up holding hands on the way back to our separate doctinations. It felt very comfortable being with him, but I wasn't sure what was going on. We exchanged business cards and said goodbye without a hint of who would ring who.

'But things happened quicker than I thought. I'd accidentally left some of my belongings in the cab. He rang the next day and I went to pick them up from his house in south London. Since then we've seen each other continuously. It's been a friendship that evolved very quickly then led to passion. It took a while to dawn on me that he was the man I'd asked for. But it was obvious as I got to know him and found my list again. He's very nurturing and just happens to be vegetarian. He often cooks for me and is very understanding of women. He always manages to lighten my day with his humour. It's the first time that I've met a man who is on my level and understands my needs. And it's the first time that I've broken the cycle of the stingy selfish types I used to attract. It's a very caring, sharing relationship and I am very much in love.

'I'm so glad that I actually took time to focus on what I was really looking for. Because there is a great truth in the saying, "You can't get what you want until you know what it is."'

Programme your dreams for help

As you know by now, your dreams provide access into your inner realms, whether your subconscious or your higher mind. They can provide you with answers on how to take the next step in finding the love you want or shed light on conflicts that arise in a relationship. Before you go to sleep, focus on the kind of person you want. Read the detailed description that you have written, slowly. Hold the vision of this person in your mind and think about them and then write down the question that you want to ask. It could be, 'Tell me the next step to take in finding my perfect partner,' or 'How do I solve this conflict arising in my relationship?'

As soon as you wake up write down your dreams as quickly as possible. Once again, as I mentioned in chapter eight on dreams, set your alarm fifteen minutes earlier if you think it will give you more time, before the early morning rush. And be prepared. Sometimes dreams will wake you up in the middle of the night to relay an important message, so keep pen and paper handy by the side of the bed. Even if you can't remember specific events in the dreams, write down any words that you heard in your dream or feelings you had.

How you feel on waking will also give you some indication

of the next step. You may be told that you need to contact a certain person, an old or new friend, and arrange to go out. Or perhaps go to an event that will lead you to your ideal partner. Perhaps you will be told to trust and wait for the results. Your own inner guidance will know the right timing for you. If you feel positive and ready for action, then allow your intuition to guide you to it. If you feel emotional, it could be that your subconscious needed to bring things to the surface about old negative feelings that are holding you back. These need to be cleansed before you can move forward. Simply thank the feelings that rise to the surface as you did in the previous exercises and once the toxic feelings have shifted, you will have more clarity. If you want, you can then programme your dreams again the following night to see if you can discover any other information.

Evoke your angel

Now it's time to evoke the angel of relationships. Sit quietly and say in your mind, 'Can the angel who helps with relationships please step forward.' Sense and trust that they are with you. Whatever your circumstances, whether you are looking for new love, or wanting to heal a rift, angels can work miracles and connect with other people's higher minds. They have immense compassion and can transform the most difficult circumstances and dissolve barriers that seem impenetrable. They will work with you, without judgement, and will heighten all your intuitive faculties to help you with the next step. So be prepared and act on any strong influences or intuitive urges you get. Anything could happen to ensure the success of your goal.

Trust in the outcome

As I've mentioned before, trusting that everything will happen as it should is imperative. You must let go of the outcome and believe expectantly. The more you trust, the more you allow your higher intuitive self to take over and lead you to the right person. When you don't trust, you start controlling and that is when your limited conscious mind starts imposing restrictions and expectations on how things should be. Fear starts to filter through and you forget 'your truth'. You may believe that what you want isn't possible. So keep a check on your thoughts. Every time you notice yourself veering off into disbelief, fear, impatience or self-pity that it hasn't happened as fast as it should, keep trusting that you will be guided in the right way and your life will open up in front of you to bring you your heart's desire.

Now that you've put your trust in the right person to come along, pause for a moment. This doesn't mean you should leap in head first whenever an attractive stranger appears. Sometimes, despite using your intuition, you can have a few false starts, where your conscious mind keeps getting in the way. Consequently, people you meet aren't always quite what you hoped for. This can happen when we first get our psychic equipment into gear. We need to get accustomed to using it, in the same way that we can have a few accidents when we are just learning to drive a car or ride a bike. Appearances are deceptive and the exercises in the next section on discernment will help you to take an intuitive double-check on a potential partner.

The importance of discernment

Without doubt, if you don't use your intuition you are lost when it comes to meeting new people. And you really cannot trust your logical mind. It will mislead you. Our minds tell us that someone is wonderful because they flatter our ego and boost our confidence. It tells us that attractive looks, good clothes and a prestigious job mean someone is a decent, kind person. It tells us that if someone acts as if they are nice, then they must be. How wrong has it been before? We've all been caught out. I'm sure there are plenty of men who were taken in by Jane Andrews, the Duchess of York's former dresser, because of her privileged lifestyle and status, not thinking for a second she was unbalanced and a future murderess. And think of serial killer Fred West's outward appearance. A friend of mine told me how he once came to work on a house of someone she knew. She described him as one of the sweetest, funniest men she'd ever met – until she saw the news on the television.

I've used these extreme examples because I've often spoken to people who have needlessly put their lives at risk. Many destructive and dangerous people are overtly flattering initially. It's a great manipulative technique. On the other hand there are people who are gritty and down-to-earth. They could be loyal and thoroughly trustworthy. But you might catch them on a bad day or going through stressful circumstances and prematurely judge them as someone who is irritable, grumpy or depressed. This is why it's so important to have that radar switched on.

You don't have to turn into Mother Teresa or become celibate to be discriminating in your personal relationships. A lot of people seem to prefer to live by the adage 'What you don't don't know won't hurt you', but the truth is the opposite. Being discerning about the choices you make in your personal life can save you a lot of heartache and wasted time, and can protect you from dangerous circumstances. If you discover the truth about someone from the start, you won't need to continue down a particular road. Your intuition will tell you the underlying truth, which may be the opposite to what you see.

The answer is simple. Pace yourself when you get to know someone – enough for your intuition to do its work. And be aware that if you have been drinking, taking drugs or just feeling emotionally vulnerable, you are tempting fate. Not only do you have no clarity in these circumstances, but you are under sedation. Don't be caught out by strangers. Because strange is exactly what they might turn out to be.

Exercise in discernment

When you first meet someone you are attracted to, make a note of how you feel but not what you think. Remember, our minds fool us, particularly if someone seems overly gracious, or conciliatory. Pay attention to anything about a person that stands out for no apparent reason.

One friend bitterly regretted that she didn't listen to her sixth sense. She told me that she had met someone she found attractive initially, but after she said goodbye to them, her mind kept homing in on the man's mouth and she couldn't put her finger on why. There was nothing physically wrong with it, yet there seemed to be something niggling at the back of her mind. She also heard the words 'sabre-toothed tiger'. It was an unexpected psychic reference to someone's character, and on discovering more about these prehistoric creatures, she learned that they didn't chase their prey like other wild cats. They were crafty and waited for their victims to move closer, then, once you were on their territory they pounced and ripped you to shreds. Both impressions were very accurate and valuable but unfortunately she only found out for sure when she chose not to listen to her strong intuitive hunches.

Only a short time later she discovered that despite an outwardly charming, respectful and polite appearance, this person was not what he seemed when she bumped into him near where he lived. He invited her for a coffee and, caught off guard, she forgot her earlier reservations and accepted. But she had cause to regret not paying attention to her instincts. Once she walked through his front door, this chap's Mr Nice character changed dramatically as he pounced on her, pinning her against the wall. Terrified he was going to rape her, she had to use all her strength to push him away and escape.

If only she had paid attention to her own innate wisdom she could have avoided the situation. Her sixth sense had singled out a feature, his mouth, illuminating the fact that what he said couldn't be trusted. It also gave her a very specific characteristic by naming a particular animal. She had a tremendous shock, but she could kick herself for not giving more credence to her own abilities.

You won't always be able to get a feel for someone on first impressions and sometimes there are too many other things going on for you to be aware. But you can easily check them out psychically at home or after you've met them a few times.

Begin by doing one of the visualisations illustrated in chapter three to expand your mind energy and raise your awareness. Then focus on the person you want to know more about in your mind, and ask for information about how they are as a person. You may be given a word, a symbolic picture or a feeling. Ask what will happen if you continue to see them. If it's negative, take note of the information. You don't have to dismiss them immediately, but be aware of their behaviour and watch for any warning signs.

So before you decide that Prince or Princess Charming just walked into your life, take a breath. Try to remain objective, even if your emotions are going through the ringer. All you have to do is give your intuition a chance to work for you. If you use it properly and objectively, it will tell you the real truth.

All these exercises are designed to bring you the soul mate you have always wanted. By working through them you will activate your intuitive higher mind to take the lead role in locating and attracting what you want in a partner. But now we will focus on another subject intrinsic to loving relationships – sex. By using the higher vibrations of our sexual energy we can discover how it can magnify our psychic powers. Controlling and experiencing our sexuality on a higher level of consciousness is one of the ways in which we can contact the powerful, sacred force within all of us, called Kundalini.

How Kundalini can heighten your psychic powers

Sexual energy is a potent and mystical force and, used correctly, it has the potential to raise our intuitive awareness to new heights. This is done through awakening Kundalini energy, also known as 'chi', 'prana' or 'Holy Spirit', which lies dormant in a small 'bulb' of energy in our sacrum at the base of the spine. Kundalini is associated with our sexuality as it can be awakened through control of the orgasmic state in sexual intercourse – but it is much more than that. It is the power of pure desire within us, the reservoir of life force, where psychic gifts, inspiration, creativity and revelation originate. Many mystics consider that when we fully experience the total impact of Kundalini we become enlightened as we become one with our true selves. This force is often represented as the fiery serpent, coiled three and a half times and asleep.

When the Kundalini energy awakens, just like the snake, it uncoils and rises up, like a white fluid light that flows through our six chakras until it reaches the crown chakra. The experience has been described in many ways: as a warm heat in the spine, a feeling of cool breeze that flows over the top of the head, or an explosion of joy. The strong feminine force of Kundalini is represented in Eastern teachings not just by the snake but also by the goddess Shakti. It is said that when she awakens she will sweep you up in her passionate and creative force, which has the power to transform you.

And transform is what this energy does. As this pure life force moves through our chakras like a laser, it purges any old traumas, conflicts, emotional issues, or subconscious fears in its path, bringing them to the surface. So although at times the awakening of Kundalini can be blissful, the cleansing process can evoke a temporarily strange reaction called 'kriyas' that could make a person laugh or weep within minutes, bring repressed anger or fear to the surface or make someone want to change their life radically from working as a high-flyer in the City to becoming a gardener.

Many mystics have sought enlightment by raising Kundalini through specific breathing exercises. It is a very delicate process as energy moves up through the chakras and brings old issues to the surface. If this energy is forced, an awakening can happen too quickly for your own development and old emotional residue from the past can be over-whelming, causing serious imbalance. However, for this you need supervision from an expert in Kundalini awakening, which is why I won't elaborate.

But when you work towards a higher goal, Kundalini is aroused naturally. By developing your psychic powers you have already begun to awaken Kundalini, which is your own divine power, in a safe, protective way that works at your own pace. You have done this by expanding your mind energy, raising your vibration and connecting with the powerful and subtle voice within. This is the same primitive energy source. Psychic abilities cannot exist without this life force rising up to awaken your consciousness to your higher mind.

Regular sexual intercourse can awaken and raise Kundalini to a degree, but only if it is intense and lasts a long time and both lovers need to have developed their higher minds and be very aware of each other's sexual energy. Kundalini is about the raising of pure consciousness and nothing to do with basic desires. Obviously, these higher aspects of sex must involve two people as it is to do with an exchange and transform-ation of energy. But if you are without a partner you can still focus on the sensual awareness of tantric yoga to stir this dor-mant life force into action.

The sacred art of tantric sex (which is a form of yoga) is based on awakening our Kundalini to reach a higher con-sciousness. And it will heighten all your paranormal powers of telepathy and clairvoyance and help creativity to flow as it rises up and cleanses your energy. This yoga has been made famous by the singer Sting and his wife Trudie Styler who extol its virtues. The word *tantra* is Sanskrit and means expansion. And expansion of your mind and consciousness within your sexual expression is what this yoga aims to teach. It also involves bringing a balance to our sexuality through the integration of our feminine intuitive yin and masculine pragmatic yang energy. With more balance to your energy you learn to act consciously to events in your life – with control and alertness – rather than just reacting blindly from your own point of view. Newly heightened abilities give you the insight and understanding to respond in this way.

How to increase your psychic power through tantric sex

I must point out that the subject of tantric sex is very extensive and is a whole way of life for many. But this information will give you some basic knowledge which can help to develop your psychic energy and raise Kundalini.

The basis of tantric sex is to honour and respect your partner as a cohort in a sensory adventure. You sit in front of each other and for five minutes become in sync with each other's breathing rhythm, while gazing into each other's eyes. This brings a feeling of intimacy and affinity. But the ultimate aim is to control the orgasmic state. You remain aware of the erotic energy running through you as you make love. But as the energy transmitted through lovemaking intensifies, instead of progressing to orgasm in the normal way, the man doesn't ejaculate and the woman controls her orgasm. The sexual energy is then continually transformed and builds up into an overpowering euphoria that leaves you with a long-lasting feeling of liberation and joy. When you have experienced this it is a sure sign that Kundalini has awakened. This divine ecstasy is the sought-after spiritual experience that can be attained when one reaches a state of enlightenment through meditation.

According to Dinu Roman, an expert in the field of tantric practice, a man, contrary to belief, does not need to ejaculate ever, unless he wants to start a family, yet he can still achieve an orgasm or multiple orgasms in a deeper more profound way that affects his entire body and consciousness. Dinu Roman says, 'As you become more sexually aroused, you forget the end result and immerse yourself in the feeling of how your sexual energy affects your body. Control of an orgasm brings focused strength and mastery of your sexual energy as you are maintaining this force at its height of maximum power. The results are considered life-enhancing. A man who retains his ejaculatory seed can stay powerful and strong, both physically and mentally. He can keep his stamina up to a very old age and can stay virile practically until he dies.'

Both partners can then experience more expansive and powerful orgasms that transcend the physical and take them into a spiritual awakening. This builds a stronger connection with their higher minds and with each other, creating a psychic and spiritual bond that gives a feeling of completion. In this philosophy, regular ejaculation actually weakens a man's vitality. 'A man shouldn't need to fight the point of no return,' continues Dinu Roman, 'which leads to frustration, but simply to play with his sexual energy in a relaxed way and not get to the place where it becomes uncontrollable. The semen is then taken back into the lymphatic system and recirculated into the body, feeding and strengthening all the organs. Some of the fluid is transmuted into energy, which feeds the higher aspects of the mind and the emotions.'

Over a period of time a higher telepathic communication can occur between a couple as they become more in sync with each other's thoughts and feelings. They develop a deep feeling of empathy and resonance, becoming able to understand each other's innermost feelings, even from a great distance. It seems that the subject of ejaculation creating weakness in the body is also known in medical science. Athletes are advised against having sex (with ejaculation) before competitions.

Although you cannot experience the same intense transference of sexual energy if you don't have a partner, you can still become conscious of this powerful energy which, depending on your own degree of sensitivity and awareness, can stir this life force into rising. Pick a time when you can be alone and relaxed. Focus on how your sexual energy feels and become aware of it moving through your body. Focus on your breathing as you inhale and exhale, hear and feel your heart beating and any other sensations of heat and cold. Be aware of your senses and when you get up to continue with your day, take note of your sexuality when you move, speak and respond. Do you feel more languid, do you speak more slowly and clearly and are you more tactile? Be conscious of your body when you sit down, cook a meal or get dressed. How does doing this affect the way you feel about yourself and about life? You don't have to feel ashamed about contacting this power within. Your sexuality is sacred, a creative force of life, and should never feel dirty or embarrassing. Remember the power of the mind and thoughts from chapter nine. The more you think of this energy as sacred psychic potential, the more this awareness will expand your mind energy and alter your state of consciousness. This, along with your psychic work, will help to uncoil the dormant energy within. This understanding of your own sexuality is the primitive natural and mystical force from which you are created. And it is the seat of your psychic power.

When Kundalini is triggered through a meeting of minds

There is no doubt about it: Kundalini is contagious. Its energy is powerful, healing and at times disturbing. The mere presence of a single being whose Kundalini is strong will awaken those around them. This often happens through many gurus who need only have disciples in their presence for the devotees' Kundalini to respond. But it doesn't have to be a spiritual teacher to create a reaction. Even a simple healing session has been known to set off this primitive force. One girl who had been receiving healing on a reiki course (a form of healing) suddenly jumped up during the session shouting, 'What have you done to me?' Apparently she had experienced a sudden rush of energy that felt like an entire body orgasm exploding through her. When the reiki teacher heard what had happened, she explained how healing can awaken Kundalini energy, but that she should rejoice in the mystical experience and not be afraid. Similarly, if you are in the presence of a group whose Kundalini is awakened, the same effects can be triggered within you. The story I will now share with you will also explain how Kundalini energy can be triggered through a particular energy resonance between two people and acts as a catalyst for intense spiritual learning.

I experienced the powerful effects of this energy when I met a Russian producer who was on a short trip filming and interviewing in the UK. I was being interviewed for a television programme in my capacity as a journalist. We had had several telephone conversations before we met. I thought he might be quite difficult as a person to deal with, as he always seemed abrasive and unable to speak without shouting down the phone. But, surprisingly, from the moment we met I recognised there was a mutual attraction that seemed to be creating strong reactions in both of us. There was a huge amount of positive energy flying between us and we couldn't look at each other without laughing. It was so infectious that as I was gazing into the camera lens to do the interview, both he and the sound man quickly had to leave the room as neither of them could keep a straight face.

After meeting up for drinks, several hours later we said goodbye and that seemed to be the end of the matter. Until a week later when this energy phenomenon, despite thousands of miles between us, seemed to re-emerge. As I was talking to someone on the phone in my office I suddenly had a feeling of a firm pressure on my chest, almost as if a doctor had applied a sharp jolt to a patient's chest when they are trying to restart their heart. The feeling was so strong that it actually made me stop in mid conversation and the Russian's face swam into my mind.

The next day, whatever had happened, my heart had definitely been brought to life and I was suddenly swamped by a powerful force that seemed to come from out of the blue. For the next three weeks I was the recipient of an intense energy that was one of the most difficult things I have ever had to deal with in my life. I felt as if my heart was being pulled apart, as if some strong but blissful power was surging through me and forcibly opening it up. I tried to analyse and reason my way through what was happening but I gave up, as the mind never can appreciate what it is simply to feel something. This energy also heightened my psychic awareness. As I talked on the phone to a male colleague about work I mentioned this strange energy that this man had triggered in me and suddenly in the background on the line we both heard a high melodious voice calling out the words

'Missing you'. It sounded as if the words were travelling from a long way off. We were stunned that we had both been party to hearing this mystical intervention.

At times it seemed as if I were receiving telepathic communication with the Russian as I always seemed to feel the impact of his thoughts and emotions without even trying. If he crossed my mind, I would feel a surge of heat in my heart. I was amazed by the energy dynamics and wanted to understand more about this force that had been triggered. But communication with him was always difficult. Once when he called about work, I had to hold the phone away from my ear from his barking voice. I couldn't understand how such an irascible personality could evoke such a strong reaction. But after the call I went out to interview someone and once again felt a positive energy sweep over me so strongly that I felt dizzy.

When Kundalini begins to affect you, it is like being directed by a force that you cannot control. For many people it creates an initial feeling of fear as the energy brings many emotional issues to the surface. Sometimes I felt unbelievably delicate and at other times waves of intense anger came over me. When a meeting evokes Kundalini, it is the very impact of life force. Like a laser it sears through your personality to the underlying truth of who you really are. This strong energy created between us had been the catalyst for it, almost like a positive and negative charge connecting and causing an explosion. But in this case an explosion of the Kundalini energy within. The result was that I had been completely and totally connected with my heart, as if someone had switched me into the mains. It wasn't just about emotion but a deeper compassion and pure love within. And this affected the way I felt about everything in my life, giving me a sense of a more gentle strength.

Take care, however; this kind of energy between a man and a woman can be easily confused as just a compelling sexual attraction. If you are wondering how it differs, look at it this way. This higher energy is a clear ascension. It affects you on an integral level, influencing your higher mind and your heart. It is systematically raising your vibration. That tells you the truth of what's going on.

The power of Kundalini teaches us how to love without reason. It frees us from our limited minds and egos and as it cleanses us, if we open up to it, it allows us more access to our deeper intuitive powers and spirituality.

The mystical experience that awakening Kundalini can bring is described by Swami Muktananda (the Hindu equivalent of a spiritual teacher) who says, 'The Kundalini is powerful, unstoppable, erotic, terrifying yet most beautiful. Her love is "tough" love, without sentimentality or mercy. She is our fierce mother goddess within. She loves truth and only responds to it. She melts my ego into a vapour, which can be agony, yet if I surrender to her, she always brings me great peace. She cannot be defined in words. She is an experience only.'

As you have seen more of how this primitive force works in your life, you will understand that there are many ways of awakening Kundalini. Now you have developed and strengthened your psychic muscle, and reached this stage of the book, know that Kundalini will mould, shape and transform you into a more loving, aware and powerful person. This energy teaches you that within your vulnerability lies your strength. At times you will need to accept the cleansing process as emotions rise to the surface; accept them by feeling them and letting them wash over you. And as you do so, you create a deeper understanding with yourself and build stronger bonds with your loved ones. The awakening of Kundalini brings the understanding of what spiritual masters have been teaching for centuries: that love comes from within and the divine ecstasy of enlightenment is that pure explosion of joy that lies in our hearts.

So be brave; it takes courage to be a traveller of the inner realms and realise your true intuitive potential. Once you put all these exercises into practice you will see with different eyes. You are not a victim of fate, but a creator of your own life. And the foundations are now in place. Remember, you're not waiting for anything to come along. Why? Because within your vision you are already experiencing whatever you desire *now*. And you will be a more magnetically attractive proposition as a result. Your aura will radiate a new power and clarity that comes with working on these subtle levels. Expect and trust in unconditional love and you will be ready for a transformational adventure.

12

Living a More Magical Life

Throw your dreams into space like a kite, and you do not know what it will bring back, a new life, a new friend, a new love, a new country.
Anaïs Nin, 1903–77, writer and diarist

Congratulations: you have come a long way on your psychic journey and have achieved a tremendous amount. As soon as you picked up this book you started investing in your higher self. Now the more you put in, the more you will benefit. You've got your psychic tools and you can really start living the life you want. You no longer have just five senses to help you make sense of the world. You also have a very powerful sixth sense that is heightened and ready to help you make the right choices. When our intuition leads the way magic happens and our lives begin to unfold in a new way and become one big adventure. But if we want our lives to improve we have to be ready to go out on a limb. That means having courage, taking a risk or a leap into the unknown. So, when ideas flash into your mind – act on them. When you feel creative, do something with that energy and paint, draw, or write. Be aware of your hunches, dreams and coincidences and notice if they lead you to the answers you are looking for. Be excited and expectant, because you will discover that opportunities are everywhere.

But remember psychic powers aren't about deluding yourself and creating a fantasy life. Your problems won't just disappear: you will still be disappointed, disillusioned, have conflicts and make mistakes. That's life. The difference is that now you have a new way of changing things, an opportunity to pre-empt situations that you once saw as inevitable, a chance to change the path along which your life is travelling – if you don't like it. You can have it all, a fabulous career with more money, and constructive relationships with your friends, lovers and family. What you want to achieve is now within your grasp. You've started on a journey of inner discovery and there's no going back. There is a treasure chest of knowledge within you that you now know exists. You just have to keep remembering to use it.

Has your crystal changed?

Now is the time to see how you have transformed since working your way through this book. Remember the different-shaped crystals from the visualisation on page 79 in chapter four where you had to imagine entering the crystal you most felt comfortable with?

Now return to the exercise and picture yourself going back through the forest and down into the cave of crystals. Look at the different sizes and colours of the crystals and see which one you are most drawn to. See yourself shrinking and going within the crystal and focus on how you feel. Then leave the cave as before.

The crystal represents your mind consciousness and it will be fascinating to see if it has changed. It may now be a different shape, colour or size. It could be clearer or show different facets. This will show whether you have become more spiritually and psychically aware, open-minded and freer of emotional issues. But do not judge yourself if you can't see any change. Shifts of consciousness happen gradually deep within ourselves and your crystal may only show very subtle alterations. It doesn't mean that you haven't done a huge amount of work to awaken your higher mind. Look at the notes in your psychic development diary, if you made any, and draw comparisons between the two crystals. Try this exercise every six months and note any differences.

Be a student of life and fan your psychic flames

Now that you've got this far, you need to continue developing. Our higher minds are boundless, limitless and can continually expand outwards. Which means one important thing: you can never stop learning. The more you keep your intuition in the driving seat, the more your life will flow. But however much we learn, it is all too easy to forget, and slip back into our old limited, logical ways of doing things. So I have devised some ways of keeping your psychic flame burning brightly.

Form a psychic development group

One of the best ways of keeping up with your psychic development, once you've finished this book, is to start a circle with like-minded friends. Psychic development circles are very inspiring and keep reminding you to bring your intuition to the fore. You can begin with just three people and gradually build up numbers. You could perhaps meet once a week in the evening or just once a month. And you can put these meetings to remarkable use. Once you've got a regular focused group you can keep developing your psychic powers together, or look at ways of brainstorming any problems each of you has: how to get a new job, where to buy a new house, how to get on better with your partner or children. You could bring in your dream diary and discuss any dreams you haven't been able to understand. Intuition will shed a new light on any subject.

Dedicate a room to your inner travels

Keep a specific room in your house to hold your psychic development group in. Don't get into being politically correct and holding it in different people's houses each week. It won't work. If someone is away or has got a noisy family, it will create disruption and irritable feelings. You need to make sure you have peace and quiet. Dedicate a room that is solely for the use of relaxation so that the vibrational energy of the room will remain centred and calm. You want people to feel uplifted as soon as they walk in. You are practising psychic abilities, so everyone will be sensitive to the atmosphere if a room has had noisy children in it all day or people arguing. Equally, you don't want to use a room if it has been left abandoned with piles of boxes or rubbish, as this will not help the vibrational resonance between everyone. Recall what I said in chapter four about psychometry and the effects of houses when you walk into them and how they affect you. Walls have ears, so keep the room peaceful but fed with energy by practising meditation, chanting, visualisations or psychic readings in it.

Create an inspiring atmosphere

Create the right atmosphere for psychic development with plants, flowers, candles, incense and crystals. Make sure it is not too cold or too hot and that there is enough room for everyone to sit without feeling crowded. You can also create an altar with fresh flowers, and if you wish add a picture of a wise teacher, whoever you prefer: Jesus, Buddha, Sai Baba or alternatively the great peacemakers such as Mahatma Gandhi or Nelson Mandela. This will help remind you of the evolved souls, who helped support mankind in its highest aspirations. Bear in mind what I mentioned in chapter four about objects becoming imbued with energy. When you have a focal point in the room that you treat as sacred, everyone will view it unconsciously in this way and the altar becomes a powerful focusing point for the mind. It holds the energy of the room and builds up a positive vibration. You can also dress the altar with a lit candle and keep a crystal there which will absorb the positive energy. You can then hold the crystal after a visualisation and feel its positive energy sending you healing. This will help raise the vibration in the room for any psychic work.

What to cover in your group

You can start by using some of the visualisations in chapters three, four, six, seven and nine. You can record the visualisations on tape so you can all listen to them and relax. But make sure you use someone with a clear voice who speaks at the right pace. You can use some nature sound tapes to good effect as a background sound to your recording. This is very effective with any of the beach, forest or other scenarios to help you to switch off and go into a higher mind state. You can continue your session with a mantra to help raise your mind frequency with sound. Then experiment with some of the different mind-focusing tools you've learned such as scrying and psychometry to see what each individual can pick up.

Also, give each person an opportunity to bring a particular problem to the group so everyone can tune in and give their information. Start by presenting the problem or confusing dream and then ask everyone to raise their mind energy to focus on any solutions or information they can give to the person. Take turns, but whatever you do don't allow it to develop into an ongoing counselling session where one person gets too much attention; otherwise the energy will become dissipated and other people will feel they aren't taking part. Keep it to between five and ten minutes each and let everyone know that this is the timescale.

Ground rules

Remind anyone who comes to a psychic development group that they must not take any kind of vocational drugs beforehand. It someone turns up drunk or stoned, they will affect the energy of the group. Leave any socialising until after you have finished the psychic evening, which should last for around an hour to an hour and a half. Then everyone can chat when you have a drink afterwards. If you go for a ninety-minute session, have a five-minute break in the middle. Have fun and allow for expression but keep the group focused. No chatting or giggling when someone is trying to concentrate. Otherwise people will feel they are not being taken seriously and lose confidence in their psychic powers.

Psychic exchange

Another idea for maintaining your psychic development is to find someone who is also keen on developing themselves and swop psychic readings with them. That way you can gain confidence in your intuition. This takes time. Practise asking and answering questions and seeing if what is said comes true. It is important to keep giving each other feedback – and make sure you do. Many people, in my experience, like to give a reading, but don't want to know if they've got it wrong. Take it on board and don't take it personally. Be open to learning; mistakes are how we improve on our skills and aim higher. We can only better ourselves if we know when we get things wrong.

Regular exercise

Get into a regular exercise routine. As I mentioned earlier in the book, regular exercise is essential for keeping your psychic powers flowing, whatever the exercise. Even a half-hour brisk walk each day can help to clear stress and tension from your physical body and your energy field. It will clear your mind and re-establish a strong mind–body connection, so that intuition can flow more easily.

Watch your stress levels

As you develop your psychic abilities, you are naturally awakening your Kundalini energy and creating a harmony and balance of your yin yang energies. Remember: however intuitive you become, everyday life creates stress and sometimes it is overwhelming. Don't allow it to take over. Keep a check on what's happening to *you*. If you are stressed, it will be harder to connect with your intuition and react consciously to what's going on around you. However busy you are, take some time out to relax, even if it's only for ten minutes in a tea break. Slow down, whatever the deadline or business agenda of your day. Nothing is worth putting yourself into that state for, which is quite the opposite to the alpha level that we need to harmonise with the earth's healing vibration.

But you can get back in touch with that calm state. Close your eyes and concentrate on your breathing. Visualise yourself on a beach or floating on a cloud in the sky to expand your mind energy and re-energise yourself. Or go for a walk around a park or do some exercise. When we are emotionally reactive, it is harder to make decisions from our true selves. We feel impatient and angry and we want everything our way and fast. But when we are in touch with our inner voice we see with another perspective that the world doesn't revolve around us and that our decisions affect other people's feelings and lives. We can then take responsibility for the effects we create and consciously respond to our circumstances and influence our lives beneficially.

Keep writing your psychic and dream diaries

Keep regularly writing down your dreams. It will help you to remain aware of the messages your higher mind is trying to relay, and once your inner voice knows it is being heard it will get even louder. Keep acknowledging the hunches you have, the ideas you get and any coincidences you have that lead you to the right contacts and insights. Everything will help to lead you to a bigger, more successful life.

Help your children – and encourage their intuitive intelligence

So many people associate the proof of psychic powers with spoon bending, moving objects about with telekinesis or levitating off the floor, but while being entertaining these paranormal activities remain gimmicks which teach us nothing other than that extraordinary powers exist. The real power, however, is in using this gift to transform your life and future lives. Use the information that you have learned to help develop your child's mind. They are the real potential for our future. Now you know better you can nurture this gift in them instead of dismissing it. When they tell you about special friends, feelings and strange dreams, listen to them. Give them the confidence to believe it is perfectly right that they feel this way and be positive when their imagination runs wild, for this is the bridge to a higher consciousness where our mind energy can expand and we can develop our sixth sense.

If they know you'll accept what they say, then their psychic skills will accelerate. So encourage their visualisation skills. Make sure their rooms have lots of pictures, words, crystals and toys with splashes of colour to invigorate their minds. Help to develop their higher minds by taking them on their very own story – a mental trip to the beach to play in the sand, or an aeroplane ride to the clouds – before they go to sleep. Just make sure, as in previous visualisations, that they come back to where they started, so they feel grounded at the end of their mind adventure. Enable them to be creative and to paint and write. Creative expression is interlocked with our psychic power as it comes from that same sacred energy within. If that flows, intuition flows. Show them that it is okay to believe in the feelings they have about anything – good or bad.

If you believe in them and accept the natural precious gift that is already there, their confidence in their inner voice will mature and blossom. You are giving a wonderful present to your child as well as to society: they will become adults with insight, knowledge and wisdom. It will be normal and easy for them to help themselves and tap into this higher power. With children like this we can truly enter into a golden age that can only benefit mankind.

Be confident

Keep an open mind and heart. It takes courage to be your true self, and continued confidence to keep listening to your own intuitive voice and not be blinkered by limited thoughts. But not everyone will agree with your new way of seeing things, and don't expect them to. You will even have to keep nudging your own mind into working from a different perspective. It took a lifetime of experiences to establish the logical left brain pattern in which your mind works, much as it does with too much right-brained idealism and dreaminess. It will take some time to re-educate this energy and find balance. We all have a choice in the way we act. Choose to follow your inner voice and not block opportunities to follow your heart. When we are connecting with our true intuitive inner voice, all our relationships improve, we see behind the mask of someone's personality and understand their point of view, and take time really to listen to what our psychic sense is saying.

So, let the voice of your spirit help you fly through this life and give yourself the gift of a new heightened perspective. One in which you don't need to be bogged down by problems, but can resolve them easily, see them objectively and look for the positive. Be who you are and be the best. Who knows what your future holds. But whatever it is, it will be a successful one that you truly deserve.

Stay connected

If you're interested in being informed of any new books, seminars, or tapes coming out then you can keep in touch via my website: Sherronmayes.com.

Index

Figures in *italics* indicate illustrations

Index

electroencephalograph (EEG) 34
Elle magazine 8
energy field, altering 27
  see also aura
exercise 31, 82–3, 209, 287

foods, and lucid dreaming 189
free will 153

Ghadiali, D.P.: *The Spectro Chromemetry Encyclopaedia* 58
Gibran, Kahlil 139
God 33, 37
grace 36–7
Greeks, ancient 172
groundedness 15
guides 119, 139, 140, 166, 168
  what is a guide? 141–2
  communication through dreams 181–2
  exercise in learning to communicate with your guide 145–6
  guidance on an unhappy marriage 150
  guidance to working relationships 147–8
  guidance on your career 142–3
  how to remain aware of guidance 152
  use daydreams to contact your guide 148–9
  when guides are your spiritual schoolteachers 143–5
  when guides monitor our behaviour 147
  when guides protect us from harm 151–2

harmony 27
Harry, Debbie 225–6
healing 15, 27, 83, 156, 276
  and angels 163–5
healthy eating 31
higher minds
  and children 289
  and relationships 252
homeopathy 6

ill health
  and angels' help 160–62
  and mind energy 191

imagination 35–63
  chakras 59–60, 59
  colour chart 56–7
  discover your predominant sense 38–48
  exercises to engage the imagination 48–54
  exercise one: a deep cleanse 49–51
  exercise two: rising above 51–3
  exercise three: lift off 53–4
  setting the scene 49
  find the colour you need right now 62–3
  and grace 36–7
  healing colours for your visual technique 54–6
  the history and science of colour healing 57–8
  transform your mood with a colour meditation 58–62
independence 13
inner language 85–117
  be objective 95–6
  clairaudience 90–91, 93
  clairsentience and intuition 91–3
  clairvoyance 87–90
  developing telepathic skills 101–6
  exercise in telepathic communication 103–5
  experiment with the telepathic power of thought transference 105–6
  the different psychic levels 106–7
  keep a development diary and notice your transformation 116–17
  limber up your mind with a symbol exercise 98–100
  the past, present and future link 113–16
  penetrating the armour 109–10
  practise with everything 110–13
  practise your clairvoyance, clairaudient and clairsentient abilities 108–9
  a quick frequency lift before you tune in 100
  sight, sound and feeling 86–7
  why being blind doesn't affect your inner sight 93–4
  why you need a sounding board 94
integrity 240–41

Index